THE
ELECTORAL SYSTEM
IN BRITAIN
Since 1918

THE
ELECTORAL SYSTEM
IN BRITAIN
Since 1918

By

D. E. BUTLER

FELLOW OF NUFFIELD COLLEGE
OXFORD

SECOND EDITION

OXFORD
AT THE CLARENDON PRESS

Oxford University Press, Ely House, London W. 1

GLASGOW   NEW YORK   TORONTO   MELBOURNE   WELLINGTON
CAPE TOWN   SALISBURY   IBADAN   NAIROBI   LUSAKA   ADDIS ABABA
BOMBAY   CALCUTTA   MADRAS   KARACHI   LAHORE   DACCA
KUALA LUMPUR   HONG KONG   TOKYO

FIRST EDITION 1953

REPRINTED LITHOGRAPHICALLY IN GREAT BRITAIN
AT THE UNIVERSITY PRESS, OXFORD
FROM SHEETS OF THE FIRST EDITION 1954
SECOND EDITION 1963

REPRINTED 1968

PREFACE

THIS book was first published in 1953 under the title *The Electoral System in Britain 1918–1951*. It is now brought up to date. The text of Part I remains substantially unaltered. In Part II, the only changes are those involved in extending the statistical data to cover the elections of 1955 and 1959. The Appendix dealing with Redistribution has been much expanded and a second Appendix has been added to deal with such discussion of the electoral system as has taken place in the last ten years.

I must record my indebtedness to the Warden and Fellows of Nuffield College both for enabling me to make this study a decade ago and for their continued encouragement of research into elections. I must also thank Mr. H. G. Nicholas and Mr. P. M. Williams, who once again have provided most valuable advice and criticism, and Miss Jennie Freeman and Miss Audrey Carruthers for their diligent assistance.

D. E. B.

Nuffield College
July 1962

CONTENTS

Table of Contents

LIST OF STATISTICAL TABLES

LIST OF DIAGRAMS

INTRODUCTION

I

THE British electoral system has been much neglected in academic study. It is only in the last few years that systematic investigation of the conduct of election campaigns has been attempted, while discussion of the electoral system itself has too largely been left to propagandists in the weary argument over proportional representation. Apart from textbooks on electoral law, an electoral bibliography is astonishingly void of solid fare.

This absence of academic attention perhaps helps to account for the fact that on the few occasions when the electoral system has been the subject of parliamentary debate there has been so little informed factual comment; discussion has been not so much abstract—for theories of representation have been little voiced—as vague. Therefore it seems worth while to follow the description of the evolution of the electoral system which occupies the first part of this book with an exposition of some of the facts which can be discovered about its working. In retrospect and against this background, the debates often assume a very different perspective.

To follow such an approach is to go beyond the scope of the two works to which this book is intended as a sequel. Professor Seymour in his important study of electoral reform in the nineteenth century[1] and Professor Morris in his less notable continuation[2] were content to limit themselves to parliamentary political history. For this there was good reason. From 1832 almost until 1918, electoral reform was one of the leading questions of political debate. There are many sources which reveal the views politicians held about it. To study the growth of the electoral system between 1832 and 1918 is to study a major political issue, the exposition of which can throw substantial light on the history of the period. But after 1918 electoral re-

[1] C. S. Seymour, *Electoral Reform in England and Wales* (New Haven, 1915).
[2] H. L. Morris, *Parliamentary Franchise Reform in England and Wales, from 1885 to 1918* (New York, 1921).

form became a minor question. It is very interesting to see how a great debate tailed off; occasionally, in the treatment of electoral matters a sudden illumination on the conduct of politics may be found, but, for the most part, the electoral system constituted a complete side issue in public opinion and political thinking. None the less, the system did inevitably affect the course of politics, since it provided so large a part of the constitutional framework. Even after 1918 it still offers worthwhile material for study, but the study must be less concerned with the handling of a major political issue than with the working of an established institution and with the manner in which Parliament dealt with such a subject on the occasions when it continued to come before its notice.

II

Although the academic neglect of the electoral system may be justified by the paucity of recent sources and the limited number of obscure or contentious issues, the subject is not so small that it can be comprehensively treated in a single volume. In the pages that follow only the parliamentary electoral system is discussed; local government is not touched upon. Strictly technical questions of electoral law and administration are also, as far as possible, avoided. Above all, no attempt is made to deal with the conduct of campaigns; party organization together with election issues and their impact on the ordinary voter are perforce left alone. The evolution of electoral tactics and the reaction of the public to the changing methods of political propaganda provide a fascinating study which must be left to a later date. In these pages attention is confined to a description of actual or attempted legislative changes in the electoral system and to an analysis of the statistics that are available about its working.

PART I

THE EVOLUTION OF THE SYSTEM

CHAPTER I

EVOLUTION UP TO 1918

I. THE DEVELOPMENT OF THE SYSTEM

THE Representation of the People Act of 1918 may fairly be described as a turning-point in parliamentary history. Its passage almost completed the century-long transition from one representative system, medieval in origin and diverse in operation, to another, its lineal descendant, but modern and uniform. After eighty years the demands of the Chartists were virtually satisfied. With the 1918 Act the franchise question passed out of the political arena—or at least became no more than a sideshow—and electoral reform in general assumed less and less importance in the minds of politicians.

In some ways 1885, rather than 1918, should be regarded as the climax of the evolution that began in 1832. By 1885 the principle of universal male suffrage was more or less established, grotesque anomalies in the distribution of seats no longer survived, and electoral corruption was reduced to relatively negligible proportions. The main grievances had been met, and after 1885, as social questions obtruded themselves more and more into politics, the word 'Reform' no longer naturally denoted 'Electoral Reform'; the unofficial title 'Reform Bill', which had been attached to Representation of the People Bills since 1832, was hardly to be used in the twentieth century. None the less, the Acts of 1883–5 left several important questions open; women's suffrage was the most notable, but there were as well plural voting, equality in redistribution, and some aspects of expense limitation and registration procedure. After 1918 few issues of such magnitude remained for discussion.

However, there can be no finality about electoral reform, notwithstanding the fact that each step has been regarded by

B

some as the final one—from 1832 when Grey sought a settlement which would offer 'sure ground for resistance to further innovation'[1] to 1948 when the Home Secretary introduced his Representation Bill as '[completing] the progress . . . begun by the Great Reform Bill'.[2] Several questions were left open by the Act of 1918—not least the question of whether the Act itself would be efficient. But, although for some years there was appreciable agitation for a change in the electoral system, electoral questions never seem to have loomed so large in public or parliamentary consciousness after 1918 as they had in former times. Before 1918 there is a profusion of sources available to the electoral student in the form of Parliamentary Papers, reports of petition cases, debates in the House of Commons, and references in memoirs and articles; after 1918 the material is scant indeed. None the less, the electoral system has not been devoid of interest in the last thirty years. There were four main phases of parliamentary activity—the losing battle for proportional representation; the winning battle for the equalization of the suffrage; the abortive Representation of People Bill of 1931; and the events leading up to the Representation of the People Act of 1948.

It is notable how, in these struggles, arguments about electoral reform were put in terms of precedent. The procedures followed on previous occasions were constantly cited, most frequent references being made to the events leading up to the Act of 1918. Therefore, it is necessary to preface any discussion of recent developments with a brief survey of the nineteenth-century evolution of the electoral system and with a rather more elaborate description of the legislation of 1918.

Even during the period when electoral reform was one of the most important of political issues, interest in the subject fluctuated and change came in comprehensive stages. There are five major heads under which electoral legislation can be classified: systems of voting; redistribution; suffrage; corrupt practices; and administrative machinery. The simple plurality

---

[1] C. S. Parker, *Life and Letters of Sir J. Graham* (London, 1907), vol. i, p. 120.

[2] *House of Commons Debates*, 5th Series, vol. 447, col. 839. Hereafter referred to as, e.g., *H.C. Deb. 447, c. 839*.

system of election has hardly been tampered with since the Middle Ages, but the other four questions have tended always to be dealt with collectively. Indeed, it might be said that there are only five dates in the evolution of the electoral system— 1832, 1867, 1883–5, 1918, and 1948. Apart from the Ballot Act in 1872, the Equal Franchise Act in 1928, the Representation of the People Act in 1945, and, perhaps, one or two Corrupt Practices Acts in the nineteenth century, there has been no other legislation which in any way approached major importance.

Despite this tendency to change the electoral system comprehensively at periodic intervals, the changes have never been radical enough seriously to disturb continuity or to produce sharp or immediate modifications in the way in which government has been conducted. Electoral habits have been altered gradually, and the party system has been transformed, but there has never been a sudden break in practice, and many traditions have survived, in some form or other, from pre-reform days. The issuance of writs, the process of nomination and of election by simple majority, the appointment of agents, and the custom of canvassing still continue. It may be said that much of the vocabulary, some of the formalities, and a few of the institutions are still those which prevailed in the eighteenth century.

Together with continuity in the actual working of the system, continuity has also been maintained in the approach to its reform. Reform was always on a pragmatic level; it was sponsored by those who stood to gain from it directly or by those who feared civil unrest if some sop were not offered to the demands of democracy. There were some radicals who fought for reform on grounds of high principle, but, in general, it was not argued in those terms. There were few speeches which offered any clear and consistent theory of representation. Debates tended to be either partisan and confused arguments on the implications of practical proposals or, increasingly often, discussions of the constitutional propriety of making such proposals without universal agreement, rather than attempts to clarify the criteria against which the proposals should be judged. Much of electoral reform has been non-controversial, but it is not always clear whether this is because the principles involved were commonly agreed or commonly ignored.

II. REFORMS FROM 1832 TO 1914

The passing of the Great Reform Bill was important more for introducing the idea of change than for the changes it actually effected. The electorate was not so very much modified, and, while the worst of the rotten boroughs were abolished, the representation of seventy or more 'nomination' boroughs still remained absolutely in the gift of the landlord.[1] Corruption was, if anything, stimulated by an increase in the number of constituencies where a few dozen 'free and independent' electors might decide the issue by the sale of their votes. The innovations of the Act were more important for their ultimate than their immediate effect, notably the beginnings of a standardized franchise within the boroughs and the establishment of an electoral register.

The Act of 1832, it is important to remember, was highly controversial. There was no question of its being an agreed constitutional change. The bitterness it aroused was slightly softened by concessions made to the Opposition during its passage,[2] but, whatever traditions may subsequently have developed, the first Reform Bill hardly set a precedent of gentlemanly harmony.

Grey, Russell, and many others among its sponsors regarded their Reform Bill as a final settlement, but this idea was bound soon to come under attack. At first, the main assault came from the Chartists, and their intemperate demands frightened more moderate radicals from pressing hard for further reform. Minor Bills were passed in vain attempts to improve the highly inefficient registration procedure, and, in 1854, a Corrupt Practices Act was passed which, though of no immediate effect, at least began the process of clearly defining electoral offences. Limited attempts were made in the 1850's to broaden the electorate, but it was not until 1867 that a combination of political chances led to legislation in a form more drastic than was really desired by either of the parties which were vying for the credit of first bow-

[1] C. S. Seymour, *Electoral Reform in England and Wales* (New Haven, 1915), p. 92.
[2] The most important concessions were the relaxation of the schedules of disfranchised boroughs, the acceptance of the Chandos Clause (which by giving the vote to £50 tenants-at-will in the counties did much to preserve the influence of the landowners), and the preservation of the freeman franchise.

ing to the inevitable. Under the Representation of the People Act of 1867 household suffrage was virtually established in the towns, redistribution did irrevocable damage to the nomination boroughs, and jurisdiction over election petitions was transferred from the House of Commons to the Courts. This last, in conjunction with much more rigid limits on expenses, started a real move towards electoral purity—a development much aided by the passage of the Ballot Act five years later. The Act of 1867 was not the product of formal party agreement; there was contention over many major points, particularly on fancy franchises and on the question of whether those who paid their rates by compounding should be enfranchised. Although, on one side, Lowe and the Adullamites flatly opposed the change, and, on the other, many joined with Lord Derby in expressing apprehension about this 'leap in the dark', it may be said that both parties were united in apathetic support of the change, a reluctant concession to necessity. It was an Act which plainly could have no 'finality', for it left an absurd discrepancy between borough and county franchises. None the less, it was the most far-reaching of nineteenth-century Reform Bills in that it increased the electorate by 88 per cent., compared with 67 per cent. in 1885 and 49 per cent. in 1832. It significantly fostered the growth of party organization both by the mere increase in numbers and by the short-lived device of the limited vote in the three-membered boroughs.

By the legislation of 1883–5, the electoral system was brought much nearer to its present form. The Corrupt Practices Act of 1883 really made possible the elimination of bribery, at least in its crude and direct form. The Franchise Act of 1884 went almost all the way to universal male suffrage. The Redistribution Act of 1885 made the traditional two-member seat the rare exception rather than the general rule. The Registration Act of 1885 did much to simplify the process of securing a vote.

The Franchise and Redistribution Acts were, to begin with, highly controversial. The Franchise Act was rejected by the House of Lords and a compromise was only agreed after the Liberals consented to sacrifice any advantage they might gain from an extended franchise by introducing a Redistribution Bill that could not but hurt their prospects. This legislation can

hardly be described as constitutional reform by mutual agreement between the parties, especially in view of the vehement
debates on many specific problems. However, Gladstone, by his
restraint on the radicals, curbed excessive party bitterness. He
withstood assaults on plural voting and on university representation. He repudiated the principle of precise mathematical
equality in redistribution, and he rejected demands for proportional representation and for women's suffrage. But it is
notable that, for the first time, proportional representation,
women's suffrage,[1] plural voting, and equality in redistribution
became serious political issues.

For twenty years after 1885 there was a relative lull. But, in
1905, the advent of the Liberal Government coincided with the
rapid expansion of the Women's Suffrage Societies which were
to add the most colourful chapter to the history of electoral
reform. Electoral legislation was frequently discussed in the
period between 1906 and 1914. The main assault was on plural
voting. In 1906, in 1912, and in 1913 Bills abolishing plural
voting were passed by the House of Commons, but were defeated
by the House of Lords on the ostensible ground that it was a
constitutional tradition that redistribution should accompany
franchise reform and that 'one man, one vote' was meaningless
without the corollary 'one vote, one value'. The women's suffrage
question, of course, attracted much more publicity than plural
voting and excited much deeper bitterness. If the militant
suffragettes had not overreached themselves, some measure of
female suffrage would probably have been achieved, but their
violence exacerbated fears of what women might do with the
vote if it were granted. The female suffrage question obtruded
itself into all other electoral subjects and was largely responsible
for the absence of any electoral measures among the comprehensive body of legislation which the Liberal Government put on
the Statute Book.

A notable but mysterious event was the establishment of a
Royal Commission on Electoral Systems in 1909. It reported in

---

[1] Women's suffrage had been first brought up in 1867, and after 1870 had
been raised annually in the House. In 1883, however, it received substantial
support for the first time—the House of Commons only rejecting it by 130
votes to 114.

1910,[1] but neither its appointment nor its report was the subject either of debate in Parliament or of editorial comment in *The Times*. If not its rejection of proportional representation, at least its unanimous advocacy of the alternative vote might have been expected to draw some attention. But apparently interest in the House of Lords struggle distracted all eyes from it.

III. THE 1918 ACT

War, so often the midwife of reform, led to the most comprehensive Representation of the People Act that had yet been seen. In August 1916 Mr. Long, the Home Secretary, sought to stem criticism of a Bill designed to make special provision for electoral registration in war-time by suggesting that an all-party conference should be set up to consider all questions of electoral reform. The Speaker agreed to convene and preside over the conference. The conference reported[2] in January 1917, and displayed a surprising measure of agreement; its members were divided on only one recommendation, women's suffrage; on new methods of registration, on plural voting, on university representation, on redistribution, and, astonishingly, on proportional representation complete unanimity was achieved. The recommendations of the conference were embodied in the Representation of the People Bill of 1917. The Government left women's suffrage and proportional representation to a free vote. A large part of the Bill was accepted as uncontroversial; there was some disagreement about the temporary disfranchisement of conscientious objectors, about women's suffrage, and about the university franchise, but the only serious struggle concerned the system of election.

It is worth listing the changes incorporated in the Bill. Universal suffrage for men was provided on the basis of residence; hitherto it had been linked directly or indirectly to the payment of rates, and lodgers had had to make an annual claim to be put on the register, while, in some cases, sons living at home had been disfranchised. Apart from the university vote, the only other suffrage preserved was that based on the occupancy of business premises worth £10 annually. Six months' residence, either in the constituency or in a contiguous borough or county, now

---

[1] *Cd. 5163/1910.*   [2] *Cd. 8463/1917.*

qualified an elector, whereas previously a year's residence in the division itself had been necessary. The university franchise was extended by giving the vote to graduates of provincial universities, but there was no division on the merits of university representation. The local franchise was granted to all owners or tenants but not to all residents—and this evoked only a weak protest from the Labour benches. The receipt of poor-law relief ceased to be a disqualification from voting, and so also did electoral employment.

Women over thirty were enfranchised if they were local government electors or the wives of local government electors. The age of thirty was agreed as a result of a compromise in the Speaker's Conference designed to keep women in a minority in the electorate.

Votes were given to servicemen on easier terms, as far as residence was concerned. Those who had served in the war were entitled to the vote at the age of nineteen. Conscientious objectors, on the other hand, were disfranchised for five years.

Plural voting was only allowed on different types of qualification, and no one was to vote more than twice; women were only allowed to vote once on qualifications derived from being the wife of a local government elector. Arguments about whether an elector should be allowed to vote twice in different divisions of a borough raised bitter arguments about the nature of the compromise effected at the Speaker's Conference. Some contended that the law prohibiting plural voting within a borough had only been relaxed on the assumption that proportional representation would make it of negligible importance, while others denied any such understanding. The point was not of great moment except as an illustration of the disputes and recriminations which seem to be engendered so easily by the tacit compromises of a gathering like a Speaker's Conference.

Registration procedures were completely reformed. Two registers a year instead of one were provided for. The compilation, which since 1832 had fallen to poor-law overseers, was transferred to the Clerk of the County or Borough Council. The names were to be found not from rate-books and claims but by 'house to house or other sufficient inquiry', and the cumbrous machinery of registration courts and revising barristers was abolished.[1] The party agents who, by claims and protests, had been really responsible for maintaining the accuracy of the register were relieved of this burden by the efficiency and simplicity of the new system. The number of claims which reached the county courts was altogether negligible. The registration officer was made responsible for arranging polling-districts and polling-places. A first approach was made to dealing with the problem of the absent voter; arrangements were provided for servicemen and others debarred 'by reason of the nature of their occupation ... from voting at a poll' to be put on an absent voters list. For the immediate post-war period, servicemen overseas were to be entitled to vote by post, and permanent arrangements were made for proxy voting by servicemen.

The cost of contesting elections was materially reduced by the Act. In the first place, the official administrative costs of the election were transferred from the shoulders of the candidate to those of the taxpayer. In the second place, the permitted campaign expenditure was lowered to less than half the amount permitted under the Corrupt Practices Act of 1883. Even allowing for the fact that the electorate was being more than doubled, this meant that, in most cases, a candidate's expenses would be slightly reduced in the boroughs and appreciably reduced in the counties. One free postal delivery to each elector and the free use of schools for meetings were also provided for. The law on agency was, at the same time, strengthened; it became an offence for virtually any expense to be incurred in the promotion of a candidature without the agent's express sanction. On the other hand, one potential extra cost fell upon candidates. Freak candidatures in the latter part of the war led to the institution of the £150 deposit, forfeit by all candidates who failed to secure one-eighth of the votes cast.[2]

A major change in the appearance of a general election was effected by concentrating all polls on to a single day, instead of spreading them over a fortnight or more.

A Boundary Commission was set up in 1917 to devise a

---

[1] Technically, barristers may still be appointed to assist county court judges in dealing with registration protests. The number of registration cases brought before the courts has been negligible and revising barristers have seldom been employed.   [2] For the results of this see p. 167 below.

scheme for redistribution. It was instructed to keep the number of seats at its existing level but to allot them strictly according to a population basis laid down in the recommendations of the Speaker's Conference. Thus, apart from the City of London and the university seats, the principle of equality in numbers between constituencies was, for the first time, fully accepted. It soon became apparent that it was an almost impossible ideal. The rules first proposed for the Boundary Commissioners were thought to be too strict. Parliament relaxed them, as it was to do again thirty years later. The Commissioners only accomplished their task by adding thirty-one more territorial members to the House.[1] It seems that redistribution must always be accompanied by an increase in numbers if some very hard cases are not to be left. The recommendations of the Commissioners provoked some earnest special pleading from members affected and some laments about the damage to historic traditions; in self-defence the Government allowed no amendments of substance to the redistribution proposals.

The system of election proved to be much the most controversial question in the Bill. The conference had, as a compromise, approved proportional representation, but the House voted by a majority of eight that the Boundary Commissioners should work on the assumption that P.R. would not be enacted.[2] On the committee stage of the Bill, P.R. was again defeated, this time by thirty-two votes, and the alternative vote was substituted by the narrowest possible majority.[3] After some debate P.R. was accepted for the two- and three-membered university constituencies as an essential part of the compromise by which they were preserved; P.R. was regarded as the only way of preventing

[1] Six university seats were also added.

[2] In the light of subsequent events, the division of the parties on this question is of interest. It was:

	For P.R.	Against P.R.
Conservative . . .	38	85
Liberal	77	54
Labour	12	10
Irish	14	..
	141	149

Daily Telegraph, 18 June 1917.

For footnote 3 see opposite page.

these from becoming merely safe seats for Conservatives. However, the House of Lords tried to force a more general application of the principle. Reflecting the Conservative hostility to the alternative vote, they eliminated it and substituted P.R. The House of Commons rejected the Lords' amendments by 223 votes to 113 and then by 178 votes to 170 reinstated the alternative vote. The House of Lords insisted on their amendments, although they retreated from complete to partial P.R. The House of Commons again rejected P.R. (this time by 238–141) and once more by a majority of one vote (195–194) insisted upon the alternative vote. Finally, in the last hours of the session, a compromise was arranged. The alternative vote was abandoned and the Boundary Commissioners were instructed to prepare a limited scheme of P.R. to apply to 100 seats.

When the Boundary Commission produced the scheme, it was rejected by the House of Commons. Hardly any members in the areas affected by it supported it. Thus, on the first occasion that a fundamental change in the system of election was fully considered by Parliament, nothing was accomplished, although a parliamentary conference had unanimously recommended another system and although a substantial majority of the members of each House had, at some stage during the discussion of the Bill, voted for one or other of the proposed reforms in the system. It must be admitted, however, that the House of Lords' support for P.R. was a tactical move against the alternative vote rather than a sincere acceptance of the principle of P.R.

The Representation of the People Act of 1918 was a compromise. The Speaker's Conference by judicious management, the nature of which has not been fully revealed, obtained a measure of agreement so extraordinarily wide that substantial sacrifices must have been made on all sides. The terms of the

[3] The vote was:

				For the alternative vote	*Against*
Conservative	.	.		2	113
Liberal	.	.	.	98	13
Labour	.	.	.	17	..
Irish	.	.	.	10	..
				127	126

The Times, 11 Aug. 1917.

bargains were never made clear and provoked some argument, both during the passage of the Bill and in subsequent years. Moreover, as the debates on the individual clauses showed, the fact that the conference produced agreed resolutions did not greatly inhibit backbenchers from criticism of the conference's findings or the Government from modifying its stand on several points. The argument that constitutional change should always be by general agreement does not appear to have been much used; there was merely general satisfaction that the domestic harmony engendered by the war should offer so convenient an opportunity for settling so many vexatious questions.

IV. THE LEGACY OF THE 1918 ACT

There were some forebodings about the consequences of the 1918 Act. The electorate was more than doubled,[1] and many changes in electoral arrangements had been effected. In particular, there was anxiety about how women voters would behave. But the Act proved a triumph. Although the tone of British politics changed, and with it the way in which the elections were conducted, the change, at least in the latter, was as negative as it was gradual. Elections became calmer; petitions became much rarer; registration procedure became much more efficient; party machines became stronger; and the administrative machinery worked more smoothly.

The Act of 1918 was only modified in one important respect in the following twenty-five years, when, in 1928, the franchise for men and women was put on absolutely equal terms. It was further changed immediately after the Speaker's Conference in 1944, and it was largely superseded by the Representation of the People Act of 1948. But the Act of 1948, although it covered more pages in the Statute Book than its predecessor, did not alter it very substantially. The extension of absent voting, the limitation on motor-cars, and the abolition of all plural voting were the most radical innovations. Many of the clauses re-enacted the law of 1918 with only slight modifications.

However, the durability of the Act of 1918 does not mean that it settled all questions or that there is nothing to discuss about the subsequent working of the system. There was exten-

[1] The figures were: 1915: 8,357,648; 1918: 21,392,322.

sive skirmishing before the question of women's suffrage was settled on the only terms on which final settlement was possible. There was a more prolonged battle before the abolition of plural voting. There were many who refused to regard the failure of P.R. and the alternative vote in 1918 as final, and much was to be heard on the subject; the House of Commons was again to endorse the alternative vote, and, although as time went by a change in the system of election apparently receded from the range of practical politics, it was still being seriously spoken of by the Leader of the Conservative party in 1950.

One issue, not mentioned in 1918, was to assume growing importance in a machine age, and several attempts to limit the use of cars at election time were made before this was, to some extent, achieved by the Act of 1948. Disputes inevitably recurred about the proper maximum scales of expenses or about redistribution. All these matters, together with lesser issues like postal voting and compulsory voting, were sufficient to ensure that electoral questions should receive some share of parliamentary attention.

CHAPTER II

1918–29

I. THE PROBLEMS OF THE PERIOD

THE period from 1918 to 1929 was a confused one for British politics, especially in its first half. The 'coupon' election had left the party system in some disorder. It was not until 1923 that a clear alignment was restored and not until 1924 that the return to an overwhelmingly two-party system became unquestionably apparent. The confusion fostered lively politics and some interest in political reform. However, although there were demands for proportional representation, the electoral system, on the whole, received surprisingly little attention. By-elections were followed with exceptional interest. Three general elections took place within three years. Each party had some share of triumph and disaster. But, despite these vicissitudes, no widespread movement developed to change the system which played so large a role in provoking them. Proportional representation and the alternative vote were duly debated and each attracted appreciable support, but passions both inside and outside Parliament were little aroused. Rather more heat was engendered by another aspect of the 1918 settlement—the limitation of the female franchise to those over thirty. A prolonged battle was waged on this subject before the Government of the day found itself both able and willing to end all sex distinctions in the franchise. The battle was characterized by disagreements over the understandings arrived at in the Speaker's Conference, over the constitutional traditions about constitutional change, and over the meaning of election promises, disagreements of a kind that electoral legislation seems so easily to provoke. But even these seem to have created little public excitement. There was no organized lobbying, and the columns of the newspapers are surprisingly bare of comment or correspondence.

However, in the period from 1918 to 1929, Parliament did not. altogether neglect the arrangements by which it was elected. Twelve Acts were passed; seventeen Bills were at least discussed and a number more presented; 353 questions were asked of the Government about electoral administration or the possibility of electoral legislation. The Acts, it must be admitted, were almost all trivial administrative amendments to the Representation of the People Act of 1918: only the Equal Franchise Act was of major importance. The Bills, although some were only discussed under the ten-minute rule and others perished abruptly on the second reading, attracted some revealing discussion of electoral matters; eight were primarily concerned with the equalization of the franchise, four with changes in the system of election, and five with miscellaneous proposals ranging from abolishing the spring register to compulsory voting. Parliamentary questions covered a wide variety of topics; the cost and efficiency of the system of compiling and printing the register was the most frequent, but there were also constant and unrewarded questions from proponents of proportional representation and of franchise reform. However, despite the number of questions asked on electoral administration, the answers appear to have been satisfactory, and there was not one adjournment debate devoted to electoral matters.

The study of this period falls naturally under three heads— the fight to equalize the franchise; the attempt to modify the system of election; and the miscellaneous matters of lesser importance which arose.

II. THE EQUALIZATION OF THE FRANCHISE

The Representation of the People Act had given the vote to women over thirty if they were either local government electors or the wives of local government electors. There was no inherent reason why the age of thirty should have been chosen or why the parliamentary franchise of women, unlike that of men, should have been linked to a local government qualification. These limitations were arbitrarily agreed by the Speaker's Conference which, while accepting the principle of women's suffrage, was alarmed at the prospect of women being in an absolute majority.[1] It was found that these limitations would keep about

---

[1] It was not, however, in full agreement on the question. The report ran: 'The Conference decided by a majority that some measure of woman suffrage should be conferred. A majority was also of opinion that ... the most practical form would be to confer the vote in the terms of the following resolution: Any woman on the Local Government Register who has attained a specified age and the wife of any man who is on that Register if she has attained that age,

5 million women off the register and leave men in a majority
of about 4 million. The precise arguments used in deciding
where the line was to be drawn are shrouded in the secrecy
which veils the proceedings of a Speaker's Conference.[1] Even
the zealous proponents of women's suffrage accepted the settlement fairly meekly, but obviously so arbitrary a distinction
could not long be maintained. The election of 1918 made plain
that the dire fears expressed about the way in which women
would use their vote were groundless. Not a single woman
member came to Westminster, and there was no evidence that
women had behaved very differently from men. Moreover, the
Coalition Government in its election manifesto had said: 'It
will be the duty of the new Government to remove all existing
inequalities of the law as between men and women.'[2]

Early in the new Parliament the Labour party seized an
opportunity to introduce a private member's Bill for women's
emancipation. It was a simple Bill, putting women on an equal
basis with men as far as civil and judicial appointments, the
franchise, and admission to the House of Lords were concerned.
At the second reading,[3] issue was joined entirely on the franchise
clause. Mr. Adamson, who moved the Bill for the Labour party,
found supporters on all sides. Members professed themselves
bound by their election pledges and dilated lengthily on the
heroic war-work of women. None of the seven speakers who
opposed the Bill opposed women's suffrage, and only one suggested that equalization of the franchise was not ultimately

shall be entitled to be registered and to vote as a parliamentary elector. Various
ages were discussed of which 30 and 35 received most favour.' *Cd. 8463/1917*,
Section VIII.

[1] Mr. Dickinson in the 1918 debates gave a plausible account of the
mathematics which led the conference to accept a scheme which would enfranchise just over half the women in the country. Equal franchise for all
women over thirty would have included 10 million new voters. Cautious members of the conference thought this too many, and so the local government
qualification was added in order to reduce the number to 6 million. Short of
giving the full vote, this was an acceptable compromise. 'You practically give
to women what men were first of all given in former years; you give them a
household franchise.' *H.C. Deb. 94*, cc. 1816–24.

In point of fact, the Act of 1918 gave 8½ million women the vote, while
something over 5 million were left disfranchised. See *H.C. Deb. 117*, c. 1847.

[2] *The Times*, 22 Nov. 1918.

[3] *H.C. Deb. 114*, cc. 1561 et seq.

desirable. Only two serious arguments were used. The first was that the Speaker's Conference was a compromise in which all sides had yielded some principle; its findings should not thus be put aside within a few months of their enactment. The second, which was more strongly pressed, was that a change in the franchise must constitutionally be followed by an immediate general election—which was, at that time, most undesirable; however, most of those who opposed the women's franchise clause hoped that it would be reintroduced and enacted immediately before that Parliament was dissolved. Dr. Addison, President of the Local Government Board, accepted the arguments that the passage of the clause would make a general election unavoidable and that it was improper to reopen the franchise question after a mere six months. However, he asked that the Bill should have a second reading so that it could be revised in committee and its other provisions enacted. The closure was then carried by 119 votes to 32, and the Bill was given a second reading.

In view of the Government's statement, it was a great surprise that no amendments were offered when the Bill came before Standing Committee E, and it was reported out without discussion. This could only mean that the Government intended to kill the Bill. Major Astor, Parliamentary Secretary to the Ministry of Health, made this plain when, at the third reading,[1] he moved the Bill's rejection, explaining that the Government had, on grounds of drafting, decided not to amend it but to substitute a Bill of their own on exactly the same lines but without the suffrage clause; again their case was that they could not countenance so speedy a modification of the 1918 Act or the immediate election that the change would necessitate. This statement evoked protests from all sides of the House. Only five speakers defended the Government and only one of them took the line of downright opposition to equalizing the franchise or of denying that the phrase about equality in the coalition manifesto had included the suffrage. Fourteen speakers attacked the procedure and policy of the Government over the Bill. No new arguments were adduced, but there were several appeals for a free vote on the question. Mr. H. A. L. Fisher, President of the

[1] *H.C. Deb. 117*, cc. 1283 et seq.

Board of Education, in reply, refused to take off the whips. It would be impossible to pass so ill-drafted a Bill; the election pledge did not, he claimed, apply to the franchise; that question could not be reopened now. But, to the general surprise, when the division came, the Government was defeated by 100 votes to 88. Forty-seven coalition members rebelled against the Cabinet. *The Times* took occasion to rejoice that the days were past when Governments resigned on a single defeat, but it firmly endorsed equal suffrage.[1]

On 22 July, two days before Lord Kimberley was due to move the second reading of the Bill in the House of Lords, Lord Birkenhead, the Lord Chancellor, anticipated him with a Government Bill which, as promised, contained all the provisions of the private measure except the suffrage clause.[2] Debate was mainly focused on the clause entitling peeresses to sit—a clause subsequently eliminated in committee—and the suffrage question received as scant attention as it did two days later when Lord Kimberley moved the second reading of the original Bill; Lord Birkenhead was so crushing that it was defeated without a division or any further discussion. When the Government Bill came to be considered in committee in the House of Commons in October,[3] an attempt to insert a suffrage clause was disallowed, on the ground that the vote was a qualification not a disqualification, and, therefore, could not fall within the scope of a Bill designed to remove disqualifications. So ended the first attempt to grant the franchise on equal terms.

The fight was resumed the next year. Another Labour member, Mr. Grundy, introduced a Bill which not only equalized the franchise but also abolished plural voting. In addition, it included two minor provisions—the enfranchisement of those under twenty-one who had been given a vote as servicemen in 1918 but who had lost it on demobilization, and the abolition of the registration fee for the university franchise. The second reading argument[4] was concentrated on women's enfranchisement and followed familiar lines. However, the opposition was more vocal than the year before. Many of the members who

[1] *The Times*, 5 July 1919.   [2] *H.L. Deb. 35*, c. 891.
[3] *H.C. Deb. 120*, cc. 343 et seq.
[4] *H.C. Deb. 125*, cc. 2067 et seq.

spoke for the measure specifically limited their support to the equalization clause and hoped that the business vote could be preserved at the committee stage. Those who spoke against included several frank opponents of further extension of the suffrage, together with some who protested against hiding behind petticoats to attack the business vote. A contention that the bargain arrived at in the Speaker's Conference must be honoured brought the rejoinder that any bargain there may have been was torn up by the failure to implement the proportional representation recommendations. Dr. Addison, speaking for the Government, was diffident and non-committal; perhaps the question of the business vote could be reconsidered in committee; equalization of the franchise was a big change, but the Government would allow a free vote on the question; he personally was for it. Some attempt was made to talk the Bill out, but finally the Speaker accepted a closure motion which was carried by 122 votes to 38 and the Bill was then given a second reading without a division and sent to Standing Committee D. The proceedings there[1] show the opposition to have been much stronger than the second reading debate had suggested. The Bill lingered in committee for more than three months owing, primarily, to the frankly obstructionist tactics of that past master of the art, Sir Frederick Banbury. An amendment to limit equalization to women over thirty found 13 Conservative supporters and 21 opponents drawn from all parties. A similar amendment setting the age at twenty-five occupied three meetings before being defeated by 15 votes to 6. The committee then decided to adjourn discussion of the Bill as it had no hope of passage. A storm in the Commons at the way in which the Government had aided and abetted this slaughter led to the Bill being taken up again.[2] The next sitting was devoted to the discussion of an age limit of twenty-four and the next to an age

[1] The verbatim report of the committee's proceedings is mysteriously absent both from the British Museum and from the House of Commons Library. What follows is based on the official record of their proceedings (*Parliamentary Papers 1920*, vol. viii, p. 477) and some very brief reports in *The Times*.

[2] *The Times*, 28 Apr. 1920. Sir Kingsley Wood, who represented the Government on the committee, apparently adopted a much more hostile attitude to the Bill than Dr. Addison, his superior at the Ministry of Health, had done on the second reading.

limit of twenty-three. After a few further amendments, discussion moved to proposed new clauses. Here there was even more ample scope for obstruction, and, as Sir Frederick Banbury showed no signs of tiring, Mr. Grundy finally admitted defeat and moved that the Bill be not further proceeded with.

The only consequence of the Bill was a one-clause Government Bill, which was passed into law without any discussion, enfranchising war-time ex-servicemen under twenty-one. Very few can have been affected by this Act.[1] All those who had voted in 1918 must have been twenty-one by the time of the 1922 election. At the very most a few hundred extra votes may have been cast in the by-elections of 1920 and 1921.

In the next three years no private member with a reasonable place on the ballot introduced a women's franchise Bill. The only attempts at legislation on the subject were two Bills brought in under the ten-minute rule. On 8 March 1922[2] Lord Robert Cecil introduced the question, avowedly to force a division on the subject. He charged the Government with breach of faith and said that four years' experience had clearly exploded all the old fears about the consequences of women's suffrage. His Bill was given a first reading by 208 votes to 60. On 25 April 1923[3] Mr. Isaac Foot introduced a similar Bill which, despite formal opposition, received a first reading without even a division. But, of course, it could get no farther. In 1922 and 1923 the Government was pressed a number of times at question time about its legislative intentions. The invariable answer was that equal franchise was not being considered or that it was too soon after the Act of 1918 for any change to be made.

In view of the zeal of the Labour party for equal franchise and the end of plural voting, which had been unequivocally expressed both in its party conferences and in its election manifestos for many years, it was surprising that these matters should have been left to a private member after the first Labour Government was formed in 1924. On 18 January Mr. Adamson[4]

---

[1] 10 & 11 Geo. 5, ch. 15.
[2] *H.C. Deb. 151*, c. 1286.
[3] *H.C. Deb. 163*, c. 469.
[4] Not Mr. William Adamson, M.P. for West Fife, who had introduced the 1919 Bill and who was now Secretary of State for Scotland, but Mr. William Murdoch Adamson, M.P. for Cannock.

introduced a Bill[1] providing for the equalization of the franchise for men and women, for the assimilation of the local and parliamentary franchises, and for the abolition of the business vote. He stressed that he was primarily interested in equalization and that he left the other issues to the discretion of the House; several other supporters of the Bill argued that its scope should be reduced in committee. In the debate, the proponents merely restated the case for equality at great length and pointed out that none of the forebodings about women's suffrage had been justified. Mr. Clynes, the Lord Privy Seal, said that the Government was sympathetic to the Bill but that no facilities could be promised for it, if it emerged from the committee stage. The Duchess of Atholl, leading the opposition to the Bill, moved a reasoned rejection, refusing to consider reform until another Speaker's Conference had been held. She, like subsequent opponents of the Bill, made much of the attempt to end the business vote and to assimilate the local and parliamentary franchises surreptitiously while focusing attention on votes for women. She argued that women did not want the franchise extended, and that to have more women than men on the register would be to take advantage of the 740,000 men killed in the war. Several speakers advocated equal franchise at twenty-five and not at twenty-one. Lady Astor, one of the two Conservatives to speak for the Bill, poured scorn on her own party, and, as usual in debates on this subject, provided the liveliest speech of the day. In the end, the rejection motion was defeated by 288 votes to 72. The votes against the Bill were entirely Conservative, but so were fifty of the votes in its support.

The most interesting feature of this debate was a speech by Sir William Bull, who gave a detailed but controversial account of how the compromise settlement was reached in 1917 and asserted that the compromise was binding for ten years. He claimed that, in 1917, there had appeared no real hope of the conference settling the problem, but he had been approached by a leader of the suffrage movement who, to his surprise, had said that she would be satisfied with the franchise at forty. Sir William Bull had replied: '"Is (that) the thin end of the wedge? If you get it at forty, will you immediately agitate for something

[1] *H.C. Deb. 170*, cc. 859 et seq.

further?" She said ". . . this deputation represents the leading women's franchise societies . . . there would be no agitation for a reasonable time". I think ten years was suggested.' Later, in drafting the Bill, the age had been reduced to thirty.[1] Two other M.P.s who had been at the conference pointed out that it had not agreed definitely on any age and denied that the conference findings were binding. It seems that from this uncertain account of events seven years previously the myth of a ten-year truce arose. Before this debate, no reference to it can be traced. After it, the question of women's suffrage was never discussed without some reference to the subject.[2] At first, only the opponents of equal franchise used it as an argument, but before long its advocates, while denying that any such agreement was binding, began to refer to it as an historical fact. Strong evidence can be adduced against Sir William Bull's account. After the matter had been raised during the standing committee proceedings on the Bill, Dame Millicent Fawcett wrote indignantly to *The Times*, explaining that she had led the deputation of suffrage societies to see the Prime Minister in 1917 to demand complete equality. She asserted that they had persuaded Parliament to modify the conference report and to give the vote to the wives of local government electors.[3] The inaccuracy of this statement[4] perhaps makes suspect the categorical assertion which followed: there had been no word of 'an honourable obligation to remain petrified for ten years'. She concluded her letter by pointing out that Lord Curzon, a member of the Government in 1918, had said, 'Who can expect this illogical compromise to last more than a few years?' Dame Millicent Fawcett might have quoted from later in the same speech. Lord Curzon, an opponent of

[1] *H.C. Deb. 170*, c. 898.

[2] In the standing committee discussion of the 1924 Bill no fewer than four Conservative speakers referred to the ten-year agreement as an established fact: e.g. Lt.-Col. Fremantle (*Standing Committee Reports 1924*, c. 531): 'Most of us upon this side who favour a further extension of the franchise find a difficulty in the fact that an honourable agreement was arrived at by the Speaker's Conference to keep the franchise steady for ten years'; and Lord Eustace Percy (ibid., c. 534): 'I do not think that the 1918 Act would have been passed in that form but for that understanding.'

[3] *The Times*, 6 June 1924.

[4] The conference itself had, in fact, recommended giving the vote to the wives of local government electors. See above, p. 15, note 1.

women's suffrage, went on to say that, of course, the suffrage
societies would continue agitation. The settlement could not
last. 'In my judgement not twenty, not fifteen, and not ten
years will pass' before complete equalization.[1] There is apparently no evidence whatever for the ten-year moratorium,
apart from Sir William Bull's quotation: 'I think ten years was
suggested.'[2]

The Bill occupied Standing Committee A for five days.[3] The
first meeting was devoted to open bargaining. The Conservatives said that, on the second reading, the closure had been
accepted on the understanding that the Bill would be stripped
of all except equal franchise. Mr. Adamson replied that he was
willing to abandon everything else if the Conservatives would
promise to support equal franchise *at twenty-one*. Mr. Henderson, the Home Secretary, announced that, if the Bill were reduced to workable proportions, the Government would see it
through its later stages. After some confused exchanges, the
committee adjourned for a week so that matters could be
arranged in more decent privacy. When they reassembled, Mr.
Adamson announced that everything except equal franchise had
been abandoned. Lord Eustace Percy stressed that the Conservatives were bound by no bargain and felt free to alter the age
from twenty-one. This provoked some sharp accusations of
Conservative treachery before the committee turned to the
amendments. It began by accepting, without a division, an
amendment giving the vote to the wives of business voters—
astonishingly enough without any speech or protest from Labour
about a change which would almost double the business vote.
Next, Lord Eustace Percy moved that the operation of the Bill
should be delayed until 1928 in order to honour the ten-year
understanding about the Speaker's Conference settlement. This
amendment was withdrawn after extensive charges of obstruc-
tionism had been made. He then moved that the voting age for

[1] *H.L. Deb.* 27, c. 513.
[2] Further evidence against the suggestion that the suffrage societies agreed
to a period of quiescence may be found in the message read to the Labour
Party Conference in June 1918 from the National Union of Women's Suffrage
Societies. This thanked the Labour party for its help in the struggle and
assured it of the N.U.W.S.S.'s 'firm intention of working for complete
equality'. [3] *Standing Committee Reports 1924*, cc. 490 et seq.

everyone should be raised to twenty-five, on the ground that
the electorate was growing too large, and that twenty-one was
too young for balanced judgement. His suggestion was ridiculed
by Conservatives as much as anyone, but it was only defeated
by 25 votes to 11, 10 Conservatives supporting it and 7 opposing.
Most of the rest of the committee discussion was devoted to
drafting and technical points. An attempt to allow electors to
vote on both their university and their business qualification
was defeated by 17 votes to 16. A new clause, setting up a Redistribution Commission, was defeated by 23 votes to 18, Labour
and Liberal on one side, Conservatives on the other, on the
ground that it would overload the Bill. The Conservatives made
out a case for redistribution so much more emphatic than at any
other time in the inter-war period—although, in 1924, the
anomalies were relatively small—that the charge that this was a
wrecking clause seems to have some justification. The Home
Secretary said firmly that the franchise must not be tied to redistribution, for a conference must precede the latter. A clause
to relax the law on registration for those who moved between
neighbouring constituencies was accepted, but another, designed to give two votes to those over forty, disappeared amid
general ridicule.

The Bill was reported out of committee on 19 June, but no
time for its discussion was found before the summer recess, and,
when the House reassembled in the autumn, its whole attention
was occupied with the debate on the Campbell case, which led
to the Government's defeat and to the election of 1924.

In that election, franchise questions hardly attracted attention, but Mr. Baldwin did explicitly say:

The Unionist Party are in favour of equal political rights for men
and women, and desire that the question of the extension of the
franchise should, if possible, be settled by agreement. With this in
view, they would, if returned to power, propose that the matter be
referred to a Conference of all political parties on the lines of the
Ullswater [*sic*] Committee.[1]

The Labour party seized an early opportunity to raise the
matter in the new Parliament, and, on 20 February 1925, Mr.
Whitely used his place on the ballot to move the second reading

[1] *The Times*, 18 Oct. 1924.

of a Bill whose only substantive provision was to give women the vote on the same terms as men. The debate[1] touched much less than previous ones on the merits of the question. As its opponents constantly reiterated, all parties were committed to the Bill. The argument was largely a dog-fight on political ethics—the sanctity of election promises, the sanctity of the 1917 compromise, the necessity for an inter-party conference before making any change, the necessity of an election following any change,[2] the propriety of such a change being made by a private member's Bill, and the parliamentary manners of the Government in intervening heavily on a private members' day. On the Labour and Liberal side it was denied that such a Bill need be preceded by a conference or followed by an election, just as it was denied that there was a binding ten-year moratorium agreed in 1917; it was also pointed out that, if there was such an agreement, the next election would probably not be until more than ten years after the last Representation of the People Act and that the operation of the Bill could be delayed until then. Mr. Henderson charged the Government with obstructing the Bill in order to keep to themselves at a later date the credit for enfranchising the flappers.

Sir William Joynson-Hicks moved that the House should reject a Bill: 'involving as it would a General Election . . . (and) records its opinion that a considered scheme of franchise reform should be brought before the House . . . within the lifetime of the present Parliament'.[3] He promised that a conference would be set up, not that year, but in 1926.[4] When pressed further about the Prime Minister's election pledge, he said:

'We do mean to carry out that pledge . . . the Prime Minister adheres to his statement. . . .' (Hon. members: 'When?') 'It will be carried out by this Parliament' . . .

Lady Astor: 'Does the Right Honourable Gentleman mean equal votes at twenty-one?'

The Home Secretary: 'It means exactly what it says.' (Hon.

---

[1] *H.C. Deb. 180*, cc. 1479 et seq.

[2] It is strange that this argument was not heard in 1924, although in 1919, 1920, and again in 1925 it was extensively used. The political uncertainty in 1924, or the Conservative willingness for an election since they were in opposition, presumably provides the explanation.

[3] Ibid., c. 1496.   [4] Ibid., c. 1515.

members: 'Answer.') 'No, it would be wrong for me to prejudge the views which honourable members opposite may put before the Conference. It means that a Conference will be held. . . . The Prime Minister's pledge is for equal rights and at the next election. I will say quite definitely that means no difference will take place in the ages at which men and women go to the poll at the next election.'[1]

The Government's supporters mostly professed belief in equal franchise, but many preferred twenty-five to twenty-one; it was argued that Parliament had at least four years to run and that there was no hurry. Only the Senior Burgess for Oxford University, Sir Charles Oman, came out in flat opposition to the principle of the Bill, describing the enfranchisement of women in 1918 as a villainy in which the nation was not consulted, and saying that he was not afraid of anomalies or impressed by the word equality, but that he was afraid of lowering the quality of the electorate, as this, 'the largest change ever asked for', would do. His speech is remarkable as one of the very few in the post-war era which damned the whole trend of franchise extension. Perhaps it provides an argument for the security and independent judgement made possible by university representation; for only in the House of Lords were similar views expressed. Mr. Baldwin spoke briefly at the end of the debate, saying that the Government only intervened on private members' days when private members introduced Government Bills. The House must 'wait and see' what legislation on the subject the Government intended to bring in. The Government won the day by 220 votes to 153, but Lady Astor, the only Conservative to speak for the Bill, carried nine other Conservatives with her into the lobby.

The subject attracted considerable discussion during the next two years, but, although further Bills were introduced, none was high enough on the ballot to be debated. In March 1926 the Secretary of the National Union of Societies for Equal Citizenship was protesting that the Prime Minister had not indicated whether the Home Secretary's promise of a conference in 1926 would be fulfilled.[2] A few days later the Home Secretary was speaking of the conference probably taking place the following year.[3] In April a national conference of women Unionists

---

[1] *H.C. Deb. 180*, c. 1504.   [2] *The Times*, 2 Mar. 1926.
[3] *The Times*, 5 Mar. 1926.

defeated a motion demanding equal franchise at twenty-one and substituted one demanding it at twenty-five.[1] By January 1927 the societies demanding equal citizenship were protesting more vehemently and pointing out that, with the delay involved in compiling the register, action would soon be too late for the next election. When the new session of Parliament was opened on 7 February 1927, the Address contained no reference to franchise legislation. Several Opposition speakers accused the Government of attempting to go back on their promises, while, from the Conservative side, Lady Astor[2] said that she was beginning to suspect the intentions of the Government. What had the Lord Chancellor meant by referring to it as 'a very difficult question'? The only reply from the Government was 'wait and see'. On 8 March Mr. Baldwin received a deputation led by Lady Astor on behalf of the Equal Political Rights Campaign Committee, and promised a statement before Easter. About this time a Cabinet committee to consider the question was set up under the Home Secretary. *The Times* parliamentary correspondent alleged that, despite the demand of some ministers for a higher age, it had decided that equal franchise at twenty-one must be granted.[3] On 4 April Mr. Snowden remarked in a speech that 'the matter was at the present moment causing the keenest dissension in the Cabinet, accompanied by threats of resignation'.[4] At the same time, a leading article in *The Times* reflected the lack of enthusiasm that the question excited among many on the Government side. There was not much to be said for the change, but there was nothing left for the Government but to put a good face on it.

It would be just possible, no doubt, to treat Sir William Joynson-Hicks as an eccentric and unrepresentative individual or to suppose that the Prime Minister's remarks [in 1924] foreshadowed a higher voting age all round. But whatever may have been the case two years ago, when there was time for conference and consideration, these expedients will hardly hold water now. Unless the policy with which the Unionist Party went to the country in 1924 is to be regarded as a mere expression of academic sympathy, the Prime Minister cannot now be divorced from his colleague. [A reference to the Home Secretary's pledge in 1925.]

[1] *The Times*, 30 Apr. 1926.
[2] *H.C. Deb. 202*, c. 206.
[3] *The Times*, 10 Mar. 1927.
[4] *The Times*, 5 Apr. 1927.

But *The Times* went on to remark wistfully that income-tax payer suffrage would be preferable.[1] At last, on 14 April the Government announced its intention of introducing a Bill giving equal franchise at twenty-one in the following session.

Before the decision was reached there had apparently been some private negotiations with the Labour party over the holding of a last-minute conference; the *Manchester Guardian*[2] reported that on 5 April the parliamentary Labour party had decided that 'no good purpose would be served' by a conference, and on 19 April Mr. MacDonald said in a speech: 'when Mr. Baldwin suggested that I should join in a conference on the extension of the franchise, he put it in such a way that it was almost a condition of my acceptance that I should agree to 25 instead of 21.'[3]

There is no doubt that Mr. Snowden was right when he spoke of keen dissension within the Cabinet, and it seems probable that *The Times* leader-writer had some information about its nature. There are several sources which throw light on what happened, the most remarkable being a letter from Lord Birkenhead to a recent Cabinet colleague, Lord Irwin, who was then Viceroy of India.

April 13th, 1927.

The Cabinet went mad yesterday and decided to give votes to women at the age of twenty-one. Every speaker was against the proposal on its merits. It was universally conceded that there was no demand for change in the country. We were nevertheless to be precluded from voting according to our convictions by a pledge which our light-hearted colleague, the Home Secretary, had given on a Private Member's Bill on a Friday, with the Prime Minister sitting beside him. It was not even argued that any Cabinet decision had authorised a change so dangerous and so revolutionary. But against the strong protest of Winston, myself and others, it was decided that we were such honourable men that we could not possibly fall short of a pledge which was delivered without even the pretence of consulting the Cabinet.[4]

[1] *The Times*, 11 Apr. 1927.
[2] *The Manchester Guardian*, 14 Apr. 1927.
[3] *Daily Mail*, 20 Apr. 1928.
[4] Quoted in *Frederick Edwin, Earl of Birkenhead*, by his son (London, 1935), vol. ii, p. 291.

Mr. Churchill later expressed his opinion on much the same lines:

The Conservative Party, especially its strongest elements, were much opposed to such a step. It would never have been carried through Mr. Baldwin's Cabinet if the ordinary processes of reasonable discussion and conclave had been followed. But here was a private member's Bill, debated on a Friday. No-one took it very seriously. It fell to 'Jix' to wind up the debate. Interrupted by Lady Astor, he quite unexpectedly, and without the slightest consultation with his colleagues, said that the Conservative Party would enfranchise men and women on the same terms 'at the next election'. Two years later this formidable gesture had to be redeemed. Never was so great a change in our electorate achieved so incontinently.[1]

Mr. Neville Chamberlain, too, appears to have been unhappy. Professor Feiling writes:

He [Chamberlain] had held out some prospect of an all-party settlement of the franchise, so that men and women might exercise it on equal terms. But Joynson-Hicks proceeded to enlarge this theme so generously in public that (the Cabinet) found themselves committed to votes for women at twenty-one at the very next election. Like the majority of ministers, Chamberlain deemed that there was 'no escape' but some thought this suicide for the party, while Birkenhead, who admitted the pledge, protested that he must have a 'last kick'.[2]

The Cabinet disagreements were virtually admitted in public later in the year when the Attorney-General, Sir Douglas Hogg,[3] spoke dubiously of the change as 'an immense experiment',[4] and Mr. Churchill frankly stated[5] that he would have been glad if it could have been put off until a later period, but that the Government could not allow itself to be accused of a breach of faith.[6]

[1] Article in the *Sunday Pictorial*, 9 Aug. 1931.
[2] *Life of Neville Chamberlain*, by Keith Feiling (London, 1946), p. 163.
[3] The Attorney-General was in the Cabinet at this time. During the following year Sir Douglas Hogg accepted the title of Viscount Hailsham on becoming Lord Chancellor.
[4] *The Times*, 5 Nov. 1927.   [5] *The Times*, 25 Oct. 1927.
[6] There is no doubt that Lord Birkenhead overstated the case when he said that every member of the Cabinet was opposed to the change. It is not possible to trace the attitude of each of the nineteen ministers who, according to *The Times* of 12 Apr., attended this meeting. However, in addition to the Home Secretary Sir Philip Cunliffe-Lister certainly favoured the granting of equal votes at the age of twenty-one. Sir Samuel Hoare, too, had in 1919

Sir William Joynson-Hicks's biographer denies that he was especially responsible for the Bill and says that he resented bitterly the blame which subsequently fell on him for the results of the 1929 election from those who attributed the Conservative defeat to the flapper vote. He especially resented the fact that none of his Cabinet colleagues came to his defence or acknowledged their share of responsibility for what was, after all, a Cabinet decision.[1]

It certainly seems hard that he should have been attacked. In 1925 he made no promise on age. The most that he did was to assume that Mr. Baldwin's election pledge referred to the current Parliament—and, unless otherwise stated, it is not unreasonable to assume that such a promise refers to the immediate and not to the indefinite future.[2] In any case, this was no new or revolutionary proposal, and many Conservatives had long since committed themselves to equality at twenty-one. If the Cabinet's hostility to the measure was as great as Lord Birkenhead implies, it is surprising that Mr. Baldwin should have originally made the pledge without any apparent public or private protest, and it is equally surprising that no minister should have resigned either when the pledge was confirmed in 1925 or when the Bill was decided upon in 1927.

After the announcement of the Government's intentions, Lord Rothermere launched a violent campaign against 'the flapper

spoken vigorously for a similar proposal and had defied his party whips to support it; he had later voted for it in 1924. There is no reason to suppose that he had changed his views. On the other hand, from reports of speeches and other sources, there seems ground for believing that Lord Birkenhead's attitude had some support from Mr. Churchill, Sir Douglas Hogg, Lord Eustace Percy, Sir Laming Worthington-Evans, Mr. Neville Chamberlain, and Mr. Amery. Of those whose attitude on this question cannot be traced, it is not unreasonable to suppose that a majority, including Lord Salisbury and Sir Austen Chamberlain, were also reluctant to make the change. But there must have been varying degrees of reluctance. Only a few can have been, like Lord Birkenhead and Mr. Churchill, so irreconcilably hostile to the proposal that they were seriously prepared to repudiate the pledges which had been given or to launch upon the unpopular course of disfranchising men between twenty-one and twenty-five.

[1] See H. A. Taylor, *Jix, Viscount Brentford* (London, 1933), pp. 280–5.

[2] It should perhaps be mentioned, for what it is worth, that one member of the 1925 Cabinet recalls that the Home Secretary went to the 1925 debate without Cabinet instructions on equal franchise because, owing to lunch, that part of the Cabinet agenda had never been reached.

vote' in the *Daily Mail*, while in the more genteel columns of
The Times many correspondents advocated raising the age from
twenty-one to twenty-five.

In the autumn discussion of the subject flared up once more.
On 4 October *The Times* again took the Government to task for
having set up no conference or inquiry into the question. But it
went on to justify the proposed legislation on the ground that
the Conservatives might just as well anticipate a policy which
their opponents would inevitably enact if they got power. On
6 October the Conservative Annual Conference rejected a motion
for raising the age to twenty-five and endorsed the Government's action.[1] But, in the following month, several Conservative leaders found it necessary to refer to feeling against the
flapper vote, to 'grousing', and to 'misunderstanding and exaggeration'.

In March 1928 the Bill was finally introduced. The National
Union of Societies for Equal Citizenship, which had so long
viewed Mr. Baldwin with unveiled suspicion, cheered him
heartily at a demonstration held in Queen's Hall to mark the
occasion. *The Times* had, by now, adopted a much less equivocal
position. 'There has never been anything logically defensible in
withholding the vote from women under thirty since the day
when enfranchisement was granted', it commented, and it added
an unwitting commentary on the Representation of the People
Act to be passed twenty years later when it said that the Equal
Franchise Act would be 'the last of the political Reform Acts.
No other in this succession is possible. . . .'[2]

The Bill, as introduced, had two substantive provisions. The
first two clauses gave the parliamentary and local franchises on
equal terms to men and women; and the fourth clause provided
that women could vote on their husbands' business qualification.

The Bill received its second reading on 29 March.[3] Sir
William Joynson-Hicks, in moving the Bill, set the lofty but
slightly uncertain tone which characterized the whole debate.
This was not an Act of expediency but of justice: there was no
'women's vote', so that there was no reason to worry about

[1] *The Times*, 7 Oct. 1927.   [2] *The Times*, 14 Mar. 1928.
[3] *H.C. Deb. 215*, cc. 1359 et seq.

having a majority of women in the electorate; of the 5½ million women to be enfranchised, one-third were over thirty,[1] and half the remainder had the responsibilities of marriage; if some of the young women were uneducated, it would not be the first time there had been uneducated people on the register. On the Labour side, the Bill received a slightly ironical welcome. Mr. Snowden twitted the Conservatives for their past and present lack of enthusiasm for it and for securing equality by giving the business vote to spouses of business voters rather than by abolishing the business vote. For the diehards, Sir George Cockerill moved a reasoned rejection, regretting a Bill which gave women a majority in the electorate and which contained no provision for comprehensive franchise reform or for redistribution. The debate was one of the least inspired of the many debates on female suffrage. The opposition, although few in number, was given its full opportunity, and eight of the twelve members who finally divided the House against the Bill spoke in defence of their action. Their arguments were conflicting, but, in the main, were protests against women being put in a permanent majority and against an action for which there was no mandate; one or two were for equal franchise at twenty-five, and several regretted the absence of any clauses disfranchising undesirable voters, such as the recipients of poor relief. The supporters of the Bill merely produced the expected eulogies of women and offered widely divergent opinions about how the newly enfranchised electors would vote. Several members were concerned about election expenses, which would be proportionately increased by the increase in electorate.[2] Mr. Henderson criticized the Government for being so dilatory; if the Bill had been introduced earlier, there would have been time for redistribution and a better preparation of the enlarged register; a Speaker's Conference could have gone into the question of cars on election day and plural voting. Mr. Baldwin, in reply, explained that there had been no conference because the Speaker had declined to preside over one; 'as party controversy had been renewed since 1918, he felt that, in order to preserve the

---

[1] i.e. those older women who had no local government qualification either in their own right or through their husbands.

[2] See below, pp. 54–55.

impartial position of the Chair, he would prefer not to preside at such a conference'.[1] However, while some matters might usefully have been discussed by a conference, there was no need for one on the franchise question; the parties were agreed. The House then voted by 387 to 10 in favour of the Bill. Subsequent allegations of widespread Conservative abstention were convincingly refuted.[2]

When the Bill came before a committee of the whole House,[3] the Chairman ruled that any discussion of the general merits of plural voting was out of order, and only three important points arose on this stage. The first was an attempt to raise the age from twenty-one to twenty-five. There were a few vehement speeches in favour of this from the Government back benches; they ranged from those of members who did not really approve of the amendment but were willing to vote for anything that would damage a Bill enfranchising women to those of proponents of equal suffrage who none the less thought youth irresponsible. The Opposition left the Conservatives to fight among themselves, until the Home Secretary ended the argument by pointing out that the proposal would disfranchise 2½ million men; it was a prehistoric amendment which would deprive men of a right they had had for 500 years. The amendment was then defeated by 359 votes to 16.[4]

The second major committee debate arose when the Labour party sought to delete the paragraph enabling spouses of voters with business qualifications to vote twice at general elections.[5] It was argued that it was not necessary to increase plural voting by 200,000 in order to equalize the franchise. Sir John Simon, for the Liberals, pointed out that in 1918 women were put on the

---

[1] *H.C. Deb. 215*, c. 1471.

[2] *The Times*, 31 Mar. 1928.

[3] *H.C. Deb. 216*, cc. 205 et seq.

[4] This amendment was on the subject which predominated in all discussions of the Bill. Lord Rothermere's campaign and the extensive use of the phrase 'the flapper vote' helped to focus attention almost entirely on the 1½ million women under twenty-five who would gain the vote. No reference was made to the equal number between twenty-five and thirty or to the 2 million over thirty who were involved.

[5] Under the 1918 Act they had been allowed to qualify for the register wherever their husbands had a local government vote, but they were only allowed to vote once on such a qualification. That limitation was now to be removed to eliminate from the law any phrase implying inequality.

register, *qua* spouses, solely because the formula 'wives of local government electors' had offered a simple way of limiting the extension of the franchise; there was no reason now why that kind of qualification should be preserved, let alone extended. The Government rejected the amendment on the ground that it would take away an existing right; moreover, if a bachelor with a business vote married, his responsibilities doubled, and it was right that his family voting strength should be doubled too. Despite further opposition protests, the amendment was defeated by 208 votes to 138.[1]

The third matter, and the one which occupied most of the committee's time, was the question of election expenses. This is dealt with in a later section.[2]

At the report stage, Mr. Snowden moved an amendment, which had been out of order in committee, to abolish all plural voting except for the universities. In 1885 the property qualification had given way to the residential qualification; now it was more than ever out of date and it should not be retained, still less increased, as this Bill threatened. The Home Secretary replied that only 450,000 votes were involved and that the Bill could not be used as an instrument of disfranchisement. The Labour party had not objected in 1924 when the same provision had been inserted into Mr. Adamson's Bill in committee. Mr. Snowden protested that they had kept silent only in order to save the Bill.[3] However, the amendment met its inevitable defeat, 216 Conservatives overriding 78 Liberal and Labour members. Shortly afterwards the Bill received a silent third reading and was sent to the House of Lords.

On the second reading there,[4] Lord Hailsham (formerly Sir

---

[1] It is interesting to note that, in 1944, when the spouses' business qualification was again discussed, even so right-wing a Conservative as Sir Herbert Williams described it as 'logically impossible to defend' (*H.C. Deb.* 406, c. 1660). However, this provision in the 1928 Act provided the Conservatives with an extra counter to bargain with in the Speaker's Conference sixteen years later. See pp. 113–14 below.

[2] See pp. 54–55 below.

[3] See above, p. 23. Mr. Snowden's protest is not altogether convincing. It is certainly strange that no protest was made by Labour members when the provision was inserted, but there is nothing in the committee's proceedings to suggest that this was due to deliberate restraint and not to inadvertence.

[4] *H.L. Deb. 71*, cc. 160 et seq.

Douglas Hogg), who was now Lord Chancellor, explained that, owing to the impracticability of a Speaker's Conference, all contentious matters had been omitted. But, none the less, the Lords proceeded to give the Bill a much more disputed passage than the Commons had done. Lord Banbury, who as Sir Frederick Banbury had been famed as a chronic opponent of all legislative change, found substantial support for his rejection motion. Frank hostility was expressed to any increase in the electorate and to every form of female suffrage. A female electorate increased the tendency of parties to indulge in mass bribery; the Bill was a dangerous gamble; there was no mandate; the Conservative party was being committed to the change merely because of an *obiter dictum* of the Prime Minister. One peer quoted an M.P. who had told him that he was against the Bill but that the word had been given that it was not to be criticized. In reply to the debate, Lord Birkenhead could not conceal his hostility to the principle involved, and, in a remarkable speech, he illustrated the reluctance with which the Bill was welcomed. Of course, the Cabinet had not all the same degree of enthusiasm for it, but that was the case with all legislation. He was, and always had been, against female suffrage, but he had stayed in the Cabinet which had granted female suffrage in 1918 and he was now staying in the Cabinet which was extending it. One could not resign every time one was in a minority in the Cabinet. The House of Lords would commit suicide if it rejected what was an inevitable Bill. It should vote for it with 'resolute resignation'. After this endorsement of the Bill, coupled with so notable an exposition of the doctrine of Cabinet responsibility, the Bill was given a second reading by 114 votes to 35.

At the committee stage,[1] the only important discussion was on an amendment to put the age of voting for women at twenty-five. Lord Newton argued for this, on the ground that women should not be allowed to constitute a majority in the electorate and that men had had to wait 600 years for full adult suffrage, so why should women achieve it in ten? The larger the electorate, the smaller the power of the individual vote and the more disillusioned about democracy the electorate would become. Lord

[1] *H.L. Deb. 71*, cc. 407 et seq.

Cecil opposed the amendment solely on the ground that while
its substance was right it did not provide good ground on which
to join battle with the House of Commons. Several others
attacked the humiliating position in which the House of Lords
was placed, saying that they—and many members of the Lower
House besides those sixteen who had had the courage to rebel—
supported a higher age, and that they would seem ridiculous if
they did not vote with their consciences. The Lord Chancellor
found himself the only speaker to defend the virtues of equal
franchise at twenty-one. He pointed out that even if women had
to wait till twenty-five for the vote they would still outnumber
men over twenty-one; the amendment failed, therefore, in its
main purpose; but in any case it would kill the Bill. Presumably with 'resolute resignation', 87 silent peers voted with the
Government against the 41 who supported the amendment.
Immediately afterwards the House of Lords passed the Bill
unamended, and on 2 July 1928 it received the Royal Assent.[1]

Thus, sixty-one years after it had first been raised in Parliament by John Stuart Mill, the female suffrage question was
finally settled and passed from the political arena. The last ten
years of the struggle form a curious anti-climax. The Act of
1928 had been inevitable from the moment that the 1917
Speaker's Conference had put forward a compromise the only
logic of which was that it kept women in a minority. Many of the
opponents of female suffrage recognized the absurdity of the
compromise; the most remarkable feature of its subsequent
history is that it was so long honoured and that, in the end, there
was so much tacit if not open opposition to its abandonment.

In 1918 the Coalition Government had used a phrase which
could hardly be interpreted other than as a promise of equal
suffrage, and, within four months of their election, they were
defeated in the House of Commons when they attempted to go
back on that promise. A year later the House voted by 122 votes
to 38 in favour of equal suffrage. Moreover, many of those who
opposed it in 1919 and 1920 said that they hoped that it would
be enacted in time for the next election. Once again, in 1922,
the House voted for it by a large majority. However, the matter
lapsed, and, although in 1924 hardly anyone objected to the

[1] 18 & 19 Geo. 5, ch. 12.

principle of equal suffrage in Mr. Adamson's Bill, the measure appeared to evoke much less enthusiasm than five years before. In 1925 the reform was rejected on the ground that it should be preceded by a conference, but when the Speaker refused to preside a conference was no longer regarded as indispensable, although a substitute chairman could undoubtedly have been found. Finally, the Government bowed to the inevitable. But, although little opposition was then manifested in public, it is clear that many of the Government were most reluctant converts to the change, and that some of their supporters, especially in the Lords, shared their uneasiness. It seems probable that if the Cabinet had not felt bound by promises or tempted by the prospect of 'dishing the whigs', the final step might have been still further delayed.

Looking back on the last phase of the suffrage question, there is no doubt that the other parties appear in a better light than the Conservatives, if only because they had unitedly sided with the inevitable from the beginning. The Lloyd George Liberals had made little attempt to bring about the change when they had a share of power, and the Labour party, on coming to office, left the matter to be dealt with by a back-bencher, but their tactics and speeches were not nearly as inconsistent as those of the Conservatives in the period from 1924 to 1928.

Perhaps there was a case for delay. Despite the myth that grew up, that case certainly did not rest on any clear bargain for a ten-year pause. It might, however, have been based on the more general ground that fundamental constitutional change should be undertaken slowly and by stages, but, if so, it would have been much more convincing if the proponents of experimental delay had made their position clear. The abrupt way in which the 1919 Bill was killed, the more private and protracted murder of the 1920 Bill, the inconsistency between the Conservative arguments against the 1924 Bill and those which they subsequently used, the change of front over the question of a conference, and the belated attempt to link the question to a general increase in the voting age, betray the absence of any coherent policy.

There can be no doubt, of course, that, particularly in the later phases of the struggle, considerations of party advantage were not unimportant. In 1925 Labour was accused of trying to introduce a Government measure in order to steal the rewards of political gratitude, and in 1928 the charge was reversed—the Conservatives were alleged to be seeking credit for a measure which was, in fact, only opposed by their own supporters. Lord Birkenhead, with characteristic indiscretion, remarked, in a speech after the passage of the Act: 'Millions of new voters have been added to the electorate by the Conservative Party. They will have an opportunity of showing their gratitude at the General Election.'[1]

But, quite apart from the search for the rewards, if such exist, of political gratitude, the parties were also concerned about which side could expect to get most of the votes of the new electorate. Many speakers professed ignorance about the question, but there were those in all parties who claimed that the change would benefit them, and there were those who publicly feared that they would be the sufferers. However, it is clear that the Conservatives, particularly in the Upper House, seemed least confident about winning party benefits from the change. The historian can pretend to little greater wisdom about the consequences than those who were speculating in advance. There is certainly no positive evidence for the assertion made after the 1929 election that the ungrateful flappers had defeated the Conservatives. It is perhaps worth recording that when Gallup polls were introduced to England ten years later, appreciably more women than men were always found on the Conservative side.[2]

III. SYSTEMS OF VOTING

The traditional system of voting had only narrowly escaped reform under the Representation of the People Act of 1918. The Speaker's Conference had unanimously advocated proportional

---

[1] *The Times*, 22 Nov. 1928.

[2] Professor Tingsten, in chapter i of his study, *Political Behaviour* (London, 1937), found that, in every country he studied and for which evidence was available, women appeared to be more conservative in their political sympathies than men.

On pp. 144–6 below there is a more detailed consideration of the numbers affected by the 1928 Act.

representation.[1] The House of Commons had resolved in favour of the alternative vote. The House of Lords, to kill the alternative vote, had insisted on P.R., and the Commons had very reluctantly yielded and agreed to a trial of it in a hundred constituencies; later even that had been abandoned owing to the vested interests of the members in the areas affected. However, the survival of the existing system plainly expressed not so much an endorsement of its merits as a failure to agree upon the remedy for its faults. Certainly the advocates of reform, although they had missed an opportunity, were in no way bound to admit defeat. Unlike the other aspects of the 1918 settlement, the system of voting that it left had neither the imprimatur of the Speaker's Conference nor the support of overwhelming majorities in the division lobbies.

The period that followed was the most confused in the recent history of the party system, and the anomalous results produced by elections were at their most flagrant. Substantial numbers of M.P.s felt a sense of grievance and were prepared to support a change. If there had been agreement on which change to support, reform might yet have been achieved. The Royal Commission of 1910 had advocated the alternative vote, while P.R. had been chosen by the Speaker's Conference, the only other body which had officially been called upon to pass judgement on the system of voting. The alternative vote had the advantage of threatening fewer vested interests; but P.R., in addition to its intellectual appeal, had the support of the most assiduous of lobbyists, the Proportional Representation Society.[2] The omens for change were moderately propitious, and the P.R. Society cannot be accused of altogether absurd optimism when it wrote in its Annual Report for 1919–20 that 'P.R. is now treated as a serious reform, the ultimate adoption of which is not in doubt'.

From the beginning of 1919 onwards, the Government was

[1] The system proposed was the use of the single transferable vote in constituencies returning from three to seven members. Owing to its qualified support by the Royal Commission of 1910 and its full endorsement by the Speaker's Conference and the P.R. Society, it was the only version of P.R. that was seriously discussed in Britain after 1918.

[2] Its secretary, Mr. J. H. Humphreys, has left a very considerable mark on the history of the subject. It is astonishing how often in debates and articles on electoral matters, the phrase 'that able and indefatigable advocate, Mr. Humphreys' appears.

regularly asked about its intentions on electoral reform, and, while the answer was an invariable 'it is not being considered', it was known that some of the leading members of the Cabinet favoured it. Lord Birkenhead and Mr. Balfour were Vice-Presidents of the P.R. Society, and Mr. Churchill was reported to be 'very sympathetic'[1] to a change. The question first arose in legislative form in connexion with local, not parliamentary, elections. In the sessions of 1919, 1920, and 1921, Bills giving local authorities the option of being elected by P.R. passed the House of Lords.[2] The Government expressed full sympathy, and, in 1920, they even starred the Bill, but their sympathy did not extend to the point of securing parliamentary time for it. However, the principle of P.R. was publicly accepted in another context in 1920, when it was included in the Government of Ireland Act. Some opposition was expressed, but the House did not even divide against what was described as an essential safeguard for minorities.

The question of applying P.R. to British parliamentary elections was at last brought up in February 1921, when Sir Thomas Bramsdon secured time for a P.R. Bill. The P.R. Society immediately set about preparing the ground most carefully. Twenty thousand circular letters were sent out to every sort of influential person and institution. A deputation to the Prime Minister was elaborately organized, and, although it in fact never took place, Lord Birkenhead, the Lord Chancellor, agreed to introduce it. The P.R. Society's files reveal that 21 M.P.s and 8 peers were members of the Society; a rather optimistic list of sympathizers includes 223 M.P.s and 132 peers, as well as the Trades Union Congress, the Labour party, the Independent Labour party, and the Liberals.[3] The P.R. Society secured the help of the national press in a model P.R. election. Ballot forms with the names of leading politicians were published, and news-

---

[1] See *H.C. Deb. 129*, c. 22.

[2] See *H.L. Deb. 35*, c. 193, 39, c. 164, 44, c. 161, for second reading debates.

[3] Apparent authority for these claims:
  T.U.C.: Resolution of Annual Conference, 1918.
  Labour party: Resolution of Annual Conference, January 1918.
  I.L.P.: Resolution of Annual Conference, 1914.
  Liberals: Resolution of the National Liberal Federation, 1920 (favouring
    P.R. or the alternative vote).

paper readers were invited to cut them out and send them, filled
in, to the P.R. Society. Thirty-five thousand ballots were returned, and the results must have seemed comforting. Of the
seven victors, only Mr. Bonar Law was opposed to a change in
the system of voting.

In order further to demonstrate the working of P.R., another
model election was held in the House of Commons at the beginning of April, when 350 members used the single transferable
vote to decide what five newspapers were considered most indispensable. The activity of the P.R. Society and of the P.R.
Committee, which was formed in the House of Commons,
provoked a counter-movement, and the Anti-P.R. Committee,
which had flourished in 1917–18, was revived. It circulated
among members a lengthy pamphlet intemperately denouncing
P.R. and quoting evidence from countries where it had been
tried. This was answered by a careful refutation from the P.R.
Committee. In the two documents is caricatured the contrast
which ran through almost all discussions of the subject during
this period. Both sides overstated their case, but the proponents
of P.R. tended always to be better informed and more logically
coherent in their arguments. P.R. had able spokesmen and it was
only rarely that anyone did justice to the case that could undoubtedly be made against them.

Despite all the efforts of its advocates, Sir Thomas Bramsdon's
Bill did not receive a very warm welcome; it was debated on
8 April 1921[1] in the middle of a coal strike which distracted all
newspaper attention from it. Sir Thomas Bramsdon put the
orthodox arguments for P.R.—justice for minorities, mirroring
the nation, greater freedom from party discipline—and he was
supported by the speakers from all parties. The opposition
spokesmen were almost all Conservatives. Their arguments
ranged from defence of the existing system—its simplicity, its
small constituencies, its convenient by-elections, its provision of
strong government—to violent, and less justifiable, assertions
that P.R. had failed everywhere and that it fostered political
corruption. The Government announced that it would allow an
open vote on the question but that it could make no promise of
further facilities if the Bill should be accepted. It was, however,

---

[1] *H.C. Deb. 140*, cc. 613 et seq.

defeated by 186 votes to 87. If pairs and tellers are included, they were divided:[1]

	For the Bill	Against
Conservative . . .	34	178
Coalition Liberal . .	31	24
Independent Liberal . .	22	4
Labour	25	5
	112	211

The defeat seemed decisive enough to kill the question for that Parliament. However, it was soon to be reopened, though not in public. In the Cabinet crisis of March 1922, when Mr. Lloyd George offered to resign, Sir Alfred Mond, the Minister of Health, was reported to have been asked to produce a report on P.R. and the alternative vote. That there was such an inquiry was denied by the Chancellor of the Exchequer on 6 March.[2] But on 15 March Sir Alfred Mond, in answer to a question, said that he had on his own initiative had a report prepared;[3] a week later, in answer to a further question, he refused to give any indication of the contents of what was a secret Cabinet document.[4] News of this report leaked out early to the press, which used it to support rumours of the formulation of a new centre party—a union of a body of Liberals with the non-die-hard Conservatives; electoral reform, it was suggested, was a prerequisite to such a party's success. The idea was explored on 1 and 3 March in the *Daily Chronicle*, at the time reputed to be a semi-official mouthpiece of Mr. Lloyd George. But the flurry came to nothing. On 9 March *The Times* reported that the inquiry had been abandoned. It seems that the whole affair may have been no more than an experimental kite-flying by Mr. Lloyd George and his National Liberal henchman, Sir Alfred Mond. It may not even have amounted to that; Sir Alfred Mond's biographer records that in his eighteen months at the Ministry of Health he bombarded his Cabinet colleagues with no less than ninety-two memoranda covering a vast range of subjects.[5]

In the General Election of 1922, P.R. was included in the

[1] P.R. Society figures.   [2] *H.C. Deb. 151*, c. 841.
[3] *H.C. Deb. 151*, c. 2187.   [4] *H.C. Deb. 152*, c. 445.
[5] Hector Bolitho, *Alfred Mond, First Lord Melchett* (London, 1933), p. 226.

Independent Liberal manifesto, thus appearing for the first time as a plank in a party programme. The results of the election were thought by some to strengthen the case for electoral reform. The Conservatives, with 38 per cent. of the votes, secured a clear majority of seventy-nine seats. But, since the existing system had enabled both Conservatives and Labour to improve their position by comparison with the last Parliament, the prospects for electoral reform were hardly improved, and there is no evidence of any great excitement about the question.

In February 1923 a permissive Bill allowing local authorities the option of using P.R. was defeated by 169 votes to 157.[1] The Conservatives who voted were divided 155 to 25 against it, but the Labour party, it is interesting to note, favoured it by 69 to 11. Although the case for P.R. in this form is very different from, and in many ways very much stronger than, the case for P.R. in parliamentary elections, the arguments and the voting in this division seem, to a large extent, to have paralleled members' sympathies on the larger question.

In March 1923 a Liberal attempt to introduce an Alternative Vote Bill under the ten-minute rule was defeated by 208 votes to 178, and, although there was a little cross-voting, it was in the main a straight party split between a Conservative majority and a Labour and Liberal minority.[2]

The election of December 1923 inevitably provoked further discussion of the system of voting. The crude contrast between the results in 1922 and 1923 gave an exaggerated picture of the haphazard nature of the electoral system,[3] and fears that Labour might some day attain complete power on a minority vote provoked some anxiety in quarters which had been hitherto

[1] *H.C. Deb. 160*, cc. 1429 et seq.
[2] *H.C. Deb. 161*, cc. 501 et seq.
[3] The results were:

Year	Conservative		Liberal		Labour	
	Per cent.	*Seats*	*Per cent.*	*Seats*	*Per cent.*	*Seats*
1922	38	346	29	115	29½	142
1923	38	258	29½	159	30½	191

These figures are actually very deceptive. See pp. 172–8 below.

complacent about the working of the system. On the other hand, it must have been about at this time that majority opinion in the Labour party definitely turned against change. It is possible that change might yet have been accomplished if the Liberals had realized the peril in which they stood and devoted all their efforts to securing that one piece of legislation which was a precondition of their survival as a major party. But they were divided, as on so many questions, about the urgency of reform, the tactics by which it should be secured, and the form which it should take. There were members of the Cabinet who were not unsympathetic—Mr. Snowden, Mr. Clynes, and Lord Parmoor were Vice-Presidents of the P.R. Society—but, by the time that the Liberals approached them on the question, relations between the two parties had so deteriorated that any agreement was impossible.

In January 1924 a Liberal committee was set up to examine the rival merits of P.R. and the alternative vote, and in April it reported in favour of P.R. The question was due to come to a head on 2 May, when a P.R. Bill introduced by Mr. Rendall, a Liberal back-bencher, was down for debate. The moment was not auspicious. In April Mr. Lloyd George had protested at Labour's attitude to the Liberal 'patient oxen' who were keeping them in office, and Labour had resented the form of the protest. Two days before the debate the Liberals formally invited Labour to support the Bill and let it be known that the Liberal party would meet to reconsider its attitude after the vote on the Bill had been taken. There was a widespread feeling that this was intended to be an ultimatum. In a stormy meeting the next day, the parliamentary Labour party rejected a majority recommendation from the Cabinet to support P.R.[1] and decided 'by a large majority' to leave the Bill to a free vote but to give it no facilities if it passed the second reading.[2]

The debate,[3] although not of excessively high quality, was certainly the best that the system of voting ever provoked after 1918. The case for the single transferable vote was put clearly and fairly. Election results should mirror the electorate; the

[1] *Manchester Guardian*, 2 May 1924.
[2] *The Times*, 2 May 1924.
[3] *H.C. Deb. 172*, cc. 1987 et seq.

existing system was chancy; P.R. offered a practical remedy for an acknowledged evil; in view of the present parliamentary deadlock, it was absurd to object that P.R. would produce minority Governments; P.R. would certainly give greater freedom to M.P.s; the present system fostered executive dominance and public cynicism. Mr. Amery, from the Conservative front bench, supported the Bill, saying that, while it would not save the Liberal party or produce any drastic change, it would facilitate efficient and honest politics and reduce the danger of one party being in a permanent majority. Mr. Herbert Morrison gave the fullest exposition of the case on the other side. He explained that he had been converted from P.R. years earlier by a debate between the Prime Minister and Mr. Snowden; he suspected that the conversion of the Liberals had only taken place in the last few days. P.R. would foster large constituencies, unsavoury bargaining, and circus electioneering; under the present system, public opinion did get represented; its momentary weakness would soon be cured by the disappearance of the Liberal party; he preferred a bad logical Government to a well-meaning but unstable one. Other speakers said bluntly that the purpose of an election was not to choose a Parliament but to choose a Government, and that 1923 was the first time that the system had failed; P.R. would lead to internecine strife by the candidates within each party. However, many of the opponents of the Bill admitted the imperfections of the present system. Mr. Henderson, the Home Secretary, speaking for the Government, said that a free vote would be allowed but the Government could not offer further facilities. P.R. had not been put before the electorate and the parties were divided on the question. It had been rejected by the House of Commons four times in 1917–18. However, the Government were not happy about the present situation; they would have had a very different attitude if the Bill had proposed the alternative vote. But there was no time to do anything in that session. The Liberals must not be impatient with the Government. The whole question would be considered.

The Bill was then defeated by 238 votes to 144. There was a more clear-cut party division than ever before. The figures (including tellers) were:

			For	Against
Conservative	.	.	8	149
Labour	.	.	28	90
Liberal	.	.	106	1
Others	.	.	4	..
			146	240

The Cabinet were divided. Of these who voted, four supported P.R., and two opposed it. *The Times* parliamentary correspondent remarked the next day on the bitter feeling between Labour and the Liberals. Some Liberals were not sorry at Labour's refusal to support P.R., as they did not want to be too closely linked with Labour. The 'patient oxen' were uneasy.[1] There were further reverberations of the debate. On 7 May in a speech at Chelmsford, Mr. Asquith said that the Government had been told of the unanimous decision of the Liberal party in favour of P.R. and had been sympathetic, but the rank and file of the Labour party had revolted 'in forgetfulness in not a few cases of their recorded and pledged convictions'.[2] The unanimity of the Liberal party was put in some doubt by a letter in the *Manchester Guardian* on 13 May, in which Mr. Ellis Davies wrote that he was one of a number of Liberal M.P.s who were opposed to P.R. but who 'in deference to Mr. Asquith's appeal' did not vote against the Bill. He personally disliked all forms of 'coupon' election. A speech by Mr. Lloyd George some months later further illustrated Liberal disagreements on the question: 'Personally I am a believer in the old radical scheme of a second ballot. My simple mind is entirely free from subtleties. It does not rise to the appreciation, even if it rises to the comprehension, of the intricacies of P.R. . . . but I would prefer any plan to the present one.'[3] On the other hand, Mr. Asquith's allegations of a rank and file Labour revolt find some support in the votes of the Cabinet and in the remarks of Mr. Johnston, who, writing in *Forward*, said that the Bill was turned down by Labour members largely because 'we were dared by the Liberals to do other than support it'. The *Nation* commented:

The Liberal Party . . . so managed the affair as to create a widespread impression that the Government should support Mr. Rendall's Bill

---

[1] *The Times*, 3 May 1924.   [2] Ibid., 8 May 1924.
[3] *Manchester Guardian*, 12 Sept. 1924.

as the price of keeping in office. The impression was grossly erroneous and its prevalence was mainly due to distortions in the press; but there was just enough substance in it to make these distortions possible.[1]

It is certainly conceivable that if the Liberals had been more tactful, more united, or more clear-minded about their objectives, they might have secured from the Labour Government some measure of electoral reform. From the point of view of the proportional representationalists, the tragedy was that by the time the Liberals became enthusiastic converts it was just too late; the bulk of the Labour supporters of P.R. had, of course, become recusants.

However, although this opportunity had been missed, the critics of the system were not silenced. In the general election of 1924, the Conservatives secured a majority of 233 seats, although they won only 48 per cent. of the votes. If the party in power no longer had the least incentive to change the system, those in opposition had perhaps more ground for complaint. The Liberals, with a sixth of the votes, secured only forty seats, and at last became unitedly and violently in favour of electoral reform. Labour, on the other hand, although they had not secured a number of seats proportionate to their votes, saw that the Liberals were indubitably in decline and that in the existing system lay their best hope of power. They were not, of course, united on the question. In November 1925 Mr. Snowden was telling his constituents that nothing would do more than P.R. to purify politics and liberate the consciences of M.P.s.[2] At the Labour Party Conference in December 1925, the Executive, in answer to two motions, one condemning P.R. and one advocating it, announced that a committee had been set up to examine the merits of the transferable vote. It reported against it, and in October 1926 a large majority at the Annual Conference supported a resolution condemning P.R. but, by implication, supporting the alternative vote.[3] In 1927 *Forward* rebuked Mr.

---

[1] The *Nation*, 10 May 1924.   [2] *The Times*, 21 Nov. 1925.
[3] 'This Conference affirms that, while Electoral Reform is needed to remedy the existing defects, the proposals of the Proportional Representation Society, involving large constituencies and numerous representatives for each constituency, are not in the best interests of democratic government and ought to be opposed.' *Report* of Labour Party Annual Conference, 1926, p. 273.

Snowden for continuing to advocate P.R. in defiance of party policy.

Neither in the press nor in Parliament did electoral reform receive any substantial attention after 1924. While there was a likelihood of a Speaker's Conference to discuss equal franchise, pressure was maintained to include the system of voting within its terms of reference, and in March 1926 Mr. Lloyd George moved an amendment to the Address regretting the absence of any allusion to electoral reform. Apart from this, the question was the subject of debate only three times in this Parliament. A motion advocating the second ballot was discussed cursorily in the House of Lords in 1927 and a year later P.R. received similar consideration; little sympathy was expressed for either motion. In 1928 the House of Commons had an unenlightening debate on a private member's motion deploring 'the unrepresentative nature of the electoral system';[1] the advocates of reform were disunited and a Conservative amendment applauding 'the proved wisdom of the existing system' was carried by 205 votes to 41, the minority being composed of 1 Conservative, 10 Socialists, and 30 Liberals. Adequate comment is perhaps offered in two quotations. The *New Statesman* said that the lack of interest in the debate showed how 'that intellectual monstrosity (P.R.) . . . nowadays has not only few supporters but few active opponents—because the danger of its introduction is too slight to deserve serious attention';[2] *The Times* parliamentary correspondent noted that 'the remarkable feature of the debate was that a question which was a very live issue a few years ago appeared to have become largely academic'.[3] However, within two years, electoral reform was to become once again a major subject of political contention.

IV. MISCELLANEOUS QUESTIONS

Even the simplest electoral system involves elaborate administration. The compilation and printing of an electoral register, the provision of polling-places, and the payment of officials are questions over which small difficulties must constantly arise. Minor revisions of the law are likely to be sought and there are

---

[1] *H.C. Deb. 215*, cc. 1248 et seq.
[2] *The New Statesman*, 31 Mar. 1928.　　　[3] *The Times*, 29 Mar. 1928.

many opportunities for reformers to suggest legislation of every sort—from mobile polling-booths to pauper disfranchisement. During the 1920's, parliamentary attention was intermittently devoted to such matters.

In the first four years after the war, there were no fewer than seven Government Acts designed to improve electoral law, in most cases to remedy flaws which had manifested themselves in the working of the Representation of the People Act of 1918. In April 1919 an Act[1] was passed making the official costs of an election a charge on the Consolidated Fund, thus obviating the theoretical possibility that a Government might prevent an election by refusing to vote funds for it. In the same month an Act[2] was passed repealing a seventy-year-old statute which confined to barracks on election and nomination days all soldiers stationed within two miles of a polling-place. In 1920, after some agitation, the Government finally decided to abandon the postal voting provisions laid down in the Act of 1918. The special provisions delaying the count for eight days to allow for the return of ballots from servicemen overseas had been necessary enough at the end of the war, but, in the subsequent by-elections, there had been a steadily diminishing number of postal votes, and annoyance at the delay in announcing the result had grown. The Representation of the People Act (No. 2) of 1920[3] provided that postal voting should be limited to the United Kingdom. Servicemen overseas could appoint proxies. At the same time, the period between nomination and polling-day was increased to an average of seven days to allow more time for the return of postal votes at home. Apart from some expressions of anxiety about the possible abuse of proxies, the Act passed both Houses without comment. In the same year the Representation of the People Act, 1920,[4] enfranchised a very few young ex-servicemen.

The Representation of the People Act (No. 2) of 1921[5] was designed to facilitate registration by providing that up to four months' absence on business during the qualifying period should

---

[1] 9 & 10 Geo. 5, ch. 8.   [2] 9 & 10 Geo. 5, ch. 10.
[3] 10 & 11 Geo. 5, ch. 35.
[4] 10 & 11 Geo. 5, ch. 15. See p. 20 above.
[5] 11 & 12 Geo. 5, ch. 34.

not debar a person normally resident in a constituency from being placed on the register. Sir Frederick Banbury opposed what he considered to be an extension of the franchise, but otherwise the Bill slipped through uncontentiously.

In 1922 yet another Representation of the People Act[1] modified the registration time-table. Under the 1918 Act the day for qualification had been too near the day for the publication of the register to allow adequately for checking and printing. For the previous two years the dates had had to be modified by Order in Council, and now the change was to be regularized. This was a wholly uncontentious question, but an attempt was made by the Government to include in the Bill a clause which provided for an increase in the expense maximum to cover a recent increase in postal charges. This evoked a storm of protest from Labour and Liberal members,[2] and, surprisingly, it was abandoned.

The last in this series of small Representation of the People Acts, the R.P.A. (No. 2) of 1922,[3] corrected a lapse in the 1918 Act and made corporate bodies as well as individuals answerable in law for unauthorized expenditures on behalf of any candidate.

The 1918 Act had provided for the publication of two registers annually. From the first, this gave rise to trouble. Local authorities complained of the administrative nuisance and both they and economy-minded M.P.s were conscious of the waste of £250,000 a year upon an 'unnecessary' second register, which, being published in April, was too late to be of service in local elections and only of use in the event of a summer by-election or general election. For several years nothing was done about the question despite continuous badgering of successive Governments. In 1926 Mr. Churchill, as Chancellor of the Exchequer, introduced an Economy (Miscellaneous Provisions) Bill, which, among a number of other and more substantial cuts in public expenditure, provided for the abolition of the spring register; at the same time, the qualifying period was to be shortened from six months to three. The abolition would save the Exchequer and the local authorities £125,000 a year each. The

[1] 12 & 13 Geo. 5, ch. 12.   [2] *H.C. Deb. 152*, cc. 1637 et seq.
[3] 12 & 13 Geo. 5, ch. 41.

major economies in the Bill provoked wide controversy and
almost the only references to the electoral provisions came on
the committee stage—when the clauses were discussed largely
in the middle of an all-night sitting. The ending of the spring
register was denounced as 'tricking the poor of their franchise',[1]
and some members protested that an elector might now have
to wait sixteen and a half months to get on the register. An
amendment was moved to reduce the qualifying period from
three months to one. The Government replied that if there
had been a spring register ever since 1900, no general elections
and only twenty-four by-elections would have been fought on
it. As a result of the three months' reduction in the qualifying
period, the number able to vote would be increased in all elections held in the autumn and winter, that is to say in the vast
majority of cases.[2] The amendment was defeated. However,
the Government did make some concessions. Under pressure
they abandoned a clause which would have reduced the number
of presiding officers by allowing one to supervise several polling-districts when all happened to vote in the same room. They
also withdrew a clause allowing returning officers a choice between stamping and printing the official mark on ballot-papers.
There were some protests because the Government, in order to
avoid a report stage, would not accept these amendments in the
Commons; it was argued that to leave the House of Lords to
cope with Ballot Act provisions was unconstitutional. The only
other electoral provision in the Act repealed the clause in the
1918 Act which made the poll in Orkney and Shetland stay open
for two days; it was generally agreed that more polling-stations,
rather than longer polling-hours, were needed for the effective
enfranchisement of remote areas. It is interesting that the
Labour party which in 1926 protested against the abolition of
the second register merely for the sake of economy, and which
twenty-two years later reinstituted it, should itself have decided
within two years to abandon it in order to save money. But by

---

[1] *H.C. Deb. 194*, c. 702.

[2] In point of fact, in the thirteen years while registration continued to be
carried on normally under the 1918 Act, the only summer general election (in
1929) none the less took place on a new register because, following the Equal
Franchise Act of 1928, a special spring list was compiled in order to include
the new voters.

1949 the estimated Treasury saving had risen from £125,000 to £400,000.

Two Acts which extend beyond the scope of this study must not escape mention, although they are linked to the working of cabinet government as much as to the electoral system. In February 1919, when new appointments required four ministers to stand for re-election, the Government decided to abrogate the custom which had originated with the Succession to the Crown Act of 1707 and which made it necessary for members accepting certain offices to undergo a by-election. The Bill, which was rushed through Parliament in ten days, aroused considerable opposition.[1] This was due partly to the attempt to enact constitutional legislation so hurriedly and partly to the retroactive provisions which obviated the need for re-election of the four ministers immediately involved, but mainly to fundamental objections against the ending of a system which had so long exposed governments to the constant criticism of the electorate.[2] Much of the criticism was stilled when an amendment was accepted which limited the effect of the Act[3] to the first nine months after a general election. The futility of elections in the same constituency within a few weeks of one another was agreed by all except the Labour party and a few Liberals who together mustered forty-two votes against the Bill. It was ironical that the Labour party in 1924 should have proved to be the main beneficiaries of the Act.

The arguments used in 1919 were repeated more fully seven years later when Mr. Clayton, a Conservative back-bencher, moved the second reading of a Bill completely ending the custom.[4] Again there were some objections on the narrow ground of tactical propriety; Labour members protested at so fundamental a change being dealt with by a private member's Bill and without a mandate, observing that these were precisely the arguments which the Conservatives had used against

---

[1] See *H.C. Deb. 112*, cc. 614 et seq., 791 et seq.

[2] The number of times that this criticism seems to have been effective was surprisingly small. *The Times* (17 Feb. 1919) calculated that since 1868 ministerial appointments had provoked 284 by-elections, but that many ministers had had unopposed returns. There had been only eight Government defeats.

[3] 9 & 10 Geo. 5, ch. 2.   [4] *H.C. Deb. 191*, cc. 1417 et seq.

Labour's equal franchise Bills. They argued, too, that it should at least not become operative until the next election. But the debate centred mainly around the principle involved. For the measure it was contended that there were enough by-elections caused by death and resignation to show the trend of public opinion, and that there was no need to add to their number; the Prime Minister's choice of ministers was sometimes curtailed by the fear that a given appointment would necessitate a by-election in an unsafe seat; new ministers, instead of learning their jobs, had to waste time and money on campaigning; they were put under severe pressure to make pledges on departmental matters. Against the measure it was argued that although the custom was no longer needed for its original purpose, it still provided a useful check on the power of the executive by forcing by-elections in which, owing to their nature and to the publicity they attracted, the Government was peculiarly on test—although, as *The Times* remarked, 'the test is uncertain and the check is but slight'.[1] Several Conservatives joined the Labour party in opposition to the Bill and proved its most effective critics. But the Government assisted its passage and it was never seriously endangered; its third reading was carried by 183 votes to 88[2] although 21 Conservatives defied their whips to vote against it.

It is hard to resist the comment made by Mr. Bonar Law in the 1919 debate: 'Every Government would have liked to see the system abolished and every Opposition has enjoyed it.'[3] There was perhaps, as Mr. Clayton remarked in 1926, something to be said for taking two bites at the cherry.[4] But neither in 1919 nor in 1926 was a convincing case made for a rule which had long outlasted its original purpose. The most remarkable feature of the debates was the extreme faith manifested in by-elections as accurate pointers to public opinion. In 1926 much

[1] 11 June 1926. However, *The Times* did come down in opposition to the Bill. 'Why not leave it alone?' (Ibid.)

[2] *H.C. Deb. 196,* c. 1931.

[3] *H.C. Deb. 112,* c. 614.

[4] However, the experience of the intervening period offered no clear moral. Between Oct. 1919 and June 1922, 12 ministers had to present themselves for re-election; 10 won comfortably enough while 2 were defeated. Between June 1925 and the passage of the Bill 2 ministers successfully secured re-election.

use was made of the defeat of Sir Arthur Griffith-Boscawen in 1920, after his appointment as Minister of Agriculture, at a time when a particular cattle import policy was being much criticized; but there appears to be no reason to believe that the subject was of any great importance to the electors of Dudley who rejected him. In some of the Conservative opposition to the 1926 Act[1] there could be traced the honest dislike of constitutional change, but in the Labour arguments it is hard to find anything more than obedience to the maxim that 'the duty of the Opposition is to oppose'.

The only other Act[2] in this period was one passed in 1928 which enfranchised graduates of the University of Reading on the same basis as those of other provincial universities. If university suffrage was justified, the case for extending it to Reading, which had recently received a Charter, was unanswerable. The Bill was opposed by Labour members[3] as a protest against university representation and plural voting, but their protests were little more than formal, and it passed by 90 votes to 45.

The question of election expenses arose as a result of the Equal Franchise Bill of 1928. The permitted outlay of a candidate would have been raised by from £150 to £300 by the increase in the electorate. On the second reading of the Bill, a reduction of 1d. per elector was demanded by some Conservatives, while Labour members advocated an even greater cut. When the Bill came before a committee of the whole House, an instruction was moved without opposition to permit the extension of the Bill to include the question of election expenses. A new clause was sponsored by members of all parties to reduce the permitted maximum from 7d. to 6d. per elector in the counties and from 5d. to 4d. in the boroughs.[4] It encountered some opposition from Conservative borough members and, after an adjournment to discuss the question privately, the Government decided to leave it to a free vote. The clause was carried by 220 votes to 71, the Conservatives being fairly evenly divided. Sir John Simon then attempted to reduce the county maximum

---

[1] 16 & 17 Geo. 5, ch. 19.   [2] 18 & 19 Geo. 5, ch. 25.
[3] *H.C. Deb. 218*, cc. 1364 et seq.
[4] *H.C. Deb. 216*, cc. 303 et seq.

still further to 5*d*. The Home Secretary charged him with trying to out-reform reform, but he still attracted a few Conservative supporters, although defeated by 215 votes to 111. Next, some Conservative members from the boroughs moved an amendment to leave the borough maximum alone at 5*d*., and they just carried the day by 181 votes to 171. It was argued that a cut from 5*d*. to 4*d*. (20 per cent.) was a much more serious matter than a cut from 7*d*. to 6*d*. (14 per cent.). The Government remained neutral on this question, but at the report stage, when an attempt was made to reopen the question and to substitute a 4½*d*. limit (a 10 per cent. cut),[1] the whips were put on against the change. The Conservatives were divided on the issue. On one side they argued that they needed more money than Labour to put their case adequately before the electorate, as they lacked the free trade-union publicity and clerical assistance which Labour had; they also contended that there was no reason for a distinction of more than 1*d*. per elector between town and country. On the other side they argued that if there was a high maximum, pressure would always be brought upon them to spend to that limit; high election expenses often deterred their best men from standing; some shared the fear subsequently expressed by *The Economist* that '"the rich party" lay themselves open to the charge of depending on the power of the purse'[2] in refusing any reduction.

In the 1920's sporadic discussion about disillusion with democracy was heard. There were references to what Mussolini was doing in Italy, and fears were often expressed about 'direct action' by labour. Every debate on the electoral system produced remarks about public cynicism. One by-product was the expression of anxiety about non-voting. Many letters to *The Times* suggested either compulsory voting or alternatively automatic disfranchisement of non-voters. Others advocated plural votes for older people, and yet others wished to disfranchise recipients of poor-relief and to enfranchise limited liability companies. The issue of compulsory voting was raised on several occasions at question-time and twice reached debate. In 1920 a Bill introduced under the ten-minute rule was refused a first

[1] *H.C. Deb. 217*, cc. 75 et seq.
[2] *The Economist*, 12 May 1928, p. 972.

reading by 158 votes to 74—the minority being composed entirely of Conservatives.[1] In 1926, in the House of Lords, Viscount Burnham asked that an inquiry should be made into the question, but he received no support.[2]

In 1922 Colonel Archer-Shee secured a place on the ballot for a miscellaneous franchise Bill which, among other things, would have disfranchised for five years ex-convicts, conscientious objectors, and naturalized citizens, while it would have given the vote to managing directors of companies and to the wives of business voters. Some sympathy was expressed for some of his proposals, but the House was counted out before the debate was completed.[3] In 1928 it was reported that the Cabinet gave serious consideration to the inclusion of some measure of pauper disfranchisement in the Equal Franchise Bill, but finally abandoned it when less than one-quarter of those present at a 1922 Committee meeting favoured the idea.[4]

In 1925 the question of cars at elections was raised for the first time. Mr. Pethick-Lawrence was defeated by 212 votes to 122 on a ten-minute rule Bill to ban party use of cars and place on the returning officer the duty of getting the infirm to the poll.[5]

In 1925, also, a later approach to the problem of absent voters was anticipated by a private member's Bill, which, besides applying the postal vote to local elections, would have given the right to be permanent absent voters to those often kept from home by their occupation. It would also have given the vote to invalids. In the debate[6] opinion was overwhelmingly in support of the Bill and opposition manifested itself in talking-out speeches rather than in argument. The Home Secretary said that the Bill was impracticable and that postal voting threatened the secrecy of the ballot, but that the question could be discussed at the coming Speaker's Conference. The Bill was rejected by 79 votes to 76 in a non-partisan division.

On the whole, electoral administration appears to have run smoothly. Every election brought protests about the facilities for absent voters, the provision of polling-places, the delays in paying

[1] *H.C. Deb. 130*, cc. 2186 et seq.   [2] *H.L. Deb. 63*, cc. 601 et seq.
[3] *H.C. Deb. 153*, cc. 1713 et seq.
[4] See *The Times* parliamentary correspondent, 30 Jan., 8, 16, 21 Feb. 1928.
[5] *H.C. Deb. 182*, cc. 443–8.   [6] *H.C. Deb. 183*, cc. 1329 et seq.

returning officer's expenses, and minor confusions and infringe-
ments of the law.[1] But the complaints were neither numerous nor
substantial. There was general agreement that elections were more
quietly, economically, and efficiently conducted than before the
war. The large reduction in the expense maximum and the tighten-
ing of the law on corrupt practices seems to have provoked little
difficulty. In 1918 there were no election petitions. In 1922
the agent of the National Liberal candidate in Berwick on
Tweed was found to have exceeded the expense limit and to have
made a false return; the member was unseated, but the petition
judges found no evidence of widespread corrupt practices. At
the same election, a scrutiny of the ballot-papers in North East
Derbyshire—where a Labour candidate had won by five votes—
did not reverse the result, although it made plain that the victory
was due to the failure of some presiding officers to stamp some
ballot-papers. In 1923 the Liberal candidate in Oxford shared
the fate of the candidate in Berwick on Tweed the year before,
owing to a similar excess of zeal on the part of his agent. His
is the last instance of a candidate being unseated[2] for election
practices. Since then there have indeed been only two petitions
involving irregularities in the conduct of elections. An allegation
that illegal practices were committed on behalf of the Labour
candidate in the Drake division of Plymouth in 1929 was dis-
missed. Sir Oswald Mosley was equally unsuccessful in his
North Kensington petition in 1959, complaining of administrative irregularities in the conduct of the poll.

[1] In the confusion of 1918 a large number of soldiers' ballots went astray.
[2] The only successful petitions since 1924 have been those involving the
qualification of candidates. In 1955 the defeated Conservative candidate in
Fermanagh and South Tyrone successfully petitioned for the seat on the
ground that the Sinn Fein victor was ineligible, being a felon. After a by-
election, the Conservative candidate for Mid-Ulster followed suit (although
he himself was later found to be disqualified through holding 'an office of
profit under the Crown). In 1961 the Conservative defeated by Mr. Wedg-
wood Benn when the latter stood for re-election in South-East Bristol
petitioned successfully for the seat on the ground that Mr. Benn was known
to be disqualified because of his succession to the peerage.
  The only other cases of elections being declared void do not involve petitions. In 1924 the election of Mr. Preston at Walsall was declared void when
it was found that, unwittingly, he held a contract with the Post Office. In
1950 Mr. MacManaway, from West Belfast, was, after long investigation,
declared ineligible because he had been ordained in the Church of Ireland.

CHAPTER III

1929-31

A^T the general election in May 1929, no party secured a clear majority; 288 Labour members, 260 Conservatives, and 59 Liberals were returned to Parliament. In the political uncertainty which ensued, it was inevitable that attention should be devoted to the electoral system which provoked it. But the main agitation came from those who benefited from minority government rather than from those who deplored it; the Liberals—who had won 25 per cent. of the votes but less than 10 per cent. of the seats—were eager to use their pivotal position to ensure larger representation in the future. One of the main problems of the historian of the second Labour Government is to discover what action the Liberals took to exact the fullest return for their support in the division lobbies.

The question of electoral reform arose immediately Parliament met. The King's Speech included this paragraph:

At the recent General Election an extended franchise placed in the hands of the whole of My people of adult years, the grave responsibility for guarding the well-being of this nation as a constitutional democracy, and My Government propose to institute an examination of the experiences of the election so that the working of the law relating to Parliamentary elections may be brought into conformity with the new conditions.[1]

There is no evidence of any direct Liberal pressure behind this proposal.

In the debate on the Address, Mr. MacDonald was characteristically vague about the purposes of the inquiry; every aspect of the field should be covered, including the system of voting and expenditure by central party headquarters; probably a Speaker's Conference would be the best form of inquiry. His own views on the question were hardly elucidated by this passage:

There are the rival plans of a Second Ballot, an alternative vote and proportional representation and there is another group. There is a group which considers that after all an election really does not begin and end by accurate mathematical representation in this House

---

[1] *H.C. Deb.* 229, c. 49.

of the bodies of the electors who have grouped themselves to put their ballot-papers in the ballot-boxes. One view of Government is the static view where we are an exact replica, on a very small scale, of the millions of electors. That is one view, the static view. But the other view is that the real, final purpose of an election is to elect a Government—and I use the word rather apart from merely electing a House of Commons. That is another view and all these views must be considered in order to find out exactly where we are.[1]

Mr. Churchill questioned the motives behind the inquiry; was it to appease the Liberals? However, although his party would not have initiated it, they would take part in it in good faith.[2] Mr. Lloyd George pointed out the Liberal grievance against the electoral system. But did the Government really mean business? Liberal support would depend on the Government's sincerity on this. They were not trying to make conditions but they meant to use their chance to make sure that the wrong under which 5 million Liberals were suffering should be redressed.[3] Other speakers referred sympathetically to the proposal, although one Conservative remarked on the absence of enthusiasm on the Labour benches when the Prime Minister had spoken of other electoral systems.

On 10 June it was announced that a conference on the lines of the Speaker's Conference of 1917 would be set up. The Speaker and his immediate predecessor were busy, but Lord Ullswater, who as Speaker Lowther had presided in 1917, agreed to be chairman. No definite terms of reference were laid down. It was agreed that party representation in the conference should be based on party strengths in the country rather than in the House. Lord Ullswater duly chose seven M.P.s and one peer from panels submitted by the Conservative and Labour parties and four M.P.s and one peer from a Liberal party panel.[4]

The conference started work in December 1929 and sat until July 1930. Its proceedings were officially secret, but it was well known that it was making little progress. Lord Ullswater's

[1] *H.C. Deb. 229*, cc. 73–74.   [2] Ibid., c. 123.
[3] Ibid., c. 159.
[4] The Liberal peer selected was Lord Hewart, the Lord Chief Justice. His appointment provoked a sharp storm. Mr. Baldwin moved the adjournment of the House (*H.C. Deb. 232*, c. 2019) to discuss this involvement of the judiciary in political affairs. Lord Hewart immediately withdrew his name.

letter reporting to the Prime Minister[1] tells much of the story. The conference had decided that the first matter to be considered was the Liberal suggestion that some system be adopted with a view to 'securing that the composition of the House of Commons shall properly reflect the views expressed by the electorate'. They had during ten sittings heard evidence about the experience of the Dominions and other foreign countries, and they listened at length to Mr. J. H. Humphreys speaking for the Proportional Representation Society, to Mr. Clough, a former M.P., defending the alternative vote, and to Lord Craigmyle, one of their number, who submitted a memorandum favouring the alternative vote in the absence of proportional representation. Finding little hope of agreement on proportional representation, the following resolutions were put to the vote:

1. Any change in the electoral system should involve proportional representation. (Carried by 13 votes to 8, the Conservatives and Liberals supporting, Labour opposing.)
2. Certain constituencies should, in that case, remain single-membered. (Carried by 11 votes to 8, Labour opposing.)
3. In one-member seats the alternative vote should be used. (Rejected by 13 votes to 5, the five being Liberals. One Labour member[2] abstained.)
4. Provision should be made where P.R. is used for by-elections to be held in subdivisions of a multi-membered constituency. (Carried by 8 votes to none, 9 abstaining.)

The Liberals explained that failing proportional representation they would like the alternative vote. The Conservatives were opposed to the alternative vote in all circumstances. The Labour members were not for the alternative vote *per se*, but they would accept it if it was accompanied by these other reforms:

1. Reduction of expense maxima by 1*d.* per elector.
2. Publication of party political accounts.
3. Legalization of the payment of speakers.
4. Prohibition of the use of cars to convey voters to the poll, except under the supervision of the returning officer.

---

[1] *Cmd. 3636/*1930.
[2] Presumably Sir Ernest Bennett. See p. 70 below.

5. Abolition of plural voting and of the university and business franchise.
6. Reintroduction of half-yearly registers.
7. Reduction of the vote required to save the candidate's deposit from one-eighth to one-tenth of the poll.
8. Division of two-member constituencies.
9. Simplification of petition procedure.

Lord Ullswater commented in his letter to the Prime Minister that some of these questions were outside the scope of the conference, as they did not arise from experience since the Representation of the People Act of 1918.[1] The Conservatives felt that, if any questions of corrupt and illegal practices were raised, the whole field should be examined. Lord Ullswater then asked the Prime Minister whether he wanted them to continue. He left it to the conference to decide. They spent three more sittings on election expenses and party accounts. After the fifteenth sitting agreement seemed remote, at any rate during that session, so Lord Ullswater ended the conference.

It is plain that even with goodwill on all sides—and that was certainly lacking—agreement at the conference would not have been possible. On the minor issues some compromise might have been reached, but on the major problem of the system of voting the interests of the parties were too irreconcilable. The bigger parties were almost bound to lose seats, either by P.R. or the alternative vote. The Liberals were bound to gain them. The only hope that the bigger parties would attend to the Liberal demands, apart from the abstract attraction of justice, was that the critical situation in Parliament would force their hands. Labour, whose continuance in office depended on the Liberals, indicated that they might consider the alternative vote. The Conservatives gave little sign of yielding to expediency, although it appears that some members of the conference favoured the idea of P.R. in the larger boroughs as a way of lessening the danger of the Labour party winning a clear parliamentary majority. Lord Hugh Cecil, in particular, was

---

[1] The conference had, of course, no specific terms of reference. But in the King's Speech and in the debate on the Address, it was perhaps implied that the inquiry was to be confined to matters dealt with in 1918.

reported to have diverged from the party line.[1] Outside the conference, at least two of the Conservative leaders, Mr. Churchill and Mr. Amery, advocated electoral reform.

Indeed, on 27 March 1930, while the conference was sitting, Mr. Churchill had said:

> The key to the present political situation consisted in the reform of the electoral law . . . he hoped that the attitude of the Conservative party towards the reform of the electoral law would be such as to enable the two non-Socialist parties to find a certain common measure of agreement. . . . (But) he thought it was more than probable that some understanding had been reached between the Liberal and the Socialist parties behind the backs of Lord Ullswater's Conference. . . . Such an understanding . . . might mean that the electoral law would be altered in a manner most detrimental to the Conservative party.[2]

But while Mr. Churchill's fears about a deal between the other parties were certainly shared by his colleagues, his desire for reform cannot have been very widely supported.

Labour's position was much more equivocal. Lord Snowden later commented 'the conduct of the Labour members of this committee reflected no credit upon them. From the beginning of the proceedings, the Labour members deliberately set themselves to make the Conference abortive.'[3] Certainly the conditions upon which they were prepared to consider the alternative vote were wholly irrelevant to the question. There appears to have been a tug-of-war between the anti-Liberal feeling in the rank and file of the party and the desire of the leaders to stay on good terms with the Liberals—who were, after all, keeping them in power. Under pressure from above, the Labour delegates at the conference were forced to countenance discussion of a reform which almost all of them disliked.

It is impossible fully to disentangle the complications of the relationship between Liberals and Labour. Mr. Lloyd George

---

[1] See the *Daily Telegraph*, 3 May 1930.

[2] *The Times*, 28 Mar. 1930.

[3] Viscount Snowden, *Autobiography* (London, 1934), vol. ii, pp. 885–6. It is notable that when Mr. Humphreys (of the P.R. Society) appeared before the conference, he was cross-questioned at some length by the Conservatives, but that not a single query was put by Labour members.

had certainly issued a warning just after the conference met. Speaking to the Liberal Candidates Association, he said:

The third condition [of co-operation with Labour] should be an understanding that . . . members of the Liberal party should not be assailed by Government nominees in their constituencies, or . . . as an alternative, there should be a *bona fide* promise that a measure of electoral reform would be carried by the Government at an early date.[1]

Subsequent events, notably a luncheon between Mr. Lloyd George and Mr. Snowden, gave rise to rumours of growing Liberal pressure and of a 'deal'. On 4 June *The Times* parliamentary correspondent noted 'there is no doubt that the work of the conference has been made more difficult by the negotiations which have taken place between Mr. Lloyd George and representatives of the Government behind its back'.

However, from the only account of the negotiations between the Liberal and Labour parties which has been published, it would appear that formal discussion of the question of electoral reform only started between the Liberal and Labour parties after the Ullswater Conference had ended. Lord Snowden's memoirs are not perhaps altogether reliable, but he gives this circumstantial account:

On the 18th September 1930, Mr. MacDonald and myself had an important talk with him [Lloyd George] and Lord Lothian in the Cabinet room. . . . When we had finished our talk on these matters [various questions of agricultural and economic policy], Mr. Lloyd George raised the question of the future of the Parliamentary relations between the Government and the Liberal Party. He said that the Liberals could not promise to continue to support the Government in Parliament unless they could get something in return for their support. The co-operation of the Liberals in the coming session would be dependent upon a definite understanding that the Government would introduce and pass legislation for Electoral Reform. The Liberals did not want office but they did want proper Parliamentary representation. . . . He indicated that the Tories were open to bargain with him. The Tories were prepared to promise no opposition to Liberal M.P.s at the next General Election who would help them to turn out the Labour Government and in the next Parliament they would undertake to pass legislation for the introduction of a

---

[1] *The Times*, 21 Jan. 1930.

system of Proportional Representation. Mr. Lloyd George did not want to enter into any alliance with the Tories, and would prefer to continue co-operation with the Labour Government, provided we would pass such a measure of Electoral Reform. He thought it likely that the House of Lords would reject a Reform Bill, and in that case it would have to be passed under the provisions of the Parliament Act. In that case the Labour Government must be kept in office for the two years necessary to overcome the obstruction of the House of Lords. If the Labour Government would agree to his terms, the Liberals in Parliament would support the Government until Electoral Reform had been secured. . . . It was not likely that the Labour Government would introduce legislation the Liberals would oppose. The only measure which might create difficulties was the Trade Union Bill, but if such an understanding as he was suggesting could be reached, he had no doubt that the Liberals would try to avoid the defeat of the Government on this issue.[1]

Later on, Lord Snowden says:

Following upon the understanding with Mr. Lloyd George that an Electoral Reform Bill would be introduced in the new session . . . we arranged that a consultation should take place between the Liberals and ourselves as to the scope of the measure. In these consultations the Labour Government was represented by Mr. Henderson, Lord Arnold and myself, and the Liberals by Sir Herbert Samuel, Mr. Ramsay Muir and Sir Archibald Sinclair. . . . We made it clear to the Liberal members of this Consultative Committee that whatever our personal views might be there was no possibility of the Labour Party in Parliament agreeing to Proportional Representation. . . . The Liberal members of this small Committee realized our position and did not press for the introduction of Proportional Representation . . . so our conversations turned upon the possibilities of the Alternative Vote. Finally it was agreed that the Bill should include a plan for the use of the Alternative Vote.[2]

It is unfortunate that so little of Lord Snowden's narrative can be corroborated. For the reported statement of Mr. Lloyd George that the Conservatives had approached the Liberals with an offer of proportional representation there seems to be no evidence at all—although there were Conservatives who favoured such a step.[3] Sir Herbert Samuel said in a speech some months

---

[1] Op. cit., pp. 883–5.   [2] Ibid., p. 888.
[3] Sir Martin Conway, a Conservative M.P., in a letter published in *The*

later: 'The Conservative Party definitely refused to commit themselves to the introduction of any measure of electoral reform of any kind.'[1]

Nor is there much supporting evidence about the Liberal–Labour 'understanding', despite its much greater inherent plausibility. It does not seem that Mr. Lloyd George understood there to be any clear and binding agreement, for in a speech on 25 October he remarked: 'I would like to say one word to the Prime Minister. He must not presume to the extent of saying that he will not see justice done to the Liberal party electorally. . . . A party can be driven up to a point where its very self-respect will force it to hit out. . . .'[2]

That there was any bargain was certainly firmly denied in the course of subsequent debates by leaders of both the Liberal and Labour parties. Even if there was, in fact, some agreement, these denials need not all be regarded as hypocritical. Mr. Lloyd George was playing a rather lone hand in politics at this time, and on many issues he kept even his closest colleagues unaware of his plans. Mr. MacDonald also often kept his own counsel. Evidence is very hard to come by; none of the memoirs of the period, apart from Lord Snowden's, are of any assistance, and extensive private inquiries throw little further light on the matter.

It must be noted that Lord Snowden's account makes no mention of the Prime Minister's reply to Mr. Lloyd George's proposal. He makes no allegation of a clear-cut bargain. Perhaps it may be assumed that the Prime Minister, taking note of Mr. Lloyd George's remarks and being fully aware of the importance of retaining Liberal support, proceeded to sponsor the alternative vote not in fulfilment of an agreement but as a recognition of immediate political necessity. The fact that the Trade Disputes Bill was subsequently mangled by an official Liberal amendment helps to disprove any suggestion of a definite bargain, although, even if there had been one, the Government

Times on 2 Oct. 1930, said, in the course of a sweeping attack on Mr. Baldwin: 'Moreover he maintains it [the Government] in power though it has always been and still is possible to eject it at a moment's notice if he would agree to support a Reform Bill giving what is called "the Alternative Vote". To this he will not consent.'

[1] *The Times*, 15 Jan. 1931.   [2] Ibid., 27 Oct. 1930.

were by then too far committed to the Electoral Reform Bill
to withdraw it.

Lord Snowden's reference to a discussion with the Liberals
on the form of the Bill need not imply anything more than a
limited agreement on parliamentary tactics; one who was near
these events argues that the discussion merely dealt with action
in case the Conservatives should, in a diversionary move, propose
a P.R. amendment; the Liberals were then to stick to the
alternative vote.

There are many loose ends in this account. On the whole,
however, there seems no reason to disbelieve the broad outlines
of Lord Snowden's story. The Labour party would certainly not
have sponsored the alternative vote for its own sake. There can
be no doubt that the main purpose of the measure was to secure
Liberal support.

On 28 October it was announced in the King's Speech that
'a measure of Electoral Reform will be submitted'.[1] This provoked little comment during the debate on the Address. Some
questions were asked but not answered about the Bill's contents,
and some remarks were made about its dubious origin and its
irrelevance in a time of economic crisis. In December, when it
became known that the alternative vote was to be introduced,
there was much more public comment. On 5 December *The Times*
parliamentary correspondent, discussing rumours of a Liberal–
Labour pact, expressed doubt. If one existed, it was very
private. Many of the Liberal 'Shadow Cabinet' were opposed to
any formal pledge to keep Labour in office until the Electoral
Reform Bill was passed. No special enthusiasm was felt for the
alternative vote, and it would be absolutely impossible to keep
the Government in office merely to pass it over the House of
Lords. Proportional representation would be different. 'The
suggestion that the . . . bill is to be regarded as a *quid pro quo* for
Liberal support for the Trade Disputes Bill is vigorously denied
in Liberal quarters.'[2]

Mr. Lloyd George said that, although he was not for the
alternative vote, it would stop the imposition of a preventive
tariff.[2] *The Economist* commented that Mr. Lloyd George had

---

[1] *H.C. Deb. 244*, c. 7.
[2] *The Times*, 5 Dec. 1930.

been influenced to adopt an 'attitude of malevolent tolerance' towards the Government because of its 'supposed willingness' to introduce the alternative vote.

We use the word supposed advisedly because, although an electoral reform bill has been promised by the Prime Minister, there is as yet no official information as to whether it will really include provisions for a new electoral method. It must, however, be presumed that Mr. Lloyd George has some previous knowledge of the contents of the Bill.[1]

Sir Archibald Sinclair observed in a speech that there seemed to be an idea that the Electoral Reform Bill and the Trade Disputes Bill were somehow linked.

Let me say quite bluntly—from full knowledge of what is in the minds of Mr. Lloyd George and Sir Herbert Samuel—that there is no sort or kind of a pact, written or verbal, with the Labour Party by which the Electoral Reform Bill is introduced in return for our support of amendment of the Trade Disputes Act.

The Labour Government, in introducing the Bill, was under no obligation to the Liberal party.[2] Such a denial was more emphatic than comprehensive. *The Times* parliamentary correspondent reported that the parliamentary Liberal party had met and agreed to support Mr. Lloyd George in his stand on the alternative vote, favouring it, if it should be included in the new Bill. Mr. Lloyd George 'indicated once more that there is no pact or arrangement between ministers and himself and that the Liberals can pronounce no verdict on the electoral reform bill until the text is available'.[3]

Sir John Simon, who was already on the brink of breaking with the Liberal party, made his doubts public in a speech:

He was not enamoured of the alternative vote and he was a little mystified by the sudden change of opinion about its merits. Last October the National Liberal Federation declared for proportional representation and insisted on excluding from its resolution any reference to the alternative vote as a tolerable second best.[4]

[1] *The Economist*, 13 Dec. 1930, p. 1099.   [2] *The Times*, 11 Dec. 1930.
[3] *The Times*, 12 Dec. 1930.
[4] *The Times*, 15 Dec. 1930. This account does not appear fully to agree with reports of the conference of the National Liberal Federation held at Torquay; on 17 Oct. a resolution was passed calling for a better method of election, preferably P.R., but not excluding other methods. Sir John Simon's speech led to a correspondence in *The Times* between Sir Herbert Samuel and himself about his desertion of the alternative vote which he had supported in 1918.

The repeated Liberal denials of a bargain hardly convinced the Conservatives. Sir Samual Hoare said of the 'Liberal–Labour pact' that they were brazen-faced enough to call it electoral reform. It was 'nothing more than an unscrupulous and partisan attack on one political party'.[1] A leading article in *The Times* commented:

> It may be taken as certain . . . that the official view of the two parties who stand to profit most from a change in the electoral law is that the present Parliament should be kept in existence until such a change has been effected.[1]

The Labour party also had its doubts. There was gossip to the effect that if the House of Lords substituted P.R. for the alternative vote, Labour would drop the Bill. Mr. MacDonald hardly clarified the position by a speech on 12 December: 'There is talk about a combination, a bargain and so on. I am in favour of such a change in the electoral system as will prevent a party getting a majority in the House of Commons by a large minority of votes in the country. I believe in two parties' . . . but what happened in 1924 must not be repeated.[2]

On 18 December the parliamentary Labour party met; it was announced that, after Mr. Henderson had said that the alternative vote would be included in the Electoral Reform Bill, 'a lengthy discussion ensued which was concluded by a speech from the Prime Minister. The resolution (approving the proposal) was then put and declared carried by 133 votes to 20.' The twenty were mainly but not entirely from the Clydeside group. There must have been a considerable number of abstentions.

On 19 December the Bill was introduced in dummy. The long title referred to the use of the alternative vote, the division of two-member constituencies, and the abolition of university seats and the business vote; and to facilitating voting for those who moved house, 'making provision with respect to speakers at election meetings', restricting the use of cars on polling-day, reducing election expenses, and limiting the purposes for which

---

[1] *The Times*, 15 Dec. 1930.
[2] *Manchester Guardian*, 12 Dec. 1930. Mr. MacDonald does not seem to have realized that the alternative vote would not have prevented the Conservatives winning a majority of seats with a minority of votes in 1924. See p. 191 below.

party funds might be used. On 17 January the full text was published. It included no provision for the payment of speakers, for
the publication of party accounts, or for facilitating voting by
those who had moved house. It also excepted the City of London
from the abolition of the business vote. On 22 January the Under
Secretary of State for Home Affairs, when questioned in Parliament about the omissions, announced that the Government had,
since December, decided not to proceed with these questions.
To avoid any confusion they would withdraw the Bill and
introduce it again immediately with a more precise long
title.[1] As a result of this the ill-fated Bill proceeded on its way
with the cumbrous label 'The Representation of the People
(No. 2) Bill'.

The provisions of the Bill, particularly the abolition of the
university seats, were unpopular with many people, and by the
time it was debated appreciable opposition had been aroused.
On 24 February Mr. Clynes, the Home Secretary, moved the
second reading.[2] He said that the Bill was the result of the Ullswater Conference. Although the Labour party had said nothing
about voting systems in its election programme, it had reserved
the right to improve 'the political instrument'. The alternative
vote maintained and improved the single-member constituency
system and had been repeatedly endorsed in the past. Plural
voting could no longer be justified, and the Conservatives must
also be deprived of the special advantages which the ownership
of cars gave them.

Sir Samuel Hoare's reply summed up the Conservative case
against the Bill. It was irrelevant to the current economic crises.
It was only introduced to buy Liberal support. The clause on
publication of party funds had been dropped because it would
embarrass Mr. Lloyd George. The alternative vote was bad in
principle and had always proved unsatisfactory in practice.
University representation had fully justified itself. The virtues
of the business vote were admitted by the Government by their
preservation of it in the City of London. The limitation on cars
was absurd.

These opening speeches covered almost all the ground which

---

[1] *H.C. Deb.* 247, c. 344.
[2] Ibid., cc. 1467 et seq.

was subsequently crossed and recrossed in a singularly dreary two-day debate. The Prime Minister spoke with greater length than clarity about the alternative vote, devoting himself mainly to showing that there was no jugglery about second preferences and that there would be no more log-rolling than already went on. The Liberals who spoke all regretted the absence of P.R. from the Bill but welcomed the alternative vote as a great improvement of the existing system. Sir Ernest Bennett, who had been a Labour representative on the Ullswater Conference, was the only member to speak in unqualified support of the alternative vote. Several Labour members expressed doubts about it or even open hostility. One Labour member, Mr. Lang, pleaded for the university franchise in defiance of the general 'one man, one vote' arguments of his colleagues. The supporters of the Bill made small allusion to the allegations of a bargain, although one back-bencher did describe the Bill as 'the result of a bargain, but none the worse for that'. Mr. Shaw, Secretary for War, who replied to the debate, firmly denied that there had been any bargain.

The Opposition devoted themselves mainly to the defence of university representation and to the unsatisfactory nature of the alternative vote. The limitation on cars was ridiculed as a disfranchising clause, and the bargain underlying the whole Bill was repeatedly attacked, although no evidence was offered.

The Bill received a second reading by 295 votes to 230 on a strict party division. *The Times* commented that the Bill was a waste of time, but

the debate made it clear that no party except the Liberal Party really wants any change in the electoral system at all and few in any party expect that it will reach the statute book in anything like its present form. As for the Liberal Party, the incredulous laughter which greeted Sir Herbert Samuel's claim that the Liberals were not concerned with the effect of the Bill on their electoral fortunes was surely excusable. . . . Nothing said during the debate can seriously shake the conclusion that the Bill is part of a bargain . . . to keep the Unionists out.[1]

At the end of February the Trade Disputes Bill ran into considerable difficulties. The Government was defeated in

[1] *The Times*, 4 Feb. 1931.

standing committee because some Liberals had sided with the Conservatives. *The Times* parliamentary correspondent wrote:

Labour back-benchers who were annoyed at the action of the Liberals over the Trade Disputes Bill were declaring last night that they would do nothing more to support the demand of the Liberals for the alternative vote. So far, however, there is no indication that the Government will leave it to a free vote of the House—on which it would certainly be defeated. The Prime Minister devoted a considerable part of his speech on the second reading to the merits of the Alternative Vote and it is felt that . . . it would be quite impossible to abandon it now, especially as Mr. MacDonald made it clear that there was no compact with the Liberals on the subject. . . . The rank and file of the Liberal Party are delighted that the party has proved . . . that there is no compact between them and the Government.[1]

It was in this embittered atmosphere that the House proceeded to the committee stage of the Bill. On 3 March the Prime Minister moved the limitation of the discussion of five days, with two days more for the report stage and third reading. Mr. Baldwin gave the first of a prolonged and vehement series of protesting speeches; the guillotine, it was argued, was not justified by the pressure on parliamentary time, by the urgency of the legislation, or by the obstructiveness of the Opposition. Very strong language was used, but when, at the end of five and a half hours' debate, the Prime Minister agreed to offer one more day, the Opposition seems to have been almost completely mollified.[2]

The committee stage began after the Speaker had refused to accept instructions which would have allowed the discussion of redistribution of seats and of proportional representation. The first clause, providing for the alternative vote, was then debated.[3] An amendment which would apply the alternative vote to Northern Ireland was moved by the Liberals. The Conservatives accused them of still wanting to coerce Ulster, and pointed out the difficulties that the division of the two-member counties would involve. Mr. Clynes successfully appealed for the amendment not to be pressed, on the ground that it was not wanted by those concerned.[4]

---

[1] *The Times*, 27 Feb. 1931.   [2] *H.C. Deb. 249*, cc. 229 et seq.
[3] Ibid., cc. 415 et seq.
[4] While the Bill was in preparation, the Cabinet had decided that its application to Northern Ireland must be decided in consultation with the Northern

The debate on the Conservative motion to reject the whole clause provided the fullest discussion on a proposal to change the system of voting that occurred after 1918. But it did not show the House at its best; the convinced defenders of the alternative vote were very few, and the opponents were confused because, while they feared a measure which could hardly help their interests, they were not really clear what its consequences would be. The Opposition pointed out that nobody really wanted the alternative vote; that there would be wangling about the distribution of second preferences; that the alternative vote had produced disastrously unfair results in Alberta and in the Australian Senate; that it would weaken party lines and make impossible strong government; that the candidate eliminated first might be most popular on second preferences; that the alternative vote would not have prevented the Conservative minority victory in 1924; that it was too complicated for the ordinary elector to understand; and that too much power was given to second preferences. The defenders of the clause argued that the alternative vote was the best version of the second ballot and that it saved the electors in a constituency from having a member repugnant to the majority of them; there would be no wangling, for the ordinary voter would not take orders from his party; the likelihood of the candidate most popular on second preferences being eliminated on the first count was not great; it was not true that undue weight would be given to second preferences; the voter was not as stupid as the Conservatives suggested. Mr. Clynes observed that it was a simple change and that, unlike the drastic reform of proportional representation, it needed no mandate; the Government could not listen to appeals to allow a free vote since it was the main proposal of the Bill. The clause was then carried by 277 votes to 253. Despite the whips, 11 Labour and 2 Liberals voted against it and 27 Labour members were absent unpaired.[1]

Ireland Government—but that consultation would have to await the publication of the Bill, as communication with the Northern Ireland Government was tantamount to communication with the Conservative party. After the publication of the long title in December, the Northern Ireland Government wrote asking that it should not apply to the six counties. They attacked the abolition of university representation, both in general principle and because the disfranchisement of Queen's University would reduce the representation of Northern Ireland from the thirteen seats granted in 1922.

[1] *The Times*, 6 Mar. 1931.

The second clause providing for the division of the eleven
two-member constituencies[1] was less contentious. An attempt
to take the appointment of Boundary Commissioners out of the
hands of the Home Secretary in order to secure impartiality was
withdrawn when Mr. Clynes promised to follow the same procedure as in 1918. A few traditionalists pleaded for the preservation of a system which went back to 1265, but, whatever their
party, the members who sat for two-member seats were united
in welcoming their abolition, and the clause was accepted without a division.[2]

The third clause, which abolished the business vote, except
in the City of London, provoked one of the liveliest debates[3] on
the Bill. The Government were under fire from their own back-
benchers for preserving any remnant of the business vote and
from the Opposition for leaving the question of the representation of the City of London to a free vote. The tradition of City
representation, the role of the City in world prosperity, and the
importance of a place where, though few people lived, 400,000
worked were much stressed. To a Labour amendment—moved
by Mr. Oliver Baldwin—that the City should also lose the
business vote, Mr. Clynes replied that without the business vote
the City could not be preserved as a constituency; however,
those who used their business vote in the City would not be
allowed to use their ordinary residential vote as well. Mr. Amery
defended functional representation and suggested that the City
members should be retained not as relics of the past but as pre-
cursors of a much wider system of special representation in the
future. Others pointed out that the City paid one-quarter of
the income-tax in the country and that 'the man who pays the
piper calls the tune' was a better slogan than 'one man, one
vote'. Sir James Reynolds brought the question of the effect of
the Bill down to statistical terms—and was the only member
ever to do so;[4] he estimated that the Conservatives would lose
24 seats from the ending of the business vote, perhaps 30 from
the alternative vote, and 11 from the abolition of university

---

[1] There were fifteen two-member seats, but the City of London and the
three counties in Northern Ireland were not affected.

[2] *H.C. Deb.* 249, c. 656.

[3] Ibid., cc. 657 et seq. [4] Ibid., c. 692.

seats.[1] Sir Herbert Samuel said that the Liberals had no strong feelings on the question and that they, too, would allow a free vote. It was notable that although the Chairman had said that the general discussion of the merits of the business vote should take place on Mr. Oliver Baldwin's amendment, relatively little time or argument was devoted to the defence of the principle of plural voting; perhaps because it was a difficult case to present, the general merits of the occupation franchise were subordinated in discussion to the more particular and sentimental claims of the City of London. The amendment was finally defeated by 283 votes to 206. The Liberals were fairly evenly divided; the Conservatives and the embarrassed Government made up the majority, the Government's back-benchers the minority. The whole clause eliminating plural voting was then passed by 271 votes to 228 on a straight party division.

On 16 March the fourth clause, which abolished university representation, was discussed.[2] This had provoked more public attention than any other clause in the Bill, and an appreciable amount of propaganda and lobbying had been done on behalf of the universities. The members for Oxford and Cambridge had jointly circularized their constituents asking them to protest against their disfranchisement. The Senates of the provincial universities had passed resolutions expressing dismay at the clause, and many letters to the press, to M.P.s, and to the Home Secretary testified to the feeling aroused. The only amendment to the clause to be discussed was one designed to save Queen's University, Belfast, from disfranchisement, on the ground that Northern Ireland could not be deprived of any of her thirteen seats without dishonouring the Irish settlement. The Government replied that the settlement had not mentioned representation and that Belfast, with 3,300 electors, was the smallest of the university constituencies and could not possibly be exempted. The amendment was defeated by 178 votes to 168.

[1] His estimate about the business vote seems excessive (see below, pp. 147–8). His estimate about the alternative vote may have been too small rather than too big (see below, pp. 189–91). His estimate about the university seats is hardly complimentary to the two Liberals and the two Independents then representing them. There were at the time only eight university M.P.s who were Conservatives. [2] *H.C. Deb. 249*, cc. 1695 et seq.

Lord Hugh Cecil then moved the rejection of the clause in what seems to have been the most notable speech the Bill was to evoke. He poured scorn on the idea of egalitarian democracy, of 'one man, one vote'; under the present system votes were not of the same value in marginal as in safe seats; university representation was the least anomaly in an unjust system of representation; the voter could only choose between the candidates offered to him by the party oligarchy; this sacrifice to equality was a sacrifice to a false God, for equal representation had not existed and could not exist; however, the present system did represent the communities in the country, and the universities should be included among the communities. A Labour member, Major Church, seconded the opposition which thereafter was almost monopolized by university members. Only two other territorial members spoke on that side. The Opposition's case lay under five heads: university representation was an ancient tradition which should not be broken; it was expanded in 1918, and the 1918 settlement should be honoured; it had sent many distinguished men to Parliament; it was becoming less and less an upper-class franchise; and brains and technical skill had a claim to special representation. On the other side, the case was argued on the simple ground of equality; the universities were more than adequately represented by ordinary members; the educated had extra power in many ways—there was no need to give them extra votes as well; university members were not, in practice, particularly independent, and most of them could have been elected for ordinary constituencies. At the end of the debate, the Government was defeated by 246 votes to 242. The vote (including tellers and pairs) was made up:

	Cons.	Lib.	Lab.	Ind.	Total
For university representation	255	16	2	4	277
Against	..	19	254	..	273

Those absent unpaired included 3 Conservatives, 23 Liberals, and 20 Labour members.[1]

[1] *The Times*, 18 Mar. 1931.

The failure of the Liberals to give better support to the Government provoked a new crisis in the perennially delicate relations between the Liberal and Labour parties. Rumours that the Government would withdraw the Bill to punish the Liberals were quickly stilled when, on 19 March, the Government announced that it would be proceeded with after Easter. However, within the parties, as well as between them, feelings were exacerbated. In the Labour party there was some bitterness against those members whose abstention had caused the Government's defeat. In the Liberal party the split led to a meeting on 24 March, when by a vote of only 33 to 17 the Liberal M.P.s endorsed Mr. Lloyd George's policy of giving general support to the Government.[1]

The clause dealing with the restriction on cars came next. It provided that no one should be driven to the poll except by a resident member of his family or in a car voluntarily put at the disposal of the returning officer and under his orders. This clause may have been affected by a debate on 10 December 1930, a week before the contents of the Bill were announced, when Mr. Toole seized an opportunity to bring in a motion advocating a ban on the use of cars on polling-day except in special cases.[2] Conservatives then pointed out the difficulty of framing legislation on this without disfranchising many voters, but Labour members strongly supported the motion; in the end it was withdrawn on a Government assurance that the Bill would deal with the matter. It is not clear whether this debate was needed to bring action, for the reform had already been demanded by Labour members at the Ullswater Conference. When the clause was discussed in committee,[3] the Opposition spent much time effectively ridiculing it, pointing out how unenforceable it was and what hardship it would cause in country districts. Not only was it impracticable, it was injudicious; Sir Thomas Inskip remarked frankly that each party had its own special advantages at elections—the Labour party never paid for the clerical assistance it got from the trade unions; any legislation to remove one party's special advantages should be balanced on the other side. The Government and their sup-

---

[1] *The Times*, 25 Mar. 1950.   [2] *H.C. Deb. 246*, cc. 437 et seq.
[3] *H.C. Deb. 251*, cc. 985 et seq.

porters were manifestly unhappy; they made much of the unfair assistance which Conservative candidates received from car-owners, but they could not pretend that the provisions in the clause were satisfactory; in the end they made it plain that they would consider drastic amendments as long as the general purpose of the clause was realized. The committee proceedings on further amendments were chaotic and the vital amendment which would provide that each party should be allowed to use a limited number of cars—instead of their being a returning officer's pool—had not been reached by the time the guillotine fell. The principle of limiting the use of cars was endorsed by 263 votes to 229. Including pairs, the Liberals divided 33 to 10 in favour of it.[1]

The reduction in the permitted expenditure was next debated.[2] The Bill provided that the maximum in boroughs should be reduced from 5*d.* to 4*d.* per elector and in counties from 6*d.* to 5*d.* The matter was very moderately discussed. Mr. Maxton appealed for a much lower maximum, while many Conservatives supported an amendment to leave the county maximum unchanged and to reduce the borough maximum by only $\frac{1}{2}d$. It was argued that a lot of money had to be spent if the candidate and the issues were to be adequately presented to the electorate. Mr. Clynes pointed out that in 1929 only eighty candidates had in fact exceeded the proposed new maximum, and Mr. Cazalet, a Conservative, welcomed the reduction on the ground that it would shield a candidate from the extravagance of his agent. On the other hand, Mr. Majoribanks protested that while Labour could get free workers by their election promises, Conservative workers were accustomed to being paid; the maximum was only permissive, and it was well to

---

[1] After this a conference was held at the Home Office between the Home Secretary, senior officials of the Department, parliamentary draftsmen, and representatives from Transport House. It was agreed that the original draft of the clause, allotting cars to the returning officers was impracticable and that a limitation on the number of cars which could be used on behalf of each candidate would have to be substituted.

While it is not unusual for representatives of the three parties to be summoned to the Home Office for unofficial conferences, this consultation between representatives of the party sponsoring the Bill and parliamentary draftsmen is probably unprecedented and also, by current standards, improper. [2] *H.C. Deb. 251*, cc. 1177 et seq.

leave a reasonable margin. The Conservative amendment was defeated by 258 votes to 68, a number of Conservatives voting with the majority, and the clause was accepted without a division.

The remaining clauses were passed with only drafting amendments, and a new clause, proposed by Mr. Cecil Wilson,[1] which would have merged all the English university seats into a seven-membered proportional representation constituency, was ruled out of order.[2] The first Schedule of the Bill which laid down the rules for the alternative vote caused considerable trouble.[3] Sir Hilton Young, in the ablest speech to be made on the technical side of the problem, moved that the Nanson system of counting the votes should be adopted. Simply to eliminate the bottom candidate and transfer his votes might well result in the election of the least popular man. The Nanson system, although complicated, was theoretically perfect.[4] Mr. Oliver, Under Secretary at the Home Office, replied that despite its excellence the Nanson system was not quite perfect; if there were more than four candidates, to use one's second and third preferences could reduce the chances of one's first preference candidate. In any case, the system was so intricate as to be impracticable; in the second reading debate, Sir Hilton Young had admitted as much. However, the Conservatives developed an ironical enthusiasm for the amendment and several speakers advocated it, either professing a zeal for theoretic perfection or arguing that the more complicated the electoral system the more effectively it worked as an intellectual franchise test. The amendment was defeated by 242 votes to 158. The Government, in the face of some Conservative obstruction, accepted an amendment to allow the use of as many preferences as there were candidates—the Bill had provided only for the use of a

[1] Mr. Wilson was Chairman of the Executive Committee of the Proportional Representation Society.   [2] *H.C. Deb. 251*, c. 1266.
[3] *H.C. Deb. 252*, cc. 1013 et seq.
[4] This system was first propounded by Professor Nanson in 1882 in a paper which was reproduced as an Appendix to the Report of the Royal Commission on Electoral Systems (*Cd. 5163*/1910, p. 39). It provides that if there are n candidates, first preferences shall be worth $n-1$ votes, second preferences $n-2$, and so on. All preferences are included in the count. Any candidate who fails to secure an nth share of the votes is eliminated. If more than one candidate remains, the process is repeated with the surviving candidates until only one is left.

first and a second preference. Further amendments from the Conservatives to bar the transfer of votes cast for candidates who lost their deposits, to eliminate all but the first two candidates on the second count, and to count second preferences as only half a vote, were all firmly rejected, although the last attracted a number of supporters from those Labour members who were firmly opposed to the alternative vote.

The House spent two days over the report stage of the Bill. Much old ground was retraced, but, as the Government had decided to accept defeat on the university clause, only two important issues arose. The first was on a new clause which the Government added to make plain that no one might vote more than once in a general election.[1] The Conservatives put a vigorous defence of plural voting on the second reading of the new clause, and when it had been carried they moved amendments to except the City of London and the university vote from its operation. The idea that all were equal was firmly ridiculed; the claim of business to special representation was defended; the need for plural voting to make university representation effective was expounded; Miss Rathbone argued that there was a danger of permanent working-class dominance in the electorate and that the university franchise offered some check. On the Government side the 'one man, one vote' argument was obdurately repeated, and the clause was carried by 261 votes to 225.

The second issue came in connexion with the clause limiting cars.[2] A Conservative motion to allow each candidate four cars per polling-district was rejected, on the ground that the number of polling-districts was seldom proportionate to the area of the constituency. The Government then proposed that each candidate should be permitted to use one car for every thousand electors in the constituency. This was stigmatized as hopelessly inadequate and bound to disfranchise many rural voters, but it was supported by 233 votes to 205. An amendment to allow substitute cars to be used when cars were not available for the whole polling-day was rejected, but another excluding the 54 constituencies of more than 400 square miles in area from the operation of the clause was accepted.

[1] *H.C. Deb. 252*, cc. 199 et seq.   [2] Ibid., cc. 2227 et seq.

On 2 June 1931 the Bill received a third reading.[1] Little new remained to be said. Once again Sir Herbert Samuel very firmly and specifically denied that there was any Liberal–Labour bargain. Captain Bourne challenged the Government to follow precedent and to go to the country as soon as the Bill was passed. Mr. Churchill, who had hitherto been silent on the Bill, intervened with a vehement demand for proportional representation in the large cities and for more plural voting, not less. The alternative vote was the child of fraud and would become the parent of folly; however, the Lords would give the country time to think again on this measure, produced by two despairing parties, who had made an irresponsible bargain to save their own skins.[2] The Bill was passed by 278 votes to 228 and sent to meet its fate in the House of Lords.

Lord Passfield, moving the second reading there,[3] argued somewhat lukewarmly that it was a small Bill and would have small effects. His Liberal supporters were more enthusiastic, describing the alternative vote as a substantial remedy for a substantial grievance. Lord Reading gave one more denial of any Liberal bargain about the Bill. Lord Banbury, naturally, moved the rejection of the Bill, but Lord Peel, as the official Conservative spokesman, said that it would be unwise and discourteous to do this; the Bill had many faults and represented a dangerous attempt to alter the system of government for party advantage, but it should be given a full examination. Lord Ullswater intervened weightily against the Government; for fifty years the electoral system had been changed only by party agreement; this Bill disturbed the 1918 compromise on plural voting; his conference had decided by a majority that any change in the electoral system should involve proportional representation; the alternative vote made no improvement on the existing system and it would be unpopular; it failed to meet legitimate grievances. The Conservative peers were silent but allowed the Bill a second reading by 50 votes to 14.

In committee a fortnight later they proceeded to kill virtually

---

[1] *H.C. Deb. 253*, cc. 43 et seq.

[2] Ibid., cc. 100–11. It is interesting to note that, even in 1931, Mr. Churchill could say that he had a special claim to speak on elections, since he had, in fact, fought more than any man alive.

[3] *H.L. Deb. 81*, cc. 124 et seq.

all its provisions.[1] A motion to substitute P.R. in a hundred constituencies for the alternative vote in all was, in contrast to the Commons, ruled to be in order; in the debate Lord Ullswater strongly endorsed the amendment and Lord Passfield argued against P.R. with much more enthusiasm than he had argued for the alternative vote; Lord Hailsham then intervened for the Conservatives and ended the discussion by saying that although the amendment was reasonable it was outside the Bill and should be abandoned. The next amendment, moved by the Earl of Midleton, was designed to limit the application of the alternative vote to constituencies in boroughs which had a population of more than 200,000.[2] He argued that as there was no mandate for the change the alternative vote, which anyway was a bad scheme, should to begin with be applied to only a limited number of constituencies. Although Lord Passfield pointed out that the amendment would wreck the whole purpose of the Bill, it was passed by 80 votes to 29 after a very brief debate.

A week later the abolition of the business vote and of the right to vote more than once were discussed.[3] Blunter and more extreme defences of plural voting than had been heard in the Commons were uttered. Lord Passfield protested that the business vote did not go to captains of industry or to those linked to joint-stock companies, but to a very random collection of people—and their wives; he firmly denied that the 1918 settlement had any binding force. But by votes of 96 to 26 and 96 to 24 the Lords firmly rejected the 'one man, one vote' argument. After only three further speeches, they proceeded to abolish the clause limiting the use of cars. Some drafting amendments were then made, but, in view of the disapproval of the Conservative leaders, a couple of amendments further limiting the scope of the alternative vote by excluding certain votes from the second count were abandoned.[4] On the report stage Lord

[1] Ibid., cc. 565 et seq.

[2] One hundred and seventy-four constituencies fell into this category. Since it was common for Liberals to run second in three-cornered fights in the counties and occasionally in the smaller boroughs, but rare for them to be second in the large boroughs, this amendment would have excluded virtually all the seats where the alternative vote could have benefited the Liberals.

[3] *H.L. Deb. 81*, c. 701.

[4] The *Manchester Guardian* (11 July 1931) pointed out that, although the peers responsible for this mangling of the Bill were not official Conservative

Passfield announced that the Government could not accept the Lords' amendments, but that they would not fight them at the moment; they were then accepted without discussion. The Bill received its third reading on 21 July and was returned to the Commons.

The Times parliamentary correspondent, referring to the mangling of the Bill, said that the Liberals would certainly urge the Government to restore the Representation of the People Bill to its old form before the end of the month and that

they will doubtless agree to do so, but it will be without any enthusiasm, for the feeling which has prevailed among Labour backbenchers for a long time, that the alternative vote would not be of the slightest use to them, has spread to the Government Front Bench and there are Ministers who would be glad to see the Bill dropped altogether.

But probably there would be a compromise; the Government would secure the alternative vote but accept all the other demands of the Lords.[1] Two weeks later *The Times* took a much stronger line in an editorial which saw little room for compromise; the Bill was a mere pawn in the political game between the Liberals and the Socialists. By allowing the alternative vote in one-third of the constituencies the Lords had admitted the Liberal grievance to be genuine. 'Indeed by their action they have involved themselves in a considerable difficulty for, if no change ought to be made, the concession is too great, but, if there ought to be a change, then the concession is too small.' There was no logic in the selection of the constituencies to be affected. The Lords had two courses in the forthcoming negotiations between the Houses—either total rejection or full acceptance of the alternative vote. If they decided to give it a trial, three things must be made clear: the alternative vote must be the sole concession; it must be only experimental; and party consequences must not be considered.[2]

Some weeks remained before the recess, but the Government

spokesmen, their action seemed to be approved by their party leaders. The *Manchester Guardian* assumed that in rejecting so much of the Bill, the Lords were thinking of negotiations between the Houses. 'The more [the Bill] is disembowelled, the more room they have for professing concessions' in later discussions.

[1] *The Times*, 10 July 1931.   [2] Ibid., 21 July 1931.

decided not to consider the Lords' amendments until the autumn. There was no intention of abandoning it. There is no doubt that the Cabinet resolved that the Bill should be pushed through unchanged under the provisions of the Parliament Act; only pressure of business caused the postponement of debate on the Lords' amendments.[1] In August the Government fell and no more was heard about the Bill in public, although privately Sir Herbert Samuel, now Home Secretary, pressed Mr. MacDonald to pass it before going to the country in October; he received a somewhat unsympathetic negative.

So perished a Bill whose parentage was obscure and whose life had been chequered and inglorious. It had had few sincere friends and many enemies, some avowed and some secret. It seemed to bring out the worst in all who dealt with it, whether they supported or opposed it. One cannot believe that even had so dubious a Bill become an Act, it would have long survived. As it was, those who from the beginning predicted that its provisions would never be realized were amply justified.

[1] See Viscount Snowden, *Autobiography* (London, 1934), vol. ii, p. 888.

I. 1931–9

AFTER 1931 a long period ensued in which the electoral system excited virtually no interest. The Proportional Representation Society continued to campaign and the Liberal party duly protested at the injustices under which they suffered. But the Labour party had abandoned all interest in changing the system of voting, despite the fact that in 1931 they suffered the heaviest blow ever to befall a major party; their numbers were cut from 288 to 52, and for four years they remained disastrously under-represented in the House. In 1935 they still fared badly enough—40 per cent. of the votes won them less than one-quarter of the seats—but they remained loyal to the system which seemed to offer them the best chance of gaining a clear parliamentary majority. The Conservatives naturally had little interest in electoral reform: none seems publicly to have advocated making use of the opportunity to reduce by P.R. the likelihood of the Socialists ever gaining absolute power. Apart from occasional allusions to the old issues and to the growing urgency of a redistribution of seats, the period seems to have been one in which the system was accepted and ignored.

Parliamentary references to electoral matters between 1931 and 1939 were few in number. Questions were much less frequent than formerly and mostly concerned redistribution. Only one Act was passed. Sir Ian Fraser sponsored a Bill[1] to amend the procedure by which blind persons voted, and managed adroitly to manœuvre it through Parliament unopposed, having introduced it under the difficult procedure of the ten-minute rule. A certain number of Bills and motions were put down for debate, but only four Bills and three motions were actually discussed.

Under the ten-minute rule a Bill to trisect the overgrown Romford constituency received a first reading without opposi-

---

[1] Enacted in 23 & 24 Geo. 5, ch. 27.

tion in 1933[1] and leave to introduce another which disfranchised those who, without good excuse, failed to vote was granted by 90 votes to 76 a year later.[2] In 1938 Major Milner used a place in the private members' ballot to introduce a Bill which prohibited the use of cars to take voters to the poll except under the supervision of the returning officer.[3] The lesson of the 1931 clause dealing with this subject[4] seems to have been forgotten, and even if the Conservatives had been prepared to accept the principle involved in the Bill, it was too ill-drafted to have any hope of passage. In a brief debate the Conservatives treated the question flippantly, while their opponents expressed indignation at the unfair advantage cars gave to them. The Bill was talked out.[5] The only other Bill in the period was one aimed at accelerating the publication of the autumn register; it was briefly discussed in the House of Lords and withdrawn on a promise of Government consideration.[6]

The three motions discussed were of more significance. In 1933 Mr. Holdsworth, a Liberal, moved for an inquiry into electoral reform and advocated proportional representation.[7] The familiar arguments were used on both sides, but only one Liberal and one ironical Conservative supported any change. Mr. Attlee led the opposition to the motion, with a plea for strong government; when challenged by Sir Herbert Samuel on his support for the alternative vote two years earlier, he replied that it was only the result of a bargain with the Liberals and that, although he had voted for it, he had disapproved of it. The motion was, in effect, defeated by 128 votes to 32, a few Labour and Conservative members joining the Liberals in its support.

In February 1936 Sir John Train moved that the Govern-

[1] *H.C. Deb. 281*, c. 741.   [2] *H.C. Deb. 288*, c. 158.

[3] *H.C. Deb. 331*, c. 1460.

[4] It was then discovered that such a scheme was impracticable and that to allot a certain number of cars to each candidate seemed to be the only feasible way of dealing with the question. See pp. 77 and 79 above.

[5] Sir Richard Acland (*H.C. Deb. 331*, c. 1480) gave an estimate, the first of its kind in Parliament, of the effect of cars. In this last election he had had 40 cars to the Conservatives' 200. Assuming that a car took 24 people to the poll in a day, that meant that the Conservatives gained 4,800 votes to his 960 from those who received lifts. Both the accuracy and the representativeness of this estimate are perhaps questionable.

[6] *H.L. Deb. 114*, c. 258.

[7] *H.C. Deb. 283*, cc. 1725 et seq.

ment should consider redistribution.[1] He and every subsequent speaker pointed to the serious anomalies that had developed since the last redistribution in 1918, and those concerned explained the difficulties of representing and the expense of fighting the very large constituencies. The Government expressed general sympathy, but said that redistribution must wait at least until the current modification of local government areas was completed in the following year.

In the same month, a more contentious motion, advocating the abolition of university representation, was brought forward by Mr. Viant, a Labour member.[2] The motion was, it is plain, provoked by the fact that Mr. Ramsay MacDonald, defeated at the recent general election, had just been returned by the Scottish Universities. There were many criticisms of this 'abuse' of university representation, but otherwise the argument followed the lines of the 1931 debate on the subject, Lord Hugh Cecil even giving a repetition of his previous speech. As usual, the university members monopolized their own defence against an attack which was perhaps more personal than before. These 'pocket boroughs of reaction', it was alleged, had defeated many good men and returned instead members who seldom justified their vaunted independence. The famous names of past members were cited in reply, and the motion was duly defeated by 227 votes to 130.

There was only one investigation in the 1930's which bore even remotely on the electoral system. In 1938 a Select Committee was set up to inquire into the position of the Speaker's seat. It reported[3] unanimously that it was undesirable to create a special nominal seat for the Speaker merely to prevent his constituency from being deprived of an active representative. To do that, it was held, would reduce the Speaker to a mere official and deprive him of that special element in his authority which derives from his being just another member.

It is perhaps appropriate that this isolated investigation should have led to a complacent acceptance of the *status quo*. In the 1930's hardly anyone questioned the electoral system.

[1] *H.C. Deb. 308*, cc. 283 et seq.
[2] *H.C. Deb. 309*, cc. 469 et seq.
[3] *Parliamentary Papers*, 1938–9, vol. viii, p. 215.

11. 1939-45

The outbreak of war in September 1939 made necessary interim legislation to suspend elections and electoral registration for the time being. The complications of this stop-gap action, coupled with the war-time zeal for reform, provoked in due course a general investigation which first produced thorough-going interim legislation and ultimately bore fruit in the Representation of the People Act of 1948. However, little parliamentary or public attention was devoted to these matters until the last years of the war.

Two Acts were passed annually throughout the war to hold the electoral machinery in abeyance. The first, the Local Elections and Register of Electors (Temporary Provisions) Act, was introduced in October 1939. It suspended all local elections for the duration of the war and it provided that no further register should be compiled for the time being, but that the one which was just being completed should remain valid indefinitely. This Act[1] was passed after only the briefest debate and was renewed every autumn until 1944 without serious discussion; in 1943 its registration provisions were superseded and dropped. From 1940 onwards a Prolongation of Parliament Act[2] was passed simultaneously. This extended for one year at a time the quinquennial provision of the Parliament Act of 1911. It attracted rather more attention than its companion and the second reading debates provided a platform for those who wished to protest at the delay in improving the register and the electoral machinery, and also for the small and heterogeneous group who constituted the war-time Opposition and who had more fundamental complaints against the Government's perpetuation of its own life. But only in 1942 was there a division on the Bill; it was then carried by 215 votes to 9.[3]

Meanwhile preparations were being made for less ephemeral legislation. In January 1942 a weighty committee was set up by the Home Secretary to consider whether improved electoral machinery and methods of registration could be devised, especially for the period immediately after the war, and to examine the

[1] See 2 & 3 Geo. 6, ch. 115, for 1939 Act.
[2] See 3 & 4 Geo. 6, ch. 53, for 1940 Act.
[3] *H.C. Deb. 383*, c. 885.

technical problems involved in the redistribution of seats. Sir Sylvanus Vivian, the Registrar-General, presided over this committee which included five M.P.s, as well as official experts and the chief agents of the parties. It produced in December 1942 an unusually wordy report[1] which in due course served as a basis for the interim arrangements on registration and the permanent solution of the redistribution problem.

The pre-war system of registration, it was argued, was quite inadequate to cope with the vast war-time and post-war movement of population. It could take as much as sixteen and a half months after completing the six months' residence qualification for an elector to be placed on an effective register. A system of continuous registration based upon the war-time National Registration machinery was recommended. At any given date the names of all local residents who were of age and who had been resident for a set period could be obtained from the local Food Offices and published to form an electoral register; it would, however, be necessary for claims to be made by those who were absent on war service and by those who were entitled to business votes. A canvass would be required for local elections, so long as they were based on a limited franchise.[2]

Redistribution, it was pointed out, had never been anybody's official concern. Great anomalies had developed since the last boundary changes were made in 1918. There was no reason why redistribution should only take place at times of comprehensive electoral reform; it should be a comparatively frequent process carried out on the advice of a permanent boundary commission. However, in view of the war-time situation, the only immediate redistribution possible would be on a 1939 basis. Since then there had been a great movement of population and such a redistribution would soon have to be followed by another redrawing of boundaries. As an alternative it might, for the next election, be worth redistributing seats only among those constituencies which diverged very sharply from the average quota on a 1939 basis. The Labour members of the committee, in a

---

[1] *Cmd. 6408/1942.*

[2] In view of this, three members of the committee argued that if a canvass had to be made, it should be used for parliamentary purposes too and that the Food Office records should only be used to bring the register up to date in the event of an election.

reservation to this, argued that partial redistribution in war-time was unthinkable; the very small constituencies were mainly in the London area and were peculiarly affected by war conditions; 'it is inevitable that a partial scheme would give rise to dissatisfaction and possibly criticism on the part of any political organization or group which under a piecemeal scheme found itself at a temporary disadvantage. . . .'[1]

The report of the committee attracted little attention. However, irritation at the deplorable state of the register as revealed in by-elections was growing steadily, and there were more and more references to the desirability of another Speaker's Conference, an idea which had been mooted by some leading Liberals as early as 1940. But the Government decided to take direct action on the recommendations of the Vivian Committee. In June 1943 it was announced that a Bill would be introduced to arrange for the compilation of an electoral register on the basis of the National Register, and a month later another Bill, which would establish the general principles of redistribution and set up Boundary Commissions, was announced. At the time of these announcements in the House of Commons[2] there were many demands for a more comprehensive inquiry on electoral matters, but the Government would make no promise of a Speaker's Conference. However, the pressure appears to have been sufficient, and on 14 October Mr. Churchill announced that a Speaker's Conference would be established. It was decided to postpone the Bill on redistribution until after its report, but the registration question was immediately dealt with under the Parliament (Elections and Meeting) Bill.[3]

This Bill contained thirty-five clauses and seven schedules, but its length was due more to the precision of its drafting than to the difficulty or the number of the main principles involved. It provided that for the duration of the emergency any election should be fought upon a register specially compiled after its announcement from the Food Office data; two months' residence would be required to qualify for inclusion. For this purpose,

[1] *Cmd. 6408/1942*, p. 32. For a fuller discussion of the question of redistribution see p. 205 below.
[2] *H.C. Deb. 390*, c. 1311; *391*, c. 1049.
[3] Enacted as 6 & 7 Geo. 6, ch. 48.

elections would be delayed until thirty-six days after the issue of the writ. The Bill also provided for a civilian and a service absent voters' list and for a business voters' list; it would be necessary to make a claim to be included in these lists. The Treasury was to bear the full cost of compiling the register.

At the second reading on 26 October 1943,[1] the Bill was generally welcomed, although there were some protests at the difficulties placed in the way of service and business voters. At the committee stage,[2] only small points were raised. Northern Ireland members objected to the enfranchisement of war-workers from Eire. Conservatives grumbled at the limitation on the business vote involved by the claiming procedure. Some members asked for postal facilities for invalids and for improvements in the arrangements for servicemen. All the amendments were negatived on the ground that they were impracticable, and the Bill was passed without any division. Throughout its passage, however, there was considerable evidence of party friction; some Labour speakers implied that the Conservatives were not eager to enfranchise servicemen, while some Conservatives suggested that an indirect attack on the business vote was in progress.

Unexpected complications arose in applying the Act, and eight months later it was amended by the Parliamentary Electors (War-time Registration) Act.[3] It had been found that there would be great difficulty in applying the new procedure in by-elections. This was not surprising since the procedure was based on the findings of the Vivian Committee which had in fact only been considering how to cope with a general election. There was a shortage of competent staff and it was not easy to find which electors satisfied the two months' residence provision. Therefore, until the end of 1945 it was proposed to abolish the qualifying period. This would enable the 1943 Act to come into operation almost at once. The Bill was somewhat reluctantly accepted as an unfortunate necessity. It was interesting that markedly more hesitation at the abandonment of the residence qualification was shown by Conservative than by Labour members; considerations of party advantage may have

---

[1] *H.C. Deb. 393*, cc. 58 et seq.
[2] Ibid., cc. 685 et seq.　　　　　　　[3] 7 & 8 Geo. 6, ch. 24.

influenced their attitude, but in the main it appears to have been due to a sentimental attachment to the tradition that residence was the basis of the franchise.

A motion welcoming the establishment of the Speaker's Conference was the subject of a two-day debate on 1 and 2 February 1944.[1] This provides the only example in the last thirty years of a general discussion of the electoral system; but it was notable for harmony rather than enlightenment. Mr. Morrison, the Home Secretary, introducing the motion, referred to the successful precedent of 1917, but observed that this time the issues were not so great. The main questions at issue were the principles of redistribution and the fusion of the local government and parliamentary franchise; he did not think that there would be much interest in proportional representation. In fact, however, proportional representation was the main issue on which the debate showed any great difference of opinion. On all sides the need for redistribution and the need to cut down election expenses was expressed. The sending out of poll-cards by returning officers and the desirability of allowing Wales and Scotland to keep a disproportionate number of seats were advocated without consideration of party. Mild opinions for and against the university and business franchises were put forward by the two main parties, but, apart from a deviationist on each side, they were united in opposition to the demands for proportional representation from the Liberals, from Common Wealth, and from Mr. Pritt and Mr. Gallacher. Perhaps the most notable remarks came from Mr. Woodburn, who asked for redistribution to be postponed until after the resettlement of population, and who specifically excluded the City of London from a demand for the abolition of the business vote.

The motion was agreed to without a division, and in this general aura of harmony the conference began its deliberations at once. Its terms of reference were:

To examine and, if possible, submit agreed resolutions on the following matters:
(*a*) Redistribution of seats;
(*b*) Reform of franchise (both Parliamentary and local government);

[1] *H.C. Deb. 396*, cc. 1154 et seq., 1288 et seq.

(c) Conduct and costs of Parliamentary elections, and expenses falling on candidates and Members of Parliament;

(d) Methods of elections.[1]

It had 32 members besides the Speaker. There was one peer from each of the three parties. In addition there were 29 M.P.s, 17 of them Conservative, 8 Labour, 1 Liberal, 1 I.L.P., 1 Independent Labour (Mr. Pritt), and 1 Independent (Mr. Harvey). The Conservatives were led by Lord Margesson and included Sir Hugh O'Neill, Mr. Pickthorn, Mr. Turton, and Sir Herbert Williams. The Labour members were led by Mr. Pethick-Lawrence and included Mr. Parker and Mr. Woodburn. Lord Rea and Miss Lloyd George. represented the Liberals. There was no attempt at strictly proportionate representation, but an effort was made 'to secure, as far as possible, representation of various shades of opinion, different types of constituency and all parts of the country'.[2]

The conference applied itself expeditiously to work. It had been asked to report as soon as possible on the first two questions before it, but it decided at once that redistribution could not be satisfactorily discussed until methods of election had been firmly settled. Five meetings were devoted to discussing this; in the end a Liberal resolution condemning the existing system and advocating proportional representation was defeated by 25 votes to 4, and another recommending a limited experiment with proportional representation was defeated by 24 votes to 5. A third resolution in favour of the alternative vote was defeated by 20 votes to 5. The supporters of change were limited to the two Liberals and the two Independents, with Mr. Maxton for the I.L.P. supporting the alternative vote. It appears, however, that there was also sympathy for the alternative vote among some Labour members who, remembering the Popular Front, felt that only by a combination of the Liberal and Labour votes, such as the alternative vote would make possible, would the Conservatives ever be defeated. Two Labour members of the Speaker's Conference, having failed to convince their colleagues, abstained from voting on this issue.

[1] Letter from the Prime Minister to the Speaker, 8 Feb. 1944, quoted in *Cmd. 6534/1944*, p. 2.

[2] *Cmd. 6534/1944*, p. 3.

Having thus agreed that no drastic change in constituency structure would be required, the conference turned to the question of redistribution, and unanimously agreed on the solution: a temporary measure was required to deal with the most overgrown constituencies and a comprehensive revision of boundaries should follow later. Permanent machinery should be established to prevent serious anomalies arising again. To meet the immediate problem, twenty-five extra constituencies should be created by subdividing those constituencies which in 1939 had grown to more than 190 per cent. of the average size. After this subdivision, the Boundary Commissioners should turn their attention to a complete redistribution of seats. The number of seats should remain substantially unchanged, and, whatever their average electorate, Scotland and Wales should not have their numbers reduced. Northern Ireland should continue to have thirteen seats. The total electorate should be divided by the number of seats, and in general no seat should be more than 25 per cent. above or below the quota thus derived. Double member constituencies should be divided. Local boundaries should as far as possible be respected. University seats should be left alone, and the City of London should be retained as a two-member seat. (This last was the sole contested recommendation dealing with redistribution, and was only carried by 15 votes to 13.) Separate Boundary Commissions should be set up for England, Wales, Scotland, and Northern Ireland, with the Speaker as Chairman of each. Each Commission should make a general review of boundaries at intervals of not less than three or more than seven years—in effect, once during the life of each normal Parliament—and should have power to submit special recommendations at any time. Their reports should be submitted to Parliament and the changes should be effected by Order in Council, subject to affirmative resolution of the House of Commons; however, the first general redistribution should be by Act of Parliament and not by Order in Council.

The conference recommended that the parliamentary and local government franchises should be assimilated, that the business premises vote should be retained for occupiers of business premises but not for their spouses, and that there should be no change in university representation or methods of election (except for the automatic registration of all graduates). It also recommended by a majority of 21 votes to 8 that no person should be registered for more than one residence and one business qualification. Two proposals were defeated: one suggesting that no person should vote more than once failed by 25 votes to 6, and another suggesting that the qualifying age should be reduced from twenty-one to eighteen years was rejected by 16 votes to 3.

The conference's conclusions about redistribution and the franchise were published at the end of May 1944 in the form of a letter from the Speaker to the Prime Minister.[1] A second letter in July[2] dealt with the question of 'conduct and costs of elections'. Its main recommendations were as follows:

1. Expenses should be reduced (in Great Britain only) for every candidate to £450 plus 1*d*. per elector in boroughs and 1½*d*. per elector in counties.
2. The agent's fee should be included in the maximum expenses.
3. Expenditure by any private person or body for the promotion of a candidature should be declared illegal.
4. Poll-cards should be issued by the returning officer only.
5. Payment of speakers' expenses should be permitted.
6. Provision should be made for easier relief from venial errors in returns of election expenses.
7. All state-supported schools should be available free for election meetings.
8. Substantial contributions by candidates to charities in their constituencies were to be deprecated.
9. Contributions to party organizations designed to influence the choice of candidate were to be regarded with strong disapproval.
10 and 11. The conditions of forfeiture of deposits should be slightly modified.
12 and 13. The candidate's deposit should be payable by banker's order on any day between the issue of the writ and the last day of nomination.

(A resolution to reduce the deposit from £150 to £100 was defeated by 18 votes to 4, and others to abolish the

---

[1] *Cmd. 6534/1944.*   [2] *Cmd. 6543/1944.*

deposit or to reduce the condition of forfeiture from one-eighth to one-tenth of the poll were defeated without a division.)

14–16. More polling facilities should be provided, especially in rural areas, and hours of polling should be standardized (7 a.m. to 9 p.m.).

17. Absent voting facilities should be extended to cover invalids.

18. Broadcasting from outside the United Kingdom in order to influence an election should be illegal.

19–20. Everything possible should be done to facilitate service voting, and, in particular, automatic registration should be introduced.

A resolution recommending 'some additional limitation and regulation . . . on the number of conveyances plying with voters to the polling booths' was defeated by 15 votes to 14.

Much the biggest of these changes was the recommended reduction in the maximum permitted expenses. Despite the rise in prices since the inter-war period, a cut of on the average almost one-half was unanimously advocated. It is curious to speculate upon what had convinced the Conservatives that beyond a certain point the expenditure of money did not help to win elections. The proposed change in the legal limit did not attract much public comment, and the minutes of the Speaker's Conference throw little light on party attitudes to the question. It appears, however, that pressure for lower expenses actually came from the Conservatives. During the war Labour party and Trade Union funds had grown very considerably and much more money was available for electioneering. The Conservatives, on the other hand, being accustomed to look to their candidates financing their own campaigns, felt much poorer. High taxation would make it impossible for many private individuals to pay their expenses on the pre-war scale. A movement to take all expenses off the candidate's shoulders was under way, but central party funds were also limited at that time. Everything led the Conservatives to wish for a considerable reduction, while the Labour party, feeling more affluent than formerly, and conscious of the need for campaign publicity in order to counter a predominantly Conservative press, were perhaps not so eager for change as they had been.[1]

How the decisions of the Speaker's Conference were arrived at, and how long they were binding, were to become issues of violent controversy four years later. It is more convenient to leave these questions to be dealt with at a later stage in the narrative.[2] At the time they created little stir, and a large part of the conference's recommendations were speedily enacted in two Bills.

The Redistribution Bill had its second reading on 10 October 1944. It provided for the appointment of permanent Boundary Commissioners, for the immediate division of constituencies containing more than 100,000 electors, and for general reports from the Commissioners at intervals of from three to seven years. The number of seats should remain 'substantially as at present'. In redistribution, the average electorate for England, Wales, Scotland, and Northern Ireland should be calculated separately and no constituency should be more than 25 per cent. larger or smaller than the appropriate quota. However, local government areas should be respected if possible, and permission was granted to vary these rules. The City of London and the universities were put outside the Commissioners' consideration. Mr. Morrison, moving the second reading,[3] observed that in 1917 it had been suggested that constituencies should be kept between 70 per cent. and 170 per cent. of the quota, but that, by 1941, 164 constituencies were outside even those broad limits. However, the number of M.P.s should not be increased permanently, although a temporary addition of twenty-five seats was needed to cope with the most swollen constituencies. Remarking that the Speaker's Conference had recommended by a narrow majority that two seats should be left to the City of London, he said that in view of its long history he would be sorry to see its representation abolished but that it might in due course be argued whether two seats should be allowed. Mr. Woodburn observed that the conference had worked well and its recommendations were being fully implemented; it had

---

[1] It is worth noting, however, that in 1945, in 1950, and in 1951 the Conservatives spent a larger proportion of the permitted maximum expenditure than the Labour party. See p. 170 below.

[2] See pp. 109–22 below.

[3] *H.C. Deb. 403*, cc. 1610 et seq.

achieved a good compromise on every issue except proportional representation and plural voting; it was different from the 1929 conference, which had been abortive because its members had decided 'all or nothing'; but he was glad that the question of the City of London remained open—it had no right to two members; the Labour party was also opposed to the university vote. No other especially significant contribution was made to the debate. A Liberal motion to reject the Bill because it did not include proportional representation was defeated by 202 votes to 18. Apart from the well-worn arguments on that subject, special local pleas in connexion with redistribution and arguments about the merits of the City of London attracted most attention. There was no objection to the principle of permanent redistribution machinery, although it was suggested that every seven years was too often to disturb boundaries. Several speakers thought that the rules were too tightly drawn and prophetically suggested that deviations of more than 25 per cent. from the quota would have to be allowed. Some argued that the size of the House should be increased. A few Labour speakers protested against the privileges of the City of London and against university representation.

In committee on 12 October the only important issues of contention arose over the City of London and the universities. Mr. Pritt moved an amendment[1] which would have eliminated the privileged position of the City. Mr. Morrison replied that the Bill did not decide whether the City would have one or two members, but it certainly had a claim to representation. 'I would feel regret if the political and Parliamentary identity of the ancient City of London was completely destroyed'; there was a constitutional and historic link between the City and Parliament; 'if we can possibly help it, we will not destroy its Parliamentary identity'. The number of its representatives could be settled at the general redistribution.[2] Sir George Elliston welcomed 'almost the assurances' from Mr. Morrison of its survival. But there was an odd division of opinion. Sir Percy Harris, a Liberal, and Mr. Green, a Labour member, hoped, for historic reasons, that the City would be preserved as a parliamentary entity, while Lord Winterton attacked the institution on the

[1] *H.C. Deb. 403*, cc. 1985 et seq.   [2] Ibid., c. 1994.

ground that its electors had not always been very discriminating and that its members had not always been on the side of liberty; there was much to be said for historic continuity, but this could not continue for ever. There were some conventional Labour attacks on special privilege, but an equal number argued that this was a question which should be left until the general redistribution; Mr. Peake, replying for the Government, agreed that it was for the next Parliament to decide. Mr. Pritt's amendment was defeated by 163 votes to 38, 31 Labour members being among its supporters.

Mr. Pritt then moved[1] the rejection of the clause which excluded university constituencies from the Boundary Commissioners' consideration. He argued that although some university members had been good there had never been much difference between them and ordinary M.P.s. The debate which followed centred largely on the quality of university members; the validity of the assertions on both sides could hardly be checked, since a certain reticence prevented the mentioning of names. In general, the debate was very moderate. Mr. Hogg argued that all plural qualifications should be dealt with later. Two Labour speeches indicated a change of heart. Mr. Ivor Thomas said that, judging by past M.P.s, university representation should be abolished but that the quality was now improving greatly. Mr. Pethick-Lawrence, who had led the Labour members at the conference, said that its decision on the question was the result of a compromise but that it could also be defended on its merits; university M.P.s had of late been less partisan, and so the Labour party had become less opposed to their continuance. In the end the clause was accepted by 152 votes to 16, only 10 Labour members being among the minority. The Bill[2] then passed its remaining stages in both Houses with almost no further discussion.

The Representation of the People Bill was given a second reading on 19 December 1944.[3] Its main provisions were the assimilation of the local government and parliamentary franchises, the modification of the registration machinery, and the

---

[1] *H.C. Deb. 403*, cc. 2019 et seq.
[2] Enacted as 7 & 8 Geo. 6, ch. 41.
[3] *H.C. Deb. 406*, cc. 1646 et seq.

reduction of the business vote. Mr. Morrison described the Bill as a major reconstruction measure, implementing the chief recommendations of the Speaker's Conference; several minor issues had been referred to a technical committee which he had set up under Sir Cecil Carr[1] and would have to be dealt with in the comprehensive legislation which would be needed after the war. For the time being an annual register would be published on 9 September each year, and any parliamentary election between then and 31 December would be fought on it; all other elections would be fought on a register specially compiled under the 1943 Act. But in 1945 only there would be a special register published on 7 May. Facilities for servicemen were being made as easy as possible. There were one or two Conservative protests at the assimilation of the franchise and one or two protests from the other side at the survival of business voting. But the assimilation was justified on the grounds, not only of administrative necessity, but also of equity; since taxpayers now contributed as much to the cost of local government as ratepayers, it was held to be absurd to confine the franchise to ratepayers. The survival of the business vote was excused mainly as the fruit of compromise. The second reading was not opposed.

At the committee stage[2] several amendments were proposed, including a further Conservative protest against assimilation, but the only important innovation came in Government clauses allowing servicemen overseas to vote by post (for the next election only). Lady Megan Lloyd George moved a new clause abolishing plural voting and was supported by Liberal, Labour, and Independent speakers. Mr. Pethick-Lawrence, however, said that, as a member of the Speaker's Conference, he was bound by the compromise made there over the retention of plural voting. Mr. Morrison, replying to the debate, said that Britain lived on compromises; he was opposed to all plural voting, and if he had a parliamentary majority he would abolish it; but he must accept the compromise for, at the conference, the Conservatives had given up much when it was not necessary and they must be left something. He hoped that Labour backbenchers would stand by the compromise made on their behalf.

[1] See pp. 106–7 below.
[2] *H.C. Deb.* 407, cc. 197 et seq.

They can hardly be said to have done so. The clause was only defeated by 123 votes to 51;[1] 41 Labour members voted against it and only 16 supported it. Of those 16, 4 had been members of the Speaker's Conference and 5 were members of the Government. In other words, only 7 of those Labour members who had any choice in the matter actually answered Mr. Morrison's appeal.

At the report stage a Liberal attempt to give local authorities the option of using proportional representation was defeated by 208 votes to 17. During the swift passage of the Bill through the Lords, the only noteworthy remark came from Lord Ammon, who said that he regretted the continuance of the business and university franchises, but that he was bound not to oppose them, as they were more or less agreements made at the Speaker's Conference, of which he had been a member. The Bill was enacted[2] by the end of January 1945.

As the election of 1945 approached, questions about electoral administration multiplied. This tendency grew especially in the last three weeks of the Parliament's life after the date of the election had become known—apart from 1929 this was the only occasion since the First World War when Parliament had sat after the announcement of polling-day. The questions mainly concerned voting facilities for servicemen, but there were also some objections to the polling-day selected, on the ground that it clashed with holiday weeks in some northern towns. As a result of this, the Postponement of Polling Day Act, 1945,[3] was rushed through Parliament without opposition. It delayed the poll for a week in eighteen constituencies and for a fortnight in one. It is notable that this, the only election since 1918 to clash with the holiday season, took place in the only year when a statutory delay between the poll and the counting of the votes made it possible to vary polling-days. It serves to emphasize the difficulties which in normal times stand in the way of a summer election.

The election of 1945 was remarkable for more than its result. It was fought in unique circumstances and, to some extent, under a framework of interim law. The civilian register, although

---

[1] *H.C. Deb. 407*, c. 313.   [2] As 8 & 9 Geo. 6, ch. 6.
[3] 8 & 9 Geo. 6, ch. 40.

based upon residence on 30 January 1945, a mere five months before the poll, was far from accurate, owing to the limitations of the National Registration scheme and owing to the large number of removals at the close of the war. The service register was based upon claims made by servicemen. Strenuous efforts were made by the Government to get all servicemen to complete their claim forms, and it was announced that 90 per cent. had done so.[1] This appears to have been an exaggeration, as there were apparently 4,682,000 men in the forces on 30 June 1945[2] (and hardly more than 1 million can have been under twenty-one), but only 2,895,000[3] on the service register. Of those on the service register, only 1,701,000 succeeded in recording their votes (59 per cent.). Only half of those who had appointed proxies had votes recorded on their behalf and a quarter of those who applied for postal ballots were found not to be on the service register. The need to allow for the preparation of the register and for the return on service ballots altered the pattern of the election. Its date was announced on 27 May. Parliament sat until 15 June. Polling-day was on 5 July, and the counting of the votes took place on 26 July. It was thus far the most protracted election since the institution of a single nation-wide polling-day.

[1] *H.C. Deb. 410,* c. 398.
[2] *Annual Statistical Abstract 1947*, Table 107.
[3] This figure includes women—amounting perhaps to 250,000.

CHAPTER V

THE ACT OF 1948

I. 1945–7. PREPARATION

THE election of 1945 returned Labour to power with a clear majority of 148 seats over all parties. It is interesting that the Conservatives' faith in the electoral system seems to have been in no way shaken by this, the first occasion since 1906 when it had worked heavily against them; they were willing to await the day when they once again would benefit by its natural exaggerations. Labour's victory, secured with only 48 per cent. of the votes, meant, of course, that Labour was more than ever content with the system. It also meant that a Labour Government would have to pilot through Parliament the comprehensive Representation of the People Act which had been envisaged by the Speaker's Conference and by the interim war-time Acts. There was no urgency about the question, as the better part of five years was likely to elapse before a general election, but some steps were needed to cover electoral registration in the meantime.

The Elections and Jurors Bill provided among other things for the existing register, published in September 1945, to stay in force until the end of 1946, although a supplementary register in February 1946 would do something to keep it up to date, and postal facilities would be made available to those who moved house as well as to invalids. Mr. Chuter Ede, the Home Secretary, moving the second reading on 21 November 1945,[1] said that he hoped to get back to the traditional registration by canvass in 1947. Mr. Manningham-Buller for the Conservatives moved the rejection of the Bill on the ground that it made no provision for a qualifying period; it was intolerable that a system of registration which had been universally condemned for its inefficiency at the last election should be continued indefinitely. Mr. Peake, who had been Mr. Morrison's deputy at the Home Office in 1944, also protested at the continued suspension of the qualifying period which had been imposed purely temporarily under the 1944 Act. In the Government reply, Mr. Fraser,

[1] *H.C. Deb. 416*, cc. 447 et seq.

Under Secretary for Scotland, pointed out that temporary administrative difficulties still prevented the restoration of the qualifying period or the arrangement of automatic registration for servicemen. The second reading was carried by 296 votes to 149, the Liberals supporting the Government. The Conservatives pressed their objections at the committee stage but gained no ground. However, on the third reading, Mr. Peake announced that the Conservatives now accepted the assurance privately given by the Government that it was a purely temporary measure and that the Bill[1] could now become law as an agreed measure.

An amendment to the instructions of the Boundary Commissioners led, a year later, to much more vigorous charges of bad faith which were similarly withdrawn. On 13 November 1946 Mr. Ede announced[2] that in endeavouring to keep all constituencies within 25 per cent. of the quota the Boundary Commissioners had been forced to recommend the complete dismemberment for parliamentary purposes of many unified communities; the rules guiding the Commissioners would, therefore, have to be relaxed to allow them to preserve localities intact, although they would, of course, still aim to maintain approximate numerical equality. Mr. Churchill took strong exception to this announcement and, in a heated intervention, asked if this reversal of a mature decision was not because the results of the present system were unfavourable to the Labour party. 'Is this not a case of flagrant and shameless gerrymandering?'[3] Mr. Ede replied that there had been more complaints from Conservatives than from Labour members about the Commissioners' recommendations. The Speaker intervened to say that as Chairman of the Boundary Commissions he had asked the Home Secretary for a relaxation of the rules; there was no question of gerrymandering. Prolonged exchanges followed in which Mr. Churchill accused the Government of bad faith in proposing this change without consulting the Opposition and to the last protested that they had only recommended this step because the results of the Commissioners' reports were not satisfactory to the Labour party.

[1] Enacted as 9 & 10 Geo. 6, ch. 21.
[2] *H.C. Deb. 430*, cc. 77 et seq.
[3] Ibid., c. 79.

The Times commented on this episode:

There has undoubtedly been a lack of foresight coupled with a reluctance on the part of the Government to decide much sooner on a fresh start. By no stretch of imagination, however, can their decision be fairly called, as Mr. Churchill called it yesterday, 'a case of flagrant and shameless gerrymandering'. . . . There can be no doubt that the decision to amend the Commissioners' instructions so as to enable them to give greater weight in their recommendations to local considerations will be widely popular. The decision has, in fact, been made, more than a little belatedly, in response to a popular and all-party demand.[1]

A month later, when the Bill to give effect to this change in the instructions to the Boundary Commissioners was given a second reading, there was general harmony. The Bill provided that local boundaries should, as far as practicable, be respected in drawing parliamentary boundaries, and the Commissioners should endeavour to keep the electorate of every constituency as near to the quota as was practicable having regard to that. Mr. Peake, for the Conservatives, observed that the heat a month earlier had been simply due to the absence of consultation. Since then they had met Mr. Ede and the Boundary Commissioners and they were fully satisfied that, as in 1917, the rules for redistribution were too strict; they approved of the greater latitude in constituency size and they hoped that the Boundary Commissioners would also feel free to increase the number of seats a little above the pre-war figure, if greater equity could thus be secured. Mr. Keeling observed that in the 1944 Act the recommendations of the Speaker's Conference had been misconstrued. The latter had only asked that the constituencies which diverged by more than 25 per cent. from the quota should be considered by the Commissioners and not that they should necessarily be changed. The present Bill merely righted that misunderstanding. The Bill[2] passed with no further difficulty, and the Boundary Commissioners started to go over their work again.

The heat aroused by Mr. Ede's first announcement was obviously fanned to unnecessary heights by Mr. Churchill, as

---

[1] *The Times*, 14 Nov. 1946.
[2] Enacted as 10 & 11 Geo. 6, ch. 10.

the general harmony over the subsequent Bill demonstrated. But it is a significant indication of how explosive an issue redistribution was. It was well known that the Labour party would lose seats by an equitable redrawing of boundaries. The Conservatives were very ready to suspect that Labour would try to evade inflicting this hardship upon itself. The charges of gerrymandering, utterly baseless though they proved to be, should have given the Government due warning of the trouble that would be encountered by any later proposals which could be construed as partisan.

In December 1946 another advance in the preparations for a comprehensive Representation of the People Act was made. A Home Office committee had been set up a year before to consider what arrangements should be made for electoral registration in peace conditions. In view of its deliberations, the Conservatives had been willing to allow the Home Secretary to extend by Order in Council until the end of 1947 the provisions of the November 1945 Act to which they had offered such objection. The committee, which sat under Mr. Oliver, Mr. Ede's deputy at the Home Office, and which was composed of M.P.s, party agents, and official experts, reached general agreement on the problems before it.[1] It considered that the National Registration system of compiling the register could never be as efficient as the pre-war method of canvassing. If the register was to be as up to date as possible, it was desirable permanently to abandon the requirement of a qualifying period and to include in the register the name of everyone normally resident in each constituency on a given day. The time taken in preparing the register could also be cut down from four and a half months to three and a half, and there should once again be two registers a year. There was some disagreement whether two registers a year or the abandonment of a qualifying period were desirable in Northern Ireland, where the tradition of making claims and objections would mean a great deal of administrative bother and where the register would only be of use for elections to the Imperial Parliament. It was thought that there would be little point in providing automatic registration for members of the forces, since they would, in any case, have to make a claim

[1] *Cmd. 7004/1946.*

submitting the name of their proxy; but everything should be done to help servicemen and seamen to get on to the register. It was recommended that the extended facilities for postal voting made available to civilians under the 1945 Act should be continued. No recommendation was made about service postal voting for men overseas, but the delays necessary in conducting the election, if there was to be time for ballots to be sent out and returned, was made plain. Servicemen in the United Kingdom should be allowed to vote by post or proxy as before.

Perhaps the most striking aspect of this report was the meek acceptance by the Conservative representatives on the committee of the final abandonment of the qualifying period; they seem to have realized that this change was more formal than real, for it was still required that an elector should only be qualified for his normal place of residence, and the lapse of almost four months between the date on which the register was to be compiled and the date it was to come into force would eliminate the more transient of electors. Indeed, the net effect of this change upon the result of elections was probably far less than that of the generous postal-voting facilities for civilians which were so readily endorsed.

Various technical points of electoral law were dealt with by the committee which had been set up in 1944 under Sir Cecil Carr to consider in detail what reforms in the law on corrupt and illegal practices, the conduct of the poll, and the use of schools and broadcasting were desirable. An interim report in 1945[1] had echoed the Speaker's Conference and shown that few changes in the law were required to implement its recommendations on making schools available for election meetings and increasing rural polling facilities. It found no difficulties in clarifying the law on agency, on speakers' expenses, or on relief for venial errors in expense returns. It recognized that a ban on election broadcasting from abroad would be hard to enforce but might have a valuable deterrent effect. The final report[2] was published in December 1947 and was equally modest. Apart from a number of small technical changes in the procedure prescribed for the conduct of elections, its most notable demand was for electoral law to be codified as far as possible into a single statute.

[1] *Cmd. 6606/1945.*   [2] *Cmd. 7286/1947.*

In dealing with the law on corrupt practices, it demanded that steps should be taken to reduce the obstacles to representing election petitions; at the moment the expense often might act as a deterrent to a petitioner. Wherever a *prima facie* case was made out, it was suggested that the petition should be conducted by the Treasury Solicitor. In general, the fact that so few changes were suggested was a tribute to past parliamentary draftsmen and Home Secretaries.

Between September and December 1947 the four Boundary Commissions published their reports.[1] They faithfully fulfilled their revised instructions under the 1947 Act. Only eighty constituencies were left with unchanged boundaries. Some of the remainder were merely adjusted to conform to alterations in local government areas since 1918, but others were amalgamated or drastically dismembered. In the most drastic changes, 6 new constituencies in the East End of London took the place of the former 13, while in Middlesex the number of seats, raised from 17 to 24 in the partial redistribution of 1944, was further increased to 28. Apart from 10 special cases in the remote parts of Wales and in the Highlands, none of the recommended seats had less than 40,000 electors. Only eight had more than 80,000. There were some appreciable variations from the mean of 58,000 electors, but all were justified by the need to respect local government boundaries even at the expense of mathematical equality. Even so, 2 constituencies in Northern Ireland violated county boundaries, while 57 constituencies in England intersected the limits of boroughs or of urban or rural districts. The Boundary Commission for England justified the retention of the 8 boroughs over 80,000 on the ground that if they were divided special claims would be made for boroughs just under 80,000 and that the divided seats would be abnormally small: it would 'do little to solve the general problem of equal representation'.[2] There was some criticism of this finding, but, in general, the reports of the Boundary Commissioners were welcomed as providing a just and workmanlike solution of a pressing problem.

During 1947 preparations for the comprehensive Representation of the People Act went ahead and in the King's Speech on

---

[1] *Cmd. 7231/1947*, Northern Ireland; *Cmd. 7260/1947*, England; *Cmd. 7270/1947*, Scotland; *Cmd. 7274/1947*, Wales.   [2] *Cmd. 7260/1947*, p. 5.

21 October 1947 the Government announced 'a measure to reform the franchise and electoral procedure and to give appropriate effect to recommendations of the Commissions appointed to consider the distribution of Parliamentary seats'. This attracted little attention in the debate on the Address. In the House of Lords, in answer to a query by Lord Samuel about proportional representation, the Lord Chancellor, Lord Jowitt, said that the Bill would contain provisions for electoral reform arising out of the reports of the Oliver and Carr Committees and the Speaker's Conference. 'If Lord Samuel is familiar with all the proceedings of those Committees, which I am not, he will know precisely what the Bill is going to do.'[1] After this pronouncement it came as a shock when, on 30 January 1948, the text of the Bill was published and was found to provide for the abolition of the university seats as well as of the business vote.[2]

The Bill as enacted had 81 clauses and 13 schedules, and it occupies 197 pages of the Statute Book.[3] It repealed wholly or in part 85 statutes, ranging in importance from one of 1382 imposing penalties on sheriffs who failed to return a writ of summons, to the comprehensive Representation of the People Act of 1918 which it almost wholly superseded. The greater part of the Bill was, in fact, a systematized re-enactment of existing legislation, covering the whole field of elections from Parish Council to Parliament. The substantive changes it brought to parliamentary elections can be listed briefly. A qualifying period of residence was permanently eliminated from electoral registration. Two registers a year were reinstituted. Postal voting facilities were granted to a large number of civilians—invalids, those who had moved from a district, and those whose occupation was likely to take them out of the constituency on polling-day. The procedure of nomination was made more flexible. The business and

---

[1] *H.L. Deb. 152*, c. 70.

[2] In the subsequent debates much was made of this statement of the Lord Chancellor as evidence that the Government had changed its mind at the last minute. But it is plain that Lord Jowitt misunderstood a departmental brief when replying at very short notice to Lord Samuel's question. That the Cabinet had already decided on these changes is plain from a remark of Mr. Morrison's during later debates. See *H.C. Deb. 448*, c. 1931.

[3] 11 & 12 Geo. 6, ch. 65.

university franchises were abolished. Election expense maxima were reduced. There was a comprehensive redistribution of seats. Payment of speakers was at last legalized. A considerable number of minor technical changes were also made. But the net effect of the Bill on the size of the electorate and the conduct of elections was very much less than that of any of the other major Representation of the People Bills.

II. THE 'BARGAIN'

The discussion of the Bill was focused less upon the rightness or wrongness of its provisions than upon the propriety of their introduction in view of the findings of the Speaker's Conference. The greater part of the second and third readings and much of the committee proceedings were devoted to the question of whether the Labour party was guilty of a breach of faith in departing from the recommendations made by the Speaker's Conference.

The Conservative case was launched by Mr. Churchill in the most extreme of terms, and many of his followers repeated his charges with almost equal vehemence, if with less pungency. Their argument was quite plain. At the Speaker's Conference in 1944, proposals for electoral reform were agreed between the parties. Some were immediately enacted; some had been left until this comprehensive Bill. It was grossly improper for the Labour party to alter these proposals without consulting the Opposition. In 1944 the Conservatives, although in a majority in the House and in the conference, had agreed to concede certain Labour demands. The franchise for local elections had been assimilated to that for parliamentary purposes and the vote given to the spouses of business electors had been abolished. In return, Labour had agreed neither to press for the total abolition of the business vote nor to oppose the preservation of the university seats. That was a clear, if unwritten, bargain. By breaking it, it was argued, Labour was going far to shatter the assumption of good faith between parties which was essential to the smooth working of parliamentary government.

To this accusation the Labour reply centred upon a firm denial that any bargain which had been made in 1944 was designed to be binding after the end of the war-time Parliament.

It is interesting to note the comment of *The Times*, the only newspaper to raise the question of good faith on the publication of the Bill, and before Mr. Churchill made it an issue in Parliament.

> [There is] a principle . . . that alterations in the legislative apparatus itself should, wherever possible, be founded on the agreement of parties and should never be enforced by the power of the majority unless the attempt to secure agreement has failed. . . . The rude decision to extinguish the historic representation of the City of London . . . can be explained as the consequence of [the abolition of the business premises franchise] rather than as a departure from the agreed scheme of the boundary commissioners . . . the advocacy by the Labour Party of the principle of 'one man, one vote' and their opposition to all property qualifications . . . have been clear, consistent, and undisguised since their first incursion into politics.
>
> The clause which emphatically does not satisfy the constitutional tests suggested is that which would abolish the university franchise. This proposal was unanimously rejected by the Speaker's Conference. Not only was the Labour Party, through its representatives on the conference, morally pledged against it but, in so far as there was any element of bargaining in the proceedings, it can be argued that the recommendations of the conference included concessions to Labour which would not have been obtained, if the university franchise had been opposed.[1]

This was much more moderate than any later newspaper comment on the issue. As the discussion proceeded, feelings became more aroused, and misleading statements from both sides increasingly confused a question which would, in any case, have been complicated enough. In 1944 there had been a lack of clarity about what was being settled, and, in four years, memories had become blurred and partisan; at times such wholly inaccurate accounts of what had occurred were given by those who had been personally involved that the best-intentioned of observers must have found it virtually impossible to decide just what had happened.

Was there a bargain? What issues were included in that bargain? Who was bound by it? For how long was it binding? If the Government wished to vary the Speaker's Conference

---

[1] *The Times*, 31 Jan. 1948.

findings, should they have followed some other procedure? It is worth examining each of these questions in turn.

There can be no doubt that there was a bargain. In the debates in 1944 and 1945 Mr. Woodburn, Mr. Pethick-Lawrence, and Mr. Morrison all referred to it, and in 1948 no responsible Labour member denied that there had been a bargain.

The issues that were included in the bargain present greater difficulty. At the Speaker's Conference six questions excited clear difference between the parties; their interests, and in some cases their principles, were undoubtedly opposed. The issues were the assimilation of the local government and parliamentary franchises, the abolition of the business vote, the ending of university representation, the treatment of the City of London as an ordinary constituency, the limitation of the use of cars on polling-day, and the indefinite postponement of redistribution. All of these tended to be desired by Labour and all would undoubtedly serve their narrow party advantage; all by the same token would hurt the Conservatives. Certainly all were not comprehended in the formal bargain. Although the atmosphere of conciliation and compromise which permeated the conference undoubtedly influenced the treatment of every subject, it is clear that some issues were decided independently on their merits rather than as part of a bargain.

The assimilation of the franchise was necessary if there was to be an early resumption of local government elections, for a local government register based on the pre-war franchise could not be compiled without a canvass, and a canvass was regarded as administratively impracticable at that time. Moreover, the principle that only local taxpayers should elect local authorities was somewhat invalidated when 50 per cent. of local revenue came from the Treasury and almost everyone contributed to national taxes. These arguments were put forward by Conservative members of the conference as much as by Labour and they had the support of a large majority of local authorities. The Association of Municipal Corporations reported 186 Councils in favour of the change and only 82 against. Of County Councils 30 were reported to favour and 16 to oppose it. Since a very considerable majority of local authorities were under Conservative or Independent control, it is plain that the step cannot be regarded merely as a concession to left-wing opinion. Although in the conference two Conservatives opposed it, there is no evidence in the minutes which suggests that there was a bargain on the question; it was exhaustively argued on its merits and heavily supported by all parties. Some authorities subsequently said that it was part of the bargain but, if it was, it must be observed that the Conservatives were using as a counter a concession which they were intending in any case to make for other reasons. On the Labour side it could justly be argued that a compromise is only a compromise if both sides yield something which they would not have consented to but for their desire to reach agreement.

Although redistribution was bound to hurt Labour's interests (since the great majority of the depopulated constituencies, due for abolition, were held by them), it was so obviously necessary and opposition to it was so intellectually indefensible that it could hardly have been included in a bargain on the franchise. Compromise may perhaps be seen in the agreement not to rush general redistribution (which anyway would have been very difficult administratively) and to start with only the limited stage of subdividing the largest seats.[1] But the argument over redistribution does not appear to have been conducted in partisan terms, and even in 1948 few contended that it had entered into the franchise bargain.[2]

[1] Labour erroneously believed that even this would hurt them. Actually in 1945 the 25 new seats were divided between the parties in almost exactly the same ratio as the 615 old ones.

[2] There were two speeches in 1948 by members of the Speaker's Conference which, although not strictly consistent, did suggest that there was at least a tacit bargain on redistribution. Sir Hugh O'Neill said that the Conservatives would have liked the merging of very small seats, as well as the division of very large seats, included in a partial redistribution. 'Because the Labour Party did not like that, as many of the smaller seats were held by them, the Conservative members gave way on that point in order to secure unanimity'. (*H.C. Deb. 448*, c. 1942.)

Mr. Woodburn said that the Labour party had wanted complete and the Conservatives partial redistribution. It was agreed that the latter would favour the Conservatives and 'it was certainly something upon which we might have had a bargaining point. The Labour Party gave up its demand for a complete redistribution largely on practical grounds. Eventually there was a compromise in the dividing up of the abnormal constituencies'. (*H.C. Deb.* 447, c. 1013.)

It is hard to see that either side secured the better of this bargain. In any case it was undoubtedly purely a temporary measure. No one could doubt that a comprehensive redistribution would have to follow post-war resettle-

The limitation on cars also stands outside the bargain. It arose in the Speaker's Conference two months after the franchise questions had been dealt with and under an altogether different part of the terms of reference; the Labour party was obviously not bound by the decision to leave the question alone since it had been carried by only one vote and their representatives had all opposed it.

The City of London was in a special position. The question was not settled by the Speaker's Conference. By a majority of 15 votes to 13, it was decided that the City should continue to return two members, but all the Labour members and, oddly enough, one Conservative, had opposed this. The Redistribution Bill in 1944 had only provided that the Boundary Commissioners should leave the City of London alone. Mr. Morrison pointed out at the time that this did not decide whether the City should have one member or two,[1] and Mr. Peake, replying to the debate, observed that this was a question for the next Parliament to decide. Mr. Parker does not seem to have been restrained by his membership of the Speaker's Conference from saying that the Labour party should continue to press for the City to have the same treatment as other constituencies. Indeed all this discussion seems to suggest that no excessive sanctity had yet been attached to the findings of the Speaker's Conference. Labour's case in 1948 was much more damaged by Mr. Morrison's reference in 1944 to the merits of the City of London's representation[2] than by any evidence the earlier debates offered about the 'bargain'.

It is only in connexion with plural voting that there was plainly a bargain. At the Speaker's Conference there was a vehement discussion on the merits of the business vote, 'an ideological conflict' as one member described it. This conflict was solved by a compromise under which the vote was to be limited to the occupiers of business premises and to be taken away from their spouses. The argument had been mainly

ment. If the partial redistribution was indeed included within the specific bargain, it would only support those who contend that that bargain ended with the end of the 1945 Parliament.

[1] One not unsympathetic authority referred subsequently to Mr. Morrison's having 'managed to get the question . . . left as an open one'.

[2] Quoted p. 97 above.

devoted to the merits of ensuring special representation to the dozen or so business communities where the occupation franchise was important; it was suggested that if the business vote were abolished there would be no one in Parliament to represent those interests, a contention which could hardly be supported. No one seems to have referred to the accidental way in which the spouse's qualification had developed.[1] After the question had been settled by compromise, the conference turned to university representation. It appears that no one raised the question of its merits; the discussion was confined to the secrecy of the ballot, the registration fee, and the efficiency of the register. It was resolved without discussion that provided all graduates were automatically registered without fee, university representation should be continued as before.

At the next meeting of the conference a week later, a resolution that no one should vote more than once at an election was rejected by 25 votes to 6. Mr. Pethick-Lawrence pointed out that to carry the resolution would be to make nonsense of the compromise over the business vote made a week before. Every Labour member voted with the majority. The minority was composed of the two Liberals, the three Independents, and, astonishingly, one of the Conservative group.

It seems that the only formal bargain made during the conference was this agreement to give up the spouse's business vote in return for leaving all other plural voting alone. Other issues were settled in the general spirit of compromise. Perhaps the assimilation of the franchise also came into the bargain. In 1948 Lord Margesson said that he had had private conversations with Mr. Pethick-Lawrence in advance of the conference 'to see if we could resolve some of the difficulties that were bound to come up. . . . It was agreed that I should recommend to my party that the Parliamentary and local government franchise should be assimilated and that he would recommend to his party the retention of university constituencies and some other proposals dealing with the business vote.'[2] Mr. Churchill in 1948 also said that at the time of the Speaker's Conference he had been astonished to hear that the Conservatives had given up so much, but that Lord Margesson had assured him that in return

---

[1] See pp. 33–34 above.   [2] *H.L. Deb. 157*, c. 309.

for assimilation and the spouse's vote, Labour had agreed to drop their other claims.[1] However, it must be pointed out that many Conservatives admitted that the concessions they made were, in fact, justified on their merits. Support for assimilation was widespread both inside and outside the conference, while even Sir Herbert Williams described the spouse's vote as 'logically impossible to defend'.[2] No Labour member, on the other hand, would have defended the business vote in any form and many of them were patently unhappy about university representation.

Their attitude in 1944 on this issue is of some interest as it led to one of the major confusions in 1948. Mr. Pethick-Lawrence in 1944 said that university representation was preserved as the result of a compromise but that it was a compromise which could be defended on its merits. University M.P.s had of late become less partisan and so the Labour party was less opposed to their continuance.[3] Mr. Woodburn in 1948 said: 'It might surprise everybody to know that, at that Conference, the Labour Party, by a majority, agreed to support the retention of the university vote . . . the reason was that during the war it had become apparent that the university vote was being used for the purpose for which it was destined' . . . more Independents were being returned.[4] Mr. Woodburn's remarks hardly squared with a speech which he had made four years earlier on the Redistribution Bill, when he had observed that the Labour party was, despite the conference, opposed to the university vote.[5] Indeed, Mr. Woodburn cannot be regarded as a very reliable witness. In 1948 he said 'all who were members of the Speaker's Conference . . . will remember that the argument used for the retention of the university franchise, to which we agreed, was that the university franchise . . . returned people of academic distinction and of no particular party who put forward an independent point of view'.[6] But, in fact, as Lord Margesson[7] and Mr. Pickthorn[8] recalled in 1948, there appears

---

[1] *H.C. Deb. 447*, c. 861. [2] *H.C. Deb. 406*, c. 1660.
[3] *H.C. Deb. 403*, c. 2045.
[4] *H.C. Deb. 447*, c. 1014. In point of fact, at the time of the Speaker's Conference, only one Independent had been returned for the universities in a war-time by-election.   [5] *H.C. Deb. 403*, c. 1625.
[6] *H.C. Deb. 452*, c. 187.   [7] *H.L. Deb. 157*, c. 309.
[8] *H.C. Deb. 448*, c. 1916.

to have been no discussion of the merits of university representation in the Speaker's Conference. Certainly its minutes, which are very full, contain no record of any such discussion. However, Mr. Woodburn went on to argue that since the universities were now being used to return purely party members, the Conservatives had broken the arrangements agreed at the conference.[1] This suggestion served thoroughly to confuse the issue. Thereafter the Conservatives poured a large part of their scorn on Mr. Woodburn and used his arguments to demonstrate the Labour breach of faith. If Mr. Woodburn had been right in his premises, the Conservatives would have succeeded in proving their case conclusively; but, unfortunately, as all Conservatives used as a step in their argument a wholly inaccurate statement by one of their less able opponents, the case they presented could not, in fact, prove their allegations. It seems clear that Mr. Woodburn confused the private discussions among the Labour representatives with the official proceedings of the conference. It appears safe to assume that the Labour members discussed the line that they should take on university representation; Mr. Pethick-Lawrence must have expounded the bargain that he had made with Lord Margesson and, to console the opponents of all plural voting, it must have been pointed out that the university vote had of late been used in a much less partisan way. There is no reason to believe that there was any understanding with the Conservatives that the university seats should be left to Independent candidates; it is unlikely that the matter was even mentioned.

Who were bound by the bargain? This is plain. It is obvious that the members of the conference were morally bound to support the resolutions they had voted for when these came before Parliament, at least until the next election.[2] All M.P.s who were members of the Government were also bound, at least so

[1] *H.C. Deb. 452*, c. 187. Two Conservative M.P.s who had been defeated in the 1945 election were involved. In March 1946 Mr. Strauss was victorious in the by-election caused by the death of Miss Rathbone, the Independent member for the combined English universities. A year later Mr. Walter Elliot succeeded to the Scottish universities seat which had been held by the Independent Sir John Boyd Orr.

[2] Cf. Mr. Morrison on the committee stage of the Representation of the People Bill, 1945: 'Those who were members of the Conference must stand by [its findings].' *H.C. Deb. 407*, cc. 311–12.

long as the Government lasted, to support those recommendations which it decided to implement. Other M.P.s were technically free to vote as they chose, but their party organizations
were bound to bring pressure on them to support agreements
that had been made with the party's approval by its representatives at the conference. Mr. Morrison, during the debate on
plural voting in 1945, appealed to his party on that basis, hoping
that they would 'stand by the accommodation made on their
behalf'.[1] But after those who were free had divided 41 to 7 against
the compromise on plural voting[2] there do not appear to have
been any recriminations.

How long was the bargain binding? This is the crucial
question. It is clear that the issue was never formally discussed
in 1944. If it had been the issue in 1948 would have been simple.
But, as it was, Labour members were able to argue that the
Speaker's Conference had only been drafting an immediate
legislative programme and that the bargain had lapsed with the
passage of the R.P.A. of 1945 and the election which followed.
The Conservatives for their part were able to argue that everyone had assumed a much longer life for the settlement and that
it should only have been ended after inter-party consultations.

The Speaker's Conference, it must be remembered, met in
the spring of 1944 when the war effort was reaching its climax
and when agreed compromise legislation was being passed on a
wide range of subjects. To indulge in party controversy at that
time was to endanger the Coalition Government at a critical
moment and would almost have been considered disloyal. It
was obvious that some electoral legislation had to be passed and
the Speaker's Conference was set up to agree upon the programme.[3] Everything favoured conciliation and the Speaker
testified to its presence in his letter to the Prime Minister:

The conclusions set out in this report and the amount of general
agreement that we have achieved undoubtedly represent for all a
subordination of personal opinions sincerely held which would not
have been possible unless all members of the Conference had been

[1] *H.C. Deb. 407*, c. 312.   [2] See p. 100 above.
[3] According to Mr. Woodburn, speaking in 1948, Mr. Churchill had 'laid
it down that for that Parliament no legislation which was controversial
should be introduced. The Speaker's Conference was appointed with that
guidance.' *H.C. Deb. 447*, c. 1014.

determined to tackle without bias the thorny problems which confronted us. I should like as Chairman . . . to bear witness to the admirable temper and conciliatory disposition which have been shown by all and have enabled us to reach what, I trust, will be regarded as a substantial measure of general agreement.[1]

The conference met to reach agreed conclusions. But the Conservatives were in a clear majority upon it and therefore had a very strong bargaining position. There was no point in Labour pressing for reforms which the Conservatives were not prepared to grant. They accepted, almost with gratitude, the concessions which the Conservatives made, although their back-benchers afterwards by the division on plural voting did register their disapproval of what the conference had agreed. Did the fact that the Labour members of the conference did not struggle for the abolition of plural voting, which was then unattainable, mean that they were committed for the indefinite future to accepting an institution of which they had always disapproved? In that case, the Conservatives had undoubtedly made a very good bargain. But there can surely have been no such assumption of permanence. None the less, no one on either side appears to have envisaged a reversal of the settlement within four years. There certainly seems to have been an assumption that comprehensive and lasting legislation would be enacted on the lines recommended by the Speaker's Conference. It was clear that the full redistribution proposals and much of the detailed reform of electoral law and registration procedure would have to wait for some years, almost unquestionably until another Parliament had been elected. Did anyone expect that the franchise recommendations would be modified even before all the other proposals of the conference had been enacted? If the answer to this is negative, it is partly because very few people expected that the Labour party, the only party likely to modify these recommendations, would be in office in the next Parliament. But it is also because there was some feeling in the Labour party that, at least on the universities, the compromise had intrinsic merits and that it was desirable that electoral reform should be on agreed lines. It seems unlikely that any Labour members of the conference confronted themselves with the

[1] *Cmd. 6534/1944*, p. 7.

question: 'If Labour gains absolute power in the next Parliament, will these recommendations still be binding?' But probably the answer would have been that while they would, of course, not be bound in another Parliament, it was unlikely that they would depart from these recommendations. Mr. Woodburn, it is true, did specifically remark in 1944 that 'what this Parliament does, cannot bind any future Parliament'.[1] But in the same debate Mr. Pethick-Lawrence observed that the settlements of the Speaker's Conference 'met the situation by arriving at a solution which we thought would survive'.[2]

It may be argued that the redistribution and electoral law provisions which had to await the next Parliament were quite separate from the franchise proposals which were clearly to be enacted immediately. But that attitude was never expressed at the time. The Conservatives and some Labour members evidently assumed that the Speaker's Conference provided a settlement which would last. The Conservatives, because they were content with the settlement, were more ready than Labour to regard it as having permanent binding force. They tried, on the basis of Mr. Woodburn's references to the university by-elections, to prove that the Labour party had, even after 1945, accepted that the bargain was still binding; but Mr. Woodburn's remarks were inaccurate, and neither they nor the speeches of Mr. Ede and Lord Jowitt to which the Conservatives also alluded provide any satisfactory evidence on this point. Some Labour members in 1944 may have shared the tacit assumption of the Conservatives. But there really does not seem to be any firm evidence that either the leaders or the rank and file of the party ever accepted an obligation indefinitely to continue plural voting.

What were the stages by which the Labour party came to abandon the agreements? Could they have followed any less objectionable procedure? The large majority secured in the election of 1945 gave the party a very clear sense of mandate. All the traditional objections to plural voting, dutifully ignored

[1] *H.C. Deb. 403*, c. 2014. It is strange that in the general delving into *Hansard* which characterized the 1948 debates, no Labour member unearthed this quotation. Perhaps they were shy of using Mr. Woodburn as an authority.
[2] *H.C. Deb. 403*, c. 2045.

in 1944, rose again in the breasts of those who considered the question. The replacement in March 1946 of Miss Eleanor Rathbone, so often cited as the strongest argument for university representation, by Mr. H. G. Strauss, one of the most avowedly partisan of Conservatives, can hardly have encouraged enthusiasm for the university franchise. But the issue was postponed for some time. The Committee on Electoral Registration did not finish its work until the end of 1946, and, after a false start, the Boundary Commissioners only completed their proposals in October 1947, while the Carr Committee's report was delayed until December 1947. It was in the spring of 1947 that political activity in preparation for the Bill developed. An unofficial electoral reform committee of Labour back-benchers established itself and discussed what the Bill should contain. It met Mr. Ede and pressed for the total abolition of plural voting and university representation and for some limitation on cars; an interesting argument used was that although business voters were reduced to harmless numbers —50,000—while they had to claim their votes, so long as their franchise survived at all the Conservatives at some future date might make them important again by facilitating their registration. Another argument specifically proposed that the City of London and university seats should be abolished 'as some compensation for the abolition of so many Labour constituencies'. It seems that during the summer a Cabinet sub-committee discussed what should be in the Bill and decided to abolish all plural voting. Personal inquiries lead to the conclusion that while the university by-elections had stirred up additional hostility to university representation, they were not the last straw; the camel's back would have broken anyway. Mr. Ede said quite explicitly during the debate that he would have resigned rather than introduce a Bill which provided for university representation. Even the few Labour members who sympathized with the institution must have felt the conflict between it and the principle of 'one man, one vote', for university representation without plural voting was hardly feasible. Only a very questionable obligation to the recommendations of the Speaker's Conference stood in the way of a decision to abolish every franchise except that based on residence.

Once it had been decided that plural voting was to disappear, the fate of the City of London was even more inevitable than that of the universities. Without the business vote only 4,000 electors, mostly caretakers, would be left. This was only one-tenth of the smallest English constituency. Mr. Morrison said that he would have been willing to make a substantial exception in order to preserve this historic seat but the discrepancy was too great.[1]

When the Government decided that it wished to vary the Speaker's Conference recommendations, should it have taken any steps to secure inter-party agreement? During the 1948 debates it was frequently argued that changes in electoral law had, by what had become a constitutional custom, only been carried out by such agreement. This principle, it was argued, had been followed informally in 1885 and formally in 1917 and 1944. Even in 1931 the Labour Government had introduced its Representation of the People Bill only after the Ullswater Conference had tried to secure agreement. Another Speaker's Conference should have been held. In answer to this it was argued that the recommendations of a Speaker's Conference were not comprehensive or binding. In 1917 proportional representation had been unanimously advocated but not enacted, and, on the other hand, in 1928 the franchise had been equalized without the formality of a conference. Indeed the Speaker had refused to preside over a conference at that time, on the ground that it would damage the impartial position of the Chair to do so during a period of party warfare. Subsequently, it is true, party warfare did not prevent the holding of the Ullswater Conference, but that could hardly be said to have offered a favourable precedent for such meetings. What in 1948 could a conference have achieved? The 1944 Conference and the specialist committees had dealt with all the other points at issue and nothing could have been achieved by a meeting with only plural voting on the agenda; for what compromise would have been possible?

For the attempt to vary electoral law without consulting the Opposition there were precedents enough, even excluding the nineteenth century. The Liberal Government had actively sympathized with various private members' Bills dealing with the franchise between 1906 and 1910, and in every session from 1911 to 1914 they had introduced a Bill abolishing plural voting

[1] *H.C. Deb. 448*, c. 2220.

despite vehement Conservative opposition. Like the Liberal Government in 1911, the Labour Government in 1948 were proposing a major measure to their own electoral advantage. But it is important to remember that in each case the measure was designed to deprive their opponents of a special privilege, when they themselves possessed none, and not to create one for themselves.

It may well be argued that university representation deserved to survive. But that the Labour Government were acting with gross unconstitutionality cannot be demonstrated. Despite all the vehemence of the 1948 debates, the strongest charge that can be sustained is that the Labour party in 1944 had allowed certain misconceptions about the duration of the bargain to grow up, misconceptions that some of its own members may have shared, and that in shattering those illusions it gave many people the idea that it had broken faith.[1] It is perhaps better to tolerate an unjust anomaly than to spread the idea that promises are not binding. But it is asking too much of political human nature to demand that, for the sake of appearances, an unwelcome obligation never acknowledged should be honoured.

III. THE PASSAGE OF THE ACT

The Bill was to have a turbulent passage through the House and it is surprising how mildly its publication was greeted. The only item to attract much attention in the press or before the public was the abolition of the university seats; on this issue there was no editorial comment in the national press willing to support the Government. The protests were variously but strongly phrased: 'A gratuitous piece of spiteful levelling' (*The Economist*, 7 Feb., p. 214), 'Retrograde reform' (*Sunday Times*, 1 Feb.), 'A shabby deal' (*Daily Telegraph*, 17 Feb.), 'A statistical straitjacket' (*News Chronicle*, 31 Jan.), 'A mistake' (*Manchester*

---

[1] It is perhaps worth noting the verdict of Mr. D. L. Lipson, who had been elected as an 'Independent Conservative'. On the committee stage of the Bill he said: 'I do not believe that the Government, in deciding to abolish university representation, are guilty of a breach of faith, or that this Parliament was necessarily committed by what was decided at the Speaker's Conference during the previous Parliament. I disagree profoundly with them, however, on the question of the merits or demerits of university representation' (*H.C. Deb. 448*, c. 1975).

Guardian, 14 Feb.). The *Daily Herald* did not refer to the subject. But during the passage of the Bill there were very few editorial comments, and these were mostly confined to dutiful reiterations of the arguments used in Parliament. Only in *The Times* was there any body of correspondence, and there the protests were more than once diverted on to historical side issues about past university members and elections.

It is interesting to note that *The Economist* and *The Times*, the only journals to comment extensively upon the Bill, did not serve the Conservative case very well. *The Times* justified the abolition of the business vote and the City of London representation[1] and *The Economist* wrote:

Though the abolition of the business vote was not recommended by the Speaker's Conference, it was perhaps too much to expect that a Labour Government would preserve something which looks so like a capitalist vested interest, and it would be difficult in these days to defend it on any sound political footing. The abolition of the university vote [is an altogether different matter].[2]

But if the abolition of the university vote was a breach of faith so was the abolition of the business vote. In exonerating the one breach of faith they were exonerating the other. The truth seems to be that, whatever the parliamentary reaction, the public were not very interested in the 'breach of faith'. The editors and the vocal graduates were only concerned at the abolition of the university franchise. The positive case for the universities put before the public did not differ much from that put before the House of Commons. It was felt that university representation had justified itself by providing an avenue to Parliament for distinguished men who might not otherwise have reached there. This case was allowed to make its way almost by default as far as the press was concerned; even the *New Statesman* failed to take up the challenge.

To describe the passage of the Bill separately from the dispute about the bargain is like presenting *Hamlet* without the prince. Upon this, the only occasion in the last thirty years when a question of electoral legislation has aroused deep feeling, the controversy centred upon an issue of political ethics. The debate

---

[1] See p. 110, above. [2] *The Economist*, 7 Feb. 1948, p. 214.

on the provisions of the Bill was, with the exception of two issues, a humdrum enough affair.

The second reading[1] on 17 February 1948 began in an unusual manner. The sheriffs of the City of London, exercising their ancient privilege, appeared before the House in full regalia to present a petition praying that their separate representation should remain undisturbed. Mr. Ede followed this colourful introduction with an exhaustive exposition of the Bill. He claimed that by ending all special privileges and giving everyone one vote and one vote only, it 'completed the process begun in 1832'. The redistribution proposals showed that there was nothing to Mr. Churchill's charges of underhand dealing made in 1946. He regretted that there would still be eight constituencies with over 80,000 electors. In reply, Mr. Churchill said that the Conservatives could not refuse to support a Bill which provided a much-needed redistribution and which, for the most part, conformed to the well-established tradition of electoral reform by party agreement. But he then went on to set the tone of the rest of the debate by launching the most violent attack upon the bad faith of the Government in tampering with the university and business franchises. He ended with the comment that the Labour party seemed to have decided that they had no hope of ever winning the educated vote.

In the subsequent debate, well-worn paths were followed in the intervals between post-mortems on the Speaker's Conference. On the Labour side the 'one man, one vote' argument was frequently reiterated and the charge that the abolition of university representation was a blow at education was indignantly refuted. One or two suggested that the place for university representation was in a reconstituted House of Lords.[2] Mr. Skeffington-Lodge, a lone voice, pleaded for traditionalism and the retention of some at least of the university seats. Mr. Mackay, another lone voice, pleaded for proportional representation. Other Labour speakers demanded some limitation on the use of cars on polling-day. But most Labour attention was devoted to the redistribution proposals. Members made special pleas for

[1] *H.C. Deb. 447*, cc. 839–947, 993–1118.
[2] At this time discussions about the composition of the House of Lords were going on between the leaders of the parties.

the representation of their own localities; there were protests that England would be under-represented in the new House and objections to having constituencies with more than 80,000 electors. Mr. Dalton made a notable intervention in his first back-bench speech after leaving the Exchequer. He demanded that the number of seats should be increased; over 80,000 electors in a constituency should not be tolerated; but the larger cities had also been left under-represented by the Boundary Commissioners. The quota for England was 59,000. But in Bradford it was 71,000, in Liverpool 66,000, in Birmingham 63,000, and in Plymouth 71,000. There was a very strong case for further redistribution.

On the Conservative side, 'one man, one vote' was attacked as meaningless without 'one vote, one value'. But 'one vote, one value' implied proportional representation which only the Liberals advocated. The increasing size and discrimination of the university electorate was stressed as well as the importance of preserving some avenue for independents to enter the House. The virtues of Miss Rathbone were eagerly cited. Indeed the merits of university representation occupied almost all the time the Opposition devoted to subjects other than the 1944 bargain. Of the twelve university members, six spoke, and one Conservative remarked that so many of them had talked for so long that he almost began to be opposed to university representation. Other Conservatives protested not only at the ending of the City of London's special representation but also at the insult of merging it with Shoreditch and Finsbury in the new redistribution proposals. Apart from this the Conservatives paid little attention to redistribution, although two members did defend the principle of having a larger quota for borough than for county constituencies.

The Liberals made a conventional appeal for proportional representation, but supported the Government in condemnation of all plural voting.

The Bill was given a second reading by 318 votes to 6. The Conservatives abstained, and the opposition was made up of Liberals and two of the university members.

The Bill was examined in committee of the whole House;[1]

---

[1] As being of 'first-class constitutional importance'.

it was one of the very few major Bills to be so treated by the
Labour Government. The first day in committee,[1] 16 March,
was devoted to an amendment designed to save university representation. Once again, the question of the bargain predominated
among the arguments and university members among the arguers
—six of them spoke. Labour argued mildly that a few distinguished men did not justify an illogical institution and that
the constituencies were too small. On the other side it was
contended that university representation was a safeguard of
academic freedom, that it sent independents to the House, that
it gave members of Parliament to graduates overseas, and that it
was an invaluable supplement to ordinary representation; that
tradition should be honoured and mathematical equality not be
pressed too far. On the whole, it is remarkable that the extreme
and absurd arguments for and against university representation
were less used than in former years. On the one side, lurid
attacks on the haunts of privilege were missing and, on the
other, no one now suggested that without the university seats
the professional classes would be unrepresented. The amendment was defeated by 328 votes to 198. The Liberals supported
the Government except for one who, together with one Labour
member, voted with the Conservatives.

On the following day a general debate[2] on business voting
took place on a motion designed to preserve the representation
of the City of London. The pattern set in these debates of
Conservative emphasis on the breach of faith and Labour emphasis on the merits of equality was more than ever apparent—
perhaps because the case for the business vote was not an easy
one to argue, while there were many well-tried slogans with
which to attack it. In reply to the Labour contention that fancy
franchises were indefensible, the Conservatives argued that the
business vote guaranteed representation to certain special communities and that the City of London in particular, where half
a million people worked and where a quarter of the income-tax
was raised, had a claim to a seat on the grounds both of tradition
and of justice. There were despairing pleas that people should
be given the choice of using their business or their ordinary

[1] *H.C. Deb. 448*, cc. 1892 et seq.
[2] Ibid., cc. 2015 et seq.

votes and that the City seat should be preserved in some special way, perhaps as a refuge for the Speaker or for ex-Prime Ministers. But the only concession that Mr. Ede would make to the Opposition was to say that the City could be joined to Southwark or to Westminster if there was particular objection to linking it with Shoreditch and Finsbury. The Liberals supported the Government to defeat the amendment by 323 votes to 192.

Before the committee stage was resumed a week later a new dispute broke out, almost equal in bitterness to that over university representation and the bargain. It became known that the Government had asked the Boundary Commissioners to recommend how the eight seats with more than 80,000 electors should be divided in two and how the boundaries in nine of the largest English boroughs should be redrawn in order to give each of them one more member.

The Economist commented:

Though opposition charges of gerrymandering need not be taken in this case too seriously, it is certainly unfortunate that the Government should have chosen this particular moment to bring forward amendments . . . which depart from the recommendations laid down by the Boundary Commission. For, whatever their merits, it will be difficult, after the obvious party bias shown in the abolition of the university seats and the representation of the City of London, to convince the public that they have been influenced by purely disinterested considerations. . . . It is difficult to quarrel seriously with the substance of these amendments . . . it is [only] the method and timing of their introduction which is objectionable.[1]

Mr. Ede in moving an amendment[2] to allow the increase in the total number of seats, observed that, with 625 members, the House would still be the smallest since 1801, apart from the period from 1922 to 1945. In England, even with the seventeen new seats, the quota for boroughs was still greater than for counties (57,833 compared with 55,360—a difference of 2,473). Without the seventeen seats, the discrepancy would have been more than twice as great (6,082).[3] The amendment would do

[1] *The Economist*, 27 Mar. 1948, p. 495.
[2] *H.C. Deb. 448*, cc. 3023 et seq.
[3] These figures given by Mr. Ede were, of course, like the Boundary Commissioners' recommendations, based on the relatively inaccurate figures

something to redress the under-representation of England. To this mild and mathematical argument, Mr. Churchill replied with even more violent language than he had used before. This was a disreputable job, done without statutory authority by 'the Minister of the Interior'. Such unilateral action was a breach of faith, a further repudiation of the Speaker's Conference. The Conservatives had supported the Bill, despite the earlier breach of faith, because the redistribution proposals were honoured. But now the Government had yielded to back-bench pressure and unconstitutionally approached the Boundary Commissioners, whose legal status was at an end, and asked them to draw new boundaries. Sixty-five constituencies were to be altered by private individuals; in effect, the minister himself was now drawing the boundaries—a totalitarian proceeding. The Government should feel lasting shame at their action. To this speech, Mr. Morrison replied that Mr. Churchill had not touched on the merits of the change. The Boundary Commissioners were a permanent body; the Government's procedure in approaching them may have been a bit doubtful, but the Commissioners' impartiality could not be questioned. The Government did not know who would win the extra seats. In 1945 Labour had expected, quite wrongly, that most of the twenty-five extra seats created then would go to the Conservatives; one never could tell. There was no more evidence of gerrymandering on this occasion than there was in 1946 when Mr. Churchill had previously made the charge. Mr. Morrison observed that, as he had made clear when he held the office in 1944, the Home Secretary was not bound by the recommendations of the Boundary Commissioners; in this case he had listened to the representations which had been made from all parties about the division of the boroughs with more than 80,000 electors. Government back-benchers, mostly from the areas affected, gave a warm welcome to the amendment, but from the Conservative side there were vehement protests. Redistribution

derived by the interim registration procedure. The first register compiled by canvass under the 1948 Act showed that the counties retained a rather greater advantage than Mr. Ede had suggested. The average English borough electorate was 57,319, while the average county electorate was 54,386, a difference of 2,933. In Great Britain as a whole the difference was even higher—3,954.

should only be carried out by party agreement. This was a plot to give extra seats to the Labour party. However, two Conservatives demurred; Admiral Taylor, from one of the boroughs over 80,000, welcomed its division, and Sir Patrick Hannon argued that the boundaries of Birmingham had been redrawn fairly in order to create an extra seat; he thought that the new proposals gave fair play to all concerned. Mr. Peake argued that to increase the number of seats to twenty-two more than the number suggested by the Speaker's Conference, without any consultation with the Opposition, was clearly dishonourable. It was also a breach of the agreement made privately in 1946 when the Redistribution Act was amended. It had then been settled that a 'small increase', but only a small increase, over 603 should be tolerated. Why had there been no consultation on this? Why had there been such a delay in making the change? The Boundary Commissioners had finished their job before they were asked to provide for these extra seats. Mr. Ede pointed out that the Boundary Commissioners had been asked how the seats with more than 80,000 electors should be divided before they had signed their report in October 1947. Mr. Peake agreed that the Commissioners had been acting statutorily when they dealt with those 8 seats. But what about the other 9 whose creation affected the boundaries of 56 other seats? There had been no inquiry and no opportunity for local objections. It was intolerable that this should be settled by a secret meeting of the ex-Boundary Commissioners. Mr. Ede, in his reply, observed that the Government was being attacked because it had become convinced by the arguments put forward by its own back-benchers. The Boundary Commissioners, he insisted, were a continuing body; he had gone to them quite properly to ask how the cities which were under-represented should be given an extra seat. He would ask them to consider any complaints. But he recommended the change to the House as a just measure which would reduce disparities. It was carried by 294 votes to 125. Once again the Liberals supported the Government. Later, on the motion that the clause stand part of the Bill, Mr. Peake said that there was much doubt about the statutory position of the Boundary Commissioners, and Mr. Ede replied that he did not greatly mind whether they were acting in their statutory capacity or not; the Speaker was their Chairman and their impartiality was not in doubt.

After this the House continued through an all-night sitting to discuss the more technical side of the Bill. Clauses 4 to 6 dealt with the registration of electors, and Clauses 7 to 11 with the place and manner of voting. A number of drafting amendments were made but few of the changes proposed by backbenchers were of note. A singular coalition of Ulster Unionists and anti-partitionists combined to demand that only one register a year should be compiled for Northern Ireland,[1] but the Government refused to vary the recommendations of the Oliver Committee. Mr. Piratin for the Communists vainly demanded votes at eighteen instead of twenty-one. An amendment to give postal votes to those who had moved not only from one constituency to another but even from one polling-district to another was rejected on administrative grounds, and so was one which tried to allow postal voting by those who had moved to another constituency within the same borough. The only concession won in a long and ill-tempered night of wrangling was the passage of an amendment which excepted the County of London from treatment as a single borough for electoral purposes.

A day and a half more of discussion sufficed for Clauses 13 to 75. On only two clauses was there a division or even an appreciable controversy. A Conservative attempt to reduce the condition for forfeiting the deposit from one-eighth to one-tenth of the votes in contests where there were more than three candidates—a recommendation of the Speaker's Conference—was defeated by 264 votes to 125. The last clause giving the Bill the title Representation of the People Act was more strenuously objected to by Conservatives who had put down an amendment to change its title to 'The Representation of the Labour Party Act', but the clause was carried by 242 votes to 78.[2] For once, the Liberals voted against the Government on the ground that a

---

[1] Both sides objected to having the labour of challenging the register twice a year. In Britain the number of claims and objections to the register is negligible. In Northern Ireland this Victorian custom continues and there may be some thousands of objections. See *The British General Election of 1951* (London, 1952), by D. E. Butler, p. 223.

[2] *H.C. Deb. 449*, c. 1915.

Bill which perpetuated an unjust electoral system could not be said to provide for the representation of the people.

The new clauses proved more contentious. Mr. McLeavy proposed that the use of cars to take electors to the polls should be prohibited.[1] The returning officers should provide cars to cope with casual illness but postal voting would meet most hard cases. A provision like this was needed to give fair play at elections; it had been advocated as long ago as 1883. Mr. McLeavy attracted firm support from Labour speakers, while Conservatives protested that this was a disfranchising and un-enforceable suggestion which would cause severe hardship in country areas. The clause was withdrawn after Mr. Ede had announced that he was in sympathy with the general purpose of the clause but that it would have to be redrafted and reintro-duced at the report stage. A Conservative clause giving a proxy vote to wives of servicemen who were overseas with their hus-bands was accepted. A Liberal clause providing for the alter-native vote was rejected very summarily, although it gave the Liberals a chance to twit the Government with their conversion since 1931. An Ulster Unionist clause requiring a three-months' residence qualification in Northern Ireland was negatived after a debate remarkable for the frankness with which the electoral immorality of the six counties was discussed.

On 26 and 27 April the First Schedule, specifying the new constituency boundaries,[2] came before the House. Mr. Peake asked that the seventeen new seats should not be settled until the report stage, and announced that the Conservatives had asked the Boundary Commissioners to consider new seats in other areas where the quota was high. Mr. Ede replied that everything was open until the report stage. There followed a host of amend-ments, mostly from members indulging in special pleading for their own constituencies. Mr. Ede himself moved 17 amend-ments to give effect to the Government's recommendations for new constituencies. He also accepted 12 of the 41 amendments proposed by other members. Of these 12, 8 merely changed the name of the constituency concerned and 1 changed a seat from borough to county classification; the 3 boundary changes

---

[1] *H.C. Deb. 449*, cc. 1923 et seq.
[2] *H.C. Deb. 450*, cc. 38 et seq., 217 et seq.

accepted were all of the most negligible proportions. Of the other amendments, 14 were withdrawn after Mr. Ede had explained the difficulties involved or, in some cases, had given an assurance that he would give further consideration to the point raised; 13 were negatived without a division, and 2 were defeated. Few can be regarded as of great significance. An amendment to give Plymouth three seats instead of two provoked much the most impassioned discussion of the day. West Country members of all parties pleaded that the city had special historic claims and that as it rebuilt its blitzed areas each seat would soon satisfy the full quota. Mr. Ede replied firmly that three seats would average only 47,000 electors apiece; that was 10,000 below the quota and such exceptions could not be allowed. The amendment was defeated by 189 votes to 57, Labour providing all the majority and a substantial proportion of the minority. Similar pleas for Leyton and West Ham were more expeditiously negatived. Later a sturdy fight was made on behalf of three of those singular Scottish constituencies, the Districts of Burghs, Ayr, Montrose, and Dumbarton, which were to be merged in the surrounding counties. But the only other issue to be pressed to a division arose when Mr. Mulvey, an anti-partitionist, asked that his new constituency should be called 'Mid-Ulster' and not 'North Tyrone and Magherafelt'; despite vigorous opposition, the Government reluctantly supported the amendment which was carried by 276 votes to 112. As in 1918, the Government had, throughout the discussion of the merits of individual constituencies, refused to accept any amendment of substance. In self-defence, they only allowed nominal alterations to the recommendations of the Boundary Commissioners.

Nothing further of note occurred in committee. An interval of six weeks elapsed before the next stage; this may have been determined by other pressures on the parliamentary time-table, but it also gave time for objections to the new constituencies to be heard and for a new clause on the use of cars to be carefully drafted. This clause provided that each candidate should be allowed to register with the returning officer one car for every 2,500 electors in boroughs and for every 1,500 electors in counties. No other cars would be allowed to bring to the polls any voters who were not actually resident at the owner's house.

The clause also required that a notional £2 per car should be charged against election expenses. Mr. Ede moved the second reading of this clause.[1] He observed that it followed the 1931 precedent but that, since there were more polling-stations and postal voting facilities, the permitted number of cars was set at a lower figure. The clause was warmly welcomed from the Labour benches, although some doubts were expressed about whether it could be enforced and about the £2 notional charge. One member suggested that at general elections Conservative cars outnumbered Labour by perhaps five to one and that each car was worth fifteen to twenty votes. Another objected that too few cars were to be allowed for the rural areas and suggested that the returning officer should have some cars at his disposal to meet hard cases.

The Conservatives were naturally very critical both of the purpose and detail of the clause. The disfranchisement of country people, the absurdity of the £2 expense return, the obscurity about lifts for neighbours, and the impossibility of enforcement were attacked. Lord Winterton argued that cars were of no special benefit to the Conservatives, and he was joined by others who contended that the general public rather than the Conservatives would suffer—as car ownership was now so widespread. Mr. Woodburn, in replying to the debate, got into great difficulties in explaining whether lifts would be legal or illegal, and he had to be rescued by the Attorney-General. The clause was carried by 269 votes to 114. The Liberals were evenly divided but all the Independents were against the Government. At the committee stage an attempt was made to link the number of cars to the number of polling-stations rather than to the number of electors in order to allow for more cars in scattered constituencies. It was suggested that, as in 1931, constituencies of over 400 square miles in area should be exempted. But Mr. Ede refused to make any such changes and more abruptly rejected an attempt to reduce the quota to one car per 1,000 electors. However, he pacified the Opposition a little by agreeing to abandon the notional charge of £2 per car, for which no one had had a good word.

The Opposition next proposed a new clause[2] which would

---

[1] *H.C. Deb. 452*, cc. 51 et seq.   [2] Ibid., c. 171.

allow the university electoral registers to be kept in being. This led to a brief run over the old ground. The breach of faith was attacked and denied. Professor Savory, for the third time in four years, told the House a story about an election for Belfast University, and Mr. Elliot and Sir Arthur Salter praised the independence of their electors. Mr. Eden argued that there was no mandate for disfranchising the universities and that their representatives had been distinguished. Mr. Ede replied perfunctorily that the argument about distinguished men had been used a hundred years earlier in defence of rotten boroughs. It was no answer to the case against fancy franchises. The clause was rejected by 217 votes to 88.

When the report stage took place the next day[1] some more old ground was traversed, although more swiftly than in committee. Sir Andrew Duncan moved to retain one member for the City of London. Mr. Ede regretted that he could not accept a case based solely on historic sentiment and was supported by 269 votes to 111. Mr. Peake moved that five further constituencies should be created, four in the outer suburbs of London and one in Cheshire. He argued that if the Boundary Commissioners had known that there were going to be 506 seats in England instead of 489, they would have acted differently. The Conservatives had asked them to show how nine new seats could be created in the areas now most under-represented. However, they were only now pressing five of these recommendations as the others violated local boundaries too severely. These new seats would still leave the areas concerned with a quota of M.P.s larger than in Nottingham or Leeds, where the Government had added extra seats. The sole objection to the proposals—that they would give the Conservatives two or three extra seats—was not, in fact, true.[2] Mr. Ede replied that the seventeen seats had been designed to reduce the disparity between boroughs and county quotas and to eliminate seats containing more than 80,000 electors. These new suggestions would leave even larger anomalies, but he would listen to the debate before making up his mind about them finally. There

[1] *H.C. Deb. 452*, cc. 259 et seq.
[2] But in fact it appears that, if these 5 seats had been created, at least 4 of them would, in 1950, have been won by the Conservatives.

followed a very moderate debate in which it was agreed on both sides that there was nothing sacrosanct about the total number of members. The Conservatives contended that the amendment met their worst grievances and Mr. Reid, summing up, challenged the Government to prove that their seventeen seats had been created on grounds of principle and not of self-interest by accepting these five more. Mr. Ede replied that he had heard no arguments to change his views about the individual merits of the proposed seats, all of which violated the unity of local government areas. He felt that he had been right in trying to equalize the quota between counties and boroughs. The amendment was defeated by 278 votes to 127.

The rest of the report stage saw the swift acceptance of many amendments. The most important were the transfer of the City of London from Shoreditch and Finsbury to Westminster, and the increase, by agreement between the parties, of permitted expenses by $\frac{1}{2}d$. per elector in order to allow for increased prices since the new scale had been proposed in 1944. A large number of boundary adjustments were made on the Home Secretary's recommendation and several constituencies had their status varied between borough and county.

On 23 June the third reading took place.[1] Bitterness again prevailed and the breach of faith provided the dominant theme. Mr. Ede launched the debate with a simple exposition of the changes effected by the Bill, but Mr. Churchill, in reply, moved the rejection of this 'petty, partisan' measure. The 1944 agreement for impartial electoral reform had been broken. The Socialists could not bear to lose the thirty-five seats which redistribution would cost them, and so they had decided to cheat and to abolish the universities and the City of London. But that was not enough. Twenty seats would still be lost. Therefore, seventeen more were created, and a limitation on the use of cars was thrown in for good measure.[2] They had stopped there, which

[1] *H.C. Deb. 452*, cc. 1367 et seq.
[2] This false arithmetic was echoed by many others and, oddly enough, never refuted. It is plain that 35 seats lost by redistribution must go to the other side and count for 70 in a division. But the creation of extra seats or the abolition of existing seats count only once in a division. Therefore, even granting Mr. Churchill's premises to the full, the Conservatives would still have made a net gain of 20 seats under the Act, 20 seats counting 40 in a

was surprising. In passing Mr. Churchill quite abruptly advocated compulsory voting and then, in his peroration, pledged
that the Conservatives would restore the representation of the
universities and the City of London when they returned to
power. No other new arguments or information were adduced in
the debate. Mr. Neil Maclean announced that he would vote
against the Bill because his seat had been dismembered to make
a safe refuge for the Conservatives, and Mr. Medland from
Plymouth said that he could not support the third reading
because the redistribution proposals in the south-west of
England were so much in the Conservatives' favour. On the
other side, Sir Walter Smiles protested at the broken understanding involved in the reduction of Northern Ireland representation from thirteen to twelve members by the abolition of
the Queen's University seat. Some members from rural areas
objected that lack of cars would make it harder to vote despite
the increased number of polling-places. But, apart from these
relevancies, the debate consisted of charge and denial of dishonourable conduct. The third reading was carried by 338
votes to 193. The Liberals abstained, but even the most independent of Independents voted against the Government.

The Bill passed speedily through the House of Lords without
any division and with little discussion. As Lord Salisbury explained on the second reading,[1] it was the concern of the House
of Commons. It was 'somewhat outside our sphere',[2] a principle
that certainly had not been accepted in 1931.[3] The second read-

division. But a further weakness in his argument was the assumption that all
the 17 new seats would go to Labour. In fact, in the election of 1950, the new
seats created by the division of the boroughs over 80,000 meant that Labour
won 6 more seats and the Conservatives 2; 2 of the Labour seats were
secured by very narrow majorities and in fact fell to the Conservatives in
1951. The consequence of adding 9 seats to the larger boroughs can be calculated with less certainty. It seems, however, that Labour cannot have
secured more than 6 of these extra seats; perhaps they gained only 4. Therefore, on the most extreme reckoning, Labour only gained 7 more of the extra 17
seats than the Conservatives. This, together with the abolition of the university and City of London seats, would have benefited them 21 on a division in
the House of Commons. On the other hand, the results of the 1950 election
showed that Mr. Churchill's assumption that the ordinary redistribution
proposals in the Bill would cost the Labour party 35 seats was not very far away
from the truth. This leads to the conclusion that, as a consequence of the Bill,
Labour became between 40 and 50 votes worse off in a parliamentary division.

[1] *H.L. Deb. 157*, cc. 288 et seq.   [2] Ibid., c. 295.   [3] See pp. 80–82.

ing debate was entirely concerned with the breach of faith, apart from one speech by Lord Shepherd, a former chief agent of the Labour party, who regretted that the opportunity had not been taken to consolidate all electoral law into a single Bill and who expressed doubts about the danger of abuse in postal and proxy voting. In committee the only change which was more than drafting in character was an amendment which explicitly permitted the giving of innocent lifts. The Bill, which had had such a turbulent history, passed its final stages in peace and received the Royal Assent on 30 July 1948.[1]

It seems that the whole passage of the Bill might have been almost equally tranquil had it not been for the question of 'good faith'. The great majority of the changes effected by the Act were the product of inter-party agreement and, therefore, unlikely to provoke much comment. It is significant that one of these agreed changes was to have a greater effect upon the fortunes of the parties in the ensuing election than any of the provisions which had been the subject of controversy. There can be little doubt that in 1950 the postal vote enabled the Conservatives to win a dozen seats that would otherwise have fallen to Labour. That so little attention was devoted by Parliament to this or to almost any other questions except those involving constitutional ethics is typical of all discussion of electoral matters after 1918.

Constitutional ethics occupied the major part of the debates in 1948 and much heat was generated. But the many speeches did little to clarify the problem at issue and the vehemence seems to have left little mark. Despite the strength of the language which had been used about the breach of faith, it was interesting three years later to find how far these charges had sunk into oblivion. There certainly is no evidence that the episode had done any serious or lasting harm to mutual trust between the parties or that it had made it more difficult to arrive at gentlemen's agreements. Suspicion of the motives and methods of the other side is characteristic of all politics. Whatever may have been said in 1948, in 1951 no one seemed willing to argue that 'breach of faith' over university representation had materially aggravated that suspicion.

[1] As 11 & 12 Geo. 6, ch. 65.

IV. THE AFTERMATH

The greater part of this Act which had given so much trouble was the next year noiselessly and completely repealed. A consolidation Act, combining provisions from all past electoral legislation which remained in force, was passed without any discussion as the Representation of the People Act, 1949.[1] Further consolidation measures, the House of Commons (Redistribution of Seats) Act,[2] and the Election Commissioners Act,[3] re-enacted the laws dealing with redistribution and with election petitions.

In the autumn of 1949 another Act modified one of the innovations of the 1948 Act. The devaluation crisis led to a demand for Government retrenchment. One of the lesser economy proposals decided upon was the abandonment of six-monthly registration of electors. In 1926 a similar step had been taken,[4] but this time the autumn register was to be eliminated because under the 1948 Act all local elections were to take place in the spring after the publication of the March register. The Electoral Registers Bill excited little controversy. Some speakers suggested that it should be only temporary, but it was pointed out that the postal voting facilities greatly reduced the urgency of frequent checking of the register. The only change made in the Bill[5] during its passage was an amendment, at first declared to be administratively impracticable, enabling people just under twenty-one to be placed on the register so that they could vote immediately on coming of age instead of waiting for the first register compiled after their majority.

The elections of February 1950 and October 1951 saw the new law working smoothly. The largest proportions of the electorate since the advent of universal suffrage went to the polls. The postal voting facilities were used by about 2 per cent. of the voters. The limitation on cars seems to have been observed relatively carefully. The official issue of poll-cards and the lower expense maxima did not cause much difficulty. In short, in all respects but one the electoral system showed the quiet efficiency expected of it. The exception was that, although it duly crushed

---

[1] 12, 13, & 14 Geo. 6, ch. 68.   [2] Ibid., ch. 66.
[3] Ibid., ch. 90.   [4] See pp. 50–52 above.
[5] Enacted as 12, 13, & 14 Geo. 6, ch. 86.

minor-party representation, the system failed to give a reasonable working majority to either of the major parties. Although the result of the 1950 contest led Mr. Churchill[1] to reopen the question of electoral reform, his own supporters as much as the Labour party remained as indifferent as ever to any such proposals.

[1] *H.C. Deb. 472*, c. 143. He suggested the establishment of 'a Select Committee to inquire into the whole question of electoral reform'. He wanted the committee to be composed on the basis of votes in the country rather than seats in the House. Mr. Morrison (ibid., c. 168) rejected the inquiry as unnecessary and observed that such a Select Committee so composed would be unprecedented. Only the Liberals supported Mr. Churchill's proposal. Members of his own party were silent.

Mr. Morrison seems to have forgotten that the Ullswater Conference in 1929 virtually constituted a precedent for a committee so composed.

[2] On 19 November 1952 Mr. Churchill announced: 'It remains the declared intention of Her Majesty's Government to legislate on this subject' (*H.C. Deb. 507*, c. 1869).

CHAPTER VI

CONCLUSION

FROM this narrative it becomes plain how relatively insignificant discussion of the electoral system has been in the politics of the last thirty years. The subject never loomed large enough for public opinion to be much interested in it or for individual M.P.s to make themselves specialists upon it. Therefore when it was debated, the discussion tended to consist of assertions and counter-assertions which were neither based clearly on fact nor linked to any well-formulated theory of representation. Among the majority of M.P.s there seems to have been complacency about an institution which in its way worked efficiently and with a kind of rough justice. Some minor aspects were the subject of vehement party controversy and one drastic reform, proportional representation, always had a few advocates. But, in retrospect, the scale of such disagreements only serves to emphasize the general acceptance of the system.

None the less, the history of electoral legislation and of attempts at electoral legislation since 1918 has its lessons. It is notable how the most vigorous arguments always tended to be not so much about the merits of the proposals at issue as about the propriety of putting them forward. The questions of electoral change seem often to have been submerged by those of political ethics and parliamentary manners. The battle was waged over allegations of the breach of agreements to leave things alone, of the constitutional necessity of following reform by an immediate election, of the unconstitutional motives behind proposed changes, and of the abuse of parliamentary traditions. The reputed bargain made about women's suffrage in 1917 was used as an argument against equalizing the franchise quite as often as the unfitness of young women to vote. In 1931 the 'underhand' negotiations with Mr. Lloyd George were cited against the alternative vote as much as the probable consequences of the system; and in the debates on that Bill the one on the use of the guillotine was certainly the most vehement. In 1948 the controversy over the Speaker's Conference bargain completely overshadowed all other issues. It might seem that what the Government proposed to do to the electoral system was far less important than how they did it. It is certain that the latter provided the best ground for political attack.

However, underlying all these squabbles, one issue arose repeatedly. What are the unwritten rules of the constitution? Is there an obligation to treat issues affecting the machinery of government in a different manner from the ordinary subjects of political discussion?

If the security and continuity of government is to be preserved, it is undesirable that the institutional framework within which it is conducted should be the subject of continued party controversy. But as a matter of fact and of precedent it has been the exception rather than the rule for changes in the electoral system to be agreed party measures. It is only under the unnatural circumstances of two war-time coalitions that electoral reform has been initiated by inter-party agreement. Both in the nineteenth and the twentieth centuries drastic changes have been proposed without any suggestion of inter-party agreement or even consultation. If inter-party agreement were a prerequisite to constitutional innovation, each party would have a permanent veto on all change. It is hardly realistic even to argue for inter-party consultation as a prerequisite. Apart from the vexed question of the 1944 'bargain', would a Labour Government have been bound in honour or by constitutional tradition to consult their opponents before abolishing the business vote? The views of all parties on the question were well known and surely no useful purpose would have been served by such consultation. If there is a chance of carrying through a constitutional reform by agreement every effort should be made to do so, and it behoves a party to try as far as it can to avoid any suspicions that it is rigging the constitution for its own benefit.[1] But the

---

[1] Party agreement on constitutional reform does not solve all problems even when it can be secured. Both Speaker's Conferences were succeeded by arguments over what had been agreed. In both cases the main dispute could have been avoided if the term of years during which the agreements were to be regarded as binding had been settled. But in neither case does it appear that there was any discussion, let alone agreement, on how long the parties were to honour the concessions they had made. To raise such a point would have injected contention into otherwise harmonious proceedings. But the moral of subsequent history is plain. An agreement is meaningless if its

sanction against wanton neglect of these principles lies not in unwritten rules of procedure for constitutional legislation so much as in the common sense of politicians and the curb which the next election must always place upon them. 'Unconstitutional', said Sir Austen Chamberlain, 'is a term applied in politics to the other fellow who does something that you don't like.'[1] Debates on the electoral system in the last thirty years fully justify this observation.

It does not seem that in the procedure by which electoral change was made or attempted there was any gross breach of constitutional propriety. But it is true that the constitution depends upon certain assumptions of good faith, a breach of which may be as serious as an arbitrary disregard of established procedure; it has been contended here that in no case did electoral legislation involve a serious breach of faith. It is also true that the constitution could not long survive major attempts to load it in favour of one political party. However, although, of course, no party has ever proposed electoral legislation without some consideration for its own interests, during the last thirty years no party has, in fact, created any special privileges for itself; the main battles have been over Labour attempts to abolish institutions which favoured the other side. There were perhaps two occasions when there was colour to the accusation that the Government was taking more than negative action to alter the electoral system in its own favour. In 1931 the Labour Government seem to have proposed the alternative vote in order to secure the support of the Liberals and in the belief that it would hurt the Conservatives more than themselves. In 1948 the Labour Government added seventeen seats to those proposed by the Boundary Commissioners; although a strong case could be made for the change on its merits, and although it had little net effect on party representation, the seats were all boroughs, and urban areas usually tend to favour the Labour party more than the Conservatives. Partisan spite may also be alleged in the attempts to abolish university representation or to limit the use of cars, but these proposals for the alternative vote and

duration is not understood; its duration will not be understood unless it is explicitly settled.
[1] *H.C. Deb. 261*, c. 530.

the extra seats are the only instances where it can be suggested that a Government made an attempt positively to load the system in its own favour. Since the former favoured the Liberals far more than its proposers, and since the latter was so small in scale and could so largely be justified on its own merits, it can hardly be said that there have been any gross attempts to pervert the democratic machine.

Indeed, as far as electoral matters are concerned, the democratic machine has not really been much altered since 1918. When the modifications to the framework of electoral law are set beside the parts which have remained untouched, it becomes plain how comprehensive and how lasting was the legislation of 1918. Such changes in the conduct of elections as have taken place have been in practice rather than in law. It took some time for politicians and their agents to adapt themselves to the vast increase in electorate and to the other innovations brought about by the 1918 Act. As Bagehot wrote of an earlier Reform Act: 'A new Constitution does not produce its full effect as long as all its subjects were reared under an old Constitution, as long as its statesmen were trained by that old Constitution. It is not really tested till it comes to be worked by statesmen and among a people, neither of whom are guided by a different experience.'[1] In 1950 and 1951 the parties had to cope with the minor changes in the law made in 1948; but they were also still working out the answers to the much older problem of appealing to an electorate comprising the whole adult population and of leading such vast numbers to the poll. Although the manner and matter of some of the changes since 1918 are not without importance, they have posed no such fundamental problems. The significant evolution of the electoral system now lies in the parties' use of the weapons of organization and publicity rather than in any attempts at legislation.

[1] Walter Bagehot, Introduction to the second edition of *The English Constitution* (World's Classics), p. 260.

PART II

THE WORKING OF THE SYSTEM

I. INTRODUCTION

WHEN electoral matters have been discussed in Parliament during the past thirty years there has very seldom been any allusion to the hard facts about the working of the system. Yet there existed a considerable amount of relevant information which could have been unearthed without excessive difficulty and quoted with appreciable benefit to the quality of the debate. The problem of the business vote would have appeared in a different perspective if the approximate number of contests in which it was decisive had been known. Discussions on expense maxima could have been illumined by an examination of the actual expenses incurred by the various parties. Laments at the decline of the Independent members should have been tempered by a consideration of the facts. Changes in the system of voting might have been more intelligently deliberated if more attention had been paid to the likely consequences of proportional representation or the alternative vote, and to the relation between seats and votes under the existing system. The lessons of election results could have been more usefully discussed if certain common-sense adjustments had been made to the deceptively simple aggregates of seats and votes normally published. In the pages that follow an attempt is made to set out some of the facts which are available about the working of the electoral system.

2. THE EQUALIZATION OF THE FRANCHISE

IN the debates on the Representation of the People Bill in 1928 exaggerated ideas seemed current about its possible effects. From the registers of 1928 and 1929 some idea can be derived of the number of voters involved.

The natural growth of population, together with an apparent improvement in the efficiency of the register, must account for some of the increase. On the assumption that this was in the same proportion for women as for men, it seems that 4,761,074 of the women on the 1929 register were there owing to the 1928 Act. In other words, owing to the Act the electorate was increased by 16·5 per cent.

TABLE I. *Electorate in 1928 and 1929*

Year	Total	Men	Women
1928[1]	22,855,086	12,961,200	9,893,886
1929	28,858,973	13,665,786	15,193,187
Increase	6,003,887	704,586	5,299,301

If the new voters sided overwhelmingly with any of the parties, they could decisively have influenced the 1929 election, and there are some who allege that they did. It is a contention which can be neither proved nor disproved, but there seems reason to doubt it. There is substantial evidence that those under thirty—who constituted . nearly two-thirds of those enfranchised in 1928—are the most apathetic of electors. Public opinion polls and political organizers agree that an appreciably larger proportion of young people abstain from voting than of any other age-group, just as they agree that more women than men abstain. But, more important, there is no reason to suppose that the behaviour of those who do vote differs very markedly from that of older people. In recent public opinion polls a few per cent. more of those under thirty than of their elders were regularly found to be in favour of the Labour party. On the other hand, a few per cent. more women than men have been regularly found to favour the Conservative party. If it is assumed that in 1929 5 per cent. fewer of the newly enfranchised women than of the rest of the population supported the Conservative party, it would have cost them less than 1 per cent. of the total popular vote and would be insufficient to account for their defeat. But there is no reason to accept that the 1928 Act had so adverse an effect as that on the Conservative fortunes. It may equally well have benefited them. It certainly seems that those who blamed Sir William Joynson Hicks for the

---

[1] The 1928 figures are not strictly accurate, because for Northern Ireland they are based upon the 1927 and not the 1928 register.

1929 defeat were unjust in their conclusion (even if they were not also unjust in their premise that but for him the 1928 Act would not have been passed).

3. THE BUSINESS VOTE

THE business vote was long regarded as a grievance by the Liberal and Labour parties and its abolition in 1948 was only the culmination of an extended series of debates on the question. In these debates the effect of the business vote was never specifically estimated, but there always seems to have been an exaggerated notion of the part it played in deciding the composition of the House of Commons. It is, therefore, worth examining its importance.

Under the Act of 1918 all occupiers of business premises worth more than £10 a year[1] and their wives were entitled to be placed on the register—provided that they had not already got a residential qualification in the same constituency. Until 1928 wives were only entitled to vote once in respect of a qualification derived through their husbands and must generally have exercised their residential vote. After 1928 that restriction was removed, and in addition men were given a vote in respect of their wives' business premises. But in 1944 the spouse's right to a business vote was abolished.

The business vote can never have been very fully exercised. In many cases business men had votes in several constituencies of which only one could be used, and in many others the distance between residence and business must have discouraged the use of both votes—especially by wives. It certainly seems reasonable to assume that not more than 75 per cent. of the vote can have been cast. Even this is probably an over-estimate, for when in 1944 it became necessary to claim a business vote in order to be placed on the register only one-third of the 150,000 or so who must have been eligible bothered to do so.

The figures for the business vote are necessarily incomplete because no record of the number of electors with a business qualification was kept in Scotland until 1944. The following table, therefore, refers only to England and Wales:

[1]　£5 for women.

TABLE 2. *Numbers of Business Electors*

Year	Electorate	Business vote	%
1922	18,001,692	199,904 ⎫ men	1·1
1923	18,388,833	208,694 ⎬ only	1·1
1924	18,806,842	211,257 ⎭	1·1
1929	25,095,793	371,594	1·5
1931	26,135,944	365,090	1·4
1935	27,395,836	367,797	1·3
1945	28,956,996	48,974	0·2
1950	30,176,644	None	—

It is not unreasonable to assume that the business vote was heavily Conservative. If 75 per cent. of the electors voted and cast their ballots 3 to 1 in favour of the Conservatives, the latter's share of the national vote would have been swelled by about 0·5 per cent. at general elections before 1928 and by about 0·7 per cent. afterwards as a result of the business vote. However, the effect on the composition of Parliament cannot have been very great, for in few seats did the business vote amount to as much as 1,000 votes, and most of these were Conservative strongholds in any case. It should also be pointed out that the City of London, which contributed about 10 per cent. of all business votes, was only contested in 1929 and 1945. The list of seats where on more than one occasion since 1922 the Conservatives appear to have owed their victory to the business vote is very short.

The City of London (every time). (Between 70 and 85 per cent. of its electors had a business qualification. Its very existence as a constituency obviously depended on the business vote.)
Glasgow Central (four times).
Liverpool Exchange (four times).
Manchester Exchange (four times).
Holborn (three times).
Leeds Central (twice).
Sheffield Central (twice).

It is, of course, not possible to compute the precise number of seats which the Conservatives won as the result of the business vote. Only the roughest approximation can be made as far as Scotland is concerned and the assumptions on which any calculations about English and Welsh seats are based are, to say the least, uncertain. But there are limits of probability. It is most unlikely that the Conservatives secured a clear majority of more than 60 per cent. of the total business electorate (e.g. an 85 per cent. poll, divided almost 6 to 1 in favour of the Conservatives). It seems probable, however, that they secured a majority of at least 30 per cent. of the total business electorate (e.g. 70 per cent. voting and dividing 5 to 2 in favour of the Conservatives).

TABLE 3. *Effect of the Business Vote*

Year	Number of seats won through the business vote assuming that the Conservatives won a clear majority among the business electorate of	
	30%	60%
1922	9	14
1923	6	17
1924	5	7
1929	10	14
1931	5	8
1935	8	15
1945	3	5
Average	7	11

No general election had so narrow a result that the business vote could have made a decisive difference. But it is possible that, if it had not been abolished, it would have prevented Labour from securing a clear majority in the 1950 general election.

4. UNIVERSITY REPRESENTATION, 1918–50

IT would be beyond the scope of this work to pass judgement on the quality of university representation since 1918. However, any verdict on the merits of the controversy which culminated in the abolition of the twelve[1] university seats should be preceded by a systematic examination of the election results; it is notable that no attempt to do this was made in the 1948 debates or in earlier discussions of the subject. It, therefore, seems to be worth while to set out the bare facts.

[1] In 1918 two members were elected by Dublin University and one by the National University of Ireland. With the Government of Ireland Act of 1920 these constituencies ceased to return members to Westminster and they are wholly ignored in this discussion.

In the general elections from 1918 to 1945, and in 17 by-elections, 113 university seats were filled. In 75 cases a Conservative was returned, in 18 a Liberal, and in 20 a candidate without a clear party affiliation. Forty-six different people sat as university representatives: 28 were avowed Conservatives[1] and 6 were Liberals; 12 were Independents, although 6 of these called themselves Independent Conservatives and one an Independent Socialist. It must, of course, be stressed that many of the official Conservatives showed unusual independence of mind while some Independents kept very close to the Conservative line.[2]

Here is a tabulation of the results:

TABLE 4. *University Members returned*

Year	Con.	Lab.	Lib.	Ind.
1918	9	..	3	..
1922	8	..	3	1
1923	9	..	2	1
1924	8	..	3	1
1929	8	..	2	2
1931	8	..	2	2
1935	8	..	1	3
1945	4	..	1	7

TABLE 5. *Votes for University Members*[3]

Year	Total votes				Unopposed returns	Votes for each party as % of all votes cast in seats they contested. (Number of opposed candidates shown in brackets)			
	Con.	Lab.	Lib.	Ind.		Con.	Lab.	Lib.	Ind.
1918	21,213	4,889	6,009	4,479	..	58·8 (10)	14·0 (5)	26·8 (4)	15·3 (7)
1922	14,114	2,097	5,958	3,684	4	57·4 (6)	17·6 (2)	34·5 (6)	32·0 (4)
1923	18,505	2,270	6,837	4,285	4	61·1 (6)	19·0 (2)	31·6 (4)	36·0 (3)
1924	30,666	4,308	11,583	6,443	1	62·3 (8)	14·1 (3)	29·6 (5)	31·5 (3)
1929	42,421	4,825	19,940	9,200	1	55·4 (10)	11·0 (3)	26·2 (6)	43·9 (2)
1931	18,140	..	2,229	18,065	8	59·4 (3)	..	70·1 (1)	63·5 (5)
1935	46,949	11,583	2,796	16,213	3	77·7 (7)	23·5 (4)	61·3 (1)	29·3 (2)
1945	29,497	6,274	7,111	73,765	..	51·3 (4)	13·0 (2)	17·9 (2)	63·2 (18)
Total	211,383 47·3%	36,578 8·2%	62,463 14·0%	136,134 30·5%		60·7	15·8	27·9	46·2

[1] The problem of defining parties is more than usually difficult with the university candidates. The only doubtful cases which are not here classed

For notes 1 (cont.), 2, and 3 see p. 150.

TABLE 6. *Votes in Each University*

	Party votes as % of total cast in elections which the party contested			
	Con.	Lab.	Lib.	Ind.
Oxford . .	69·4	17·6	26·1	49·9
Cambridge .	65·7	14·0	19·4	39·4 ·
London . .	49·0	18·4	30·9	61·5
Comb. English	37·4	22·8	26·3	70·9
Wales . .	11·6	32·5	66·8	31·2
Scottish . .	65·4	10·2	19·8	21·1
Belfast . .	80·1	..	..	19·9

There was, it is plain, a sharp change in the pattern of university representation after 1935. Perhaps Mr. A. P. Herbert's election for Oxford in that year marks the turn of the tide. In by-elections in 1937 Independents won Conservative seats at Oxford and the combined English universities. In 1940 the Conservatives allowed a vacancy at Cambridge to be filled by an Independent Conservative, and early in 1945 in the Scottish universities another Conservative seat fell to an Independent. In the general election of 1945 the Conservatives only contested 4 of the 12 university seats, although they had won 8 of them in the previous general election. Seven Independents were elected and the sympathies of 3 of them were unquestionably more on the left than the right.

A contrast between general elections up to 1935 and that of 1945 is revealing, as Table 7 shows.

with the Independents are the National Labour candidate for the combined English universities in 1931, three Liberal National candidates, and two National candidates (Mr. Ramsay MacDonald and Sir John Anderson) in the Scottish universities; these seem to have been too closely allied to the Conservative party for there to be any reason to make a distinction.

[2] Lord Hugh Cecil and Sir Charles Oman were perhaps outstanding among the independent Conservatives, while Sir Arthur Salter and Sir Ernest Graham-Little offer examples of conservative Independents, who offered themselves for re-election as unqualified supporters of Conservative Governments.

[3] In constituencies with proportional representation only first-preference votes are considered.

TABLE 7. *University Voting up to 1935 and in 1945*

	Conservative votes	Total votes	Con. %
1918–35	181,886	327,910	55·5
1945	29,497	116,647	25·3

Two of the seats held by Independents fell vacant in 1946 and 1947. Both were secured by Conservatives and it was alleged that there had been a reversal of the trend towards non-partisan university representation. It is worth noting that, while in the Scottish universities by-election the Conservative secured 68 per cent. of the vote, in the English universities the Independent vote was split between three candidates, and the Conservative only won on a very low minority vote—30 per cent. of the total poll.[1] Since the Conservative candidate in the Scottish universities was generally agreed to have been much the strongest of those who presented themselves, it can hardly be considered proved that the university electorate had returned to Conservative orthodoxy. It is impossible to say whether the election of 1950 would have seen a restoration of the old pattern of university representation. However, it seems probable that the Conservatives, who at the dissolution of Parliament in 1950 had the sympathy, if not the allegiance, of 9 of the 12 members, would have retained the support of a very substantial majority of university representatives. At the Conservative Conference following the election, Mr. Churchill observed:

Even the six votes of (the Government's) majority would not be theirs—on the contrary there would be six the other way—if Mr. Herbert Morrison had not thought of destroying the university representation. . . .[2]

It should also be recorded that the abolition of university representation did not deprive the country of the services of all the university representatives. Among the 12 members, 5 found territorial constituencies ready to return them.

[1] The single transferable vote was not applicable in by-elections.
[2] *Official Report* of the 71st Annual Conference of the National Union of Conservative and Unionist Associations, p. 110.

One of the criticisms made of the university constituencies was the smallness of their electorate. That argument had rapidly diminishing validity, for the university electorate changed far more than any other. In 1918 there were 4,928 electors to a university member compared with 32,822[1] electors—more than six times as many—to an ordinary member. In 1945 there were 18,114 electors to a university member compared with 52,511 electors—only three times as many—to an ordinary member. The following table shows the expansion of the university electorate:

TABLE 8. *The Expansion of the University Electorate*

Year	Electorate	Votes cast	% voting in contested seats	
1918	59,131	36,590	61·8	
1922	71,729	25,852	65·6	
1923	78,120	31,957	72·6	
1924	82,775	51,000	63·9	Average
1929	119,256	76,206	65·8	60·9
1931	137,211	28,434	69·8	
1935	164,755	77,871	58·0	
1945	217,363	116,647	53·7	

The efficiency of the university electoral register was limited[2] and there is no doubt that the smallness of the number voting was due more to the number of 'dead' names and incorrect addresses than to any lack of political consciousness on the part of graduates.

After 1918 proportional representation had its only trial in British parliamentary history in the two-membered constituencies of Oxford, Cambridge, and the combined English universities, and in the three-membered Scottish universities constituency. Since there were 8 general elections, there were thus 32 contests in which it could have been tested. But in 6 of these the candidates were returned unopposed, and in 7 of those remaining the victorious candidates each received suffi-

---

[1] Great Britain only.
[2] At Oxford, in default of other information, it was customary to leave names on the register for eighty years after matriculation before assuming the death of the elector.

cient first-preference votes to obviate any consideration of second preferences. Thus there were only 19 cases in which proportional representation was really operative and in 13 of these the victorious candidates would plainly have been successful in a direct election when each voter had one non-transferable vote for each candidate. It appears that the transfer of votes only affected the result in Oxford in 1935, in Cambridge and the Scottish universities in 1945, and in the combined English universities in 1929, 1931, and 1945. It is, of course, true that the voting system may have affected the candidatures. Moreover, it seems probable that in 1922 an Independent at Cambridge succeeded without the aid of second preferences because he had the support of just over one-third of the votes, while in the Scottish universities from 1918 to 1931 the Conservatives left one of the three seats to a Liberal who consistently secured about one-third of the first-preference votes. But it can hardly be argued that the university constituencies were of much value as test cases for the merits of proportional representation; they were so fundamentally different from territorial constituencies and none returned more than three members; the single transferable vote system really requires at least five-membered constituencies to be satisfactory.

5. THE ELECTION OF INDEPENDENT AND MINOR-PARTY MEMBERS

I T is commonly said that the British electoral system gives no chance to independents or party rebels. After almost every election the decline of the independent has been lamented; but, in point of fact, although there may have been a strengthening of party discipline and a consequent weakening of the independence of the ordinary members, there has been no very marked trend in the number of members openly dissociated from the major parties. The number of M.P.s unattached to the Conservative, Liberal, or Labour parties is listed here.[1]

---

[1] The universities are excluded throughout this section, but it should perhaps be noted that in no general election before 1935 were more than two non-party university members elected, while in 1945 seven were successful. See p. 149 above.

TABLE 9. *Minor Party and Independent M.P.s*

	Total	I. Nat.	Comm.	I.L.P.	Ind. Con.	Other
1918[1]	4	1	..	..	..	3
1922	11	3	1	..	3	4
1923	6	3	..	..	..	3
1924	4	1	1	..	..	2
1929	6	3	..	..	1	2
1931	3	2	..	..	..	1
1935	7	2	1	4	..	..
1945	15	2	2	3	2	6
1950	3	2	..	..	..	1
1951	3	2	..	..	..	1

This gives an exaggerated picture of the number who successfully defied the party machines. If only those candidates who defeated opponents from both the Conservatives and Labour parties are considered the following totals are left:[2]

1918	..	1924	..	1935	5	1951	..
1922	2	1929	1	1945	10	1955	..
1923	..	1931	1	1950	..	1959	..

It should be noted that the total of 5 for 1935 is made up of 4 Independent Labour Party members from Glasgow—where a substantial part of the Labour party had split away—and 1 Communist. Only in 1945 were any substantial numbers of fully independent candidates successful against the major parties. The figure of 10 for that year includes 4 wholly non-party men as well as 2 rebels from the Conservatives and 1 from the Labour party. It is notable that, apart from 1 Independent in 1918 and 1 independent Conservative in 1922, no independents entered Parliament for the first time at a general election; all who did get in had either entered Parliament at a by-election or had originally become members under party auspices and subsequently chosen independence.

[1] In this table, as in the rest of the book, all Irish seats are ignored for the period up to 1922.

[2] Perhaps these totals should be increased by one for 1922 to 1929, to include the Prohibitionist member for Dundee who is left out because he only had one Labour opponent in a two-member seat and he ran virtually in harness with him.

A discussion of the electoral chances of independents and candidates of minor parties should not be confined to those who were elected. The small prospect of success did not deter many from seeking election without the support of one of the major parties, as the following table shows:

TABLE 10. *Number of Candidates unsupported by one of the Major Parties*

	Total	Communists	All others
1918	151[1]	..	151
1922	51	5	46
1923	27	8	19
1924	27	8	19
1929	55	25	30
1931	70	26	44[2]
1935	47	2	45
1945	93	21	72[2]
1950	156	100	56
1951	33	10	23

It is perhaps worth considering all the instances where a candidate unattached to the major parties secured a fifth or more of the votes in his constituency. In the 7,990 contests in general and by-elections between 1918 and 1959 there were 297 such candidates. But certain of these hardly require much attention; 52 were in Northern Ireland where the political pattern is very different; and 132 more had no opposition from one of the main parties and appear to owe their strength mainly to the votes of those who would have supported an established party candidate had he presented himself; the most obvious examples are provided by those left-wing candidates who took advantage of the war-time party truce to secure the Labour vote in Conservative-held seats.

However, there remain a substantial number of cases which

[1] Party designations are particularly confused in 1918. There are many discrepancies between the various reference books. This total is based on *The Times*, 30 Dec. 1918, and includes all candidates who had neither the coalition coupon nor the title of Unionist, Liberal, or Labour.

[2] The 1931 total includes twenty-two New Party candidates. The 1945 total includes twenty-three Common Wealth candidates.

are worth setting out in more detail. They may be quite simply classified.

i. *Candidates in 1918*

In Great Britain in 1918 there were fifty candidates who had neither the coalition coupon, nor the name of one of the three major parties to support them, and who yet won a fifth of the votes in their constituencies. Twenty-two of these were the only opposition to the local coalition candidate and many of the remaining twenty plainly owed the bulk of their vote to the absence of candidates of one of the major parties. Two of the three successful candidates, Mr. Billing and Mr. Bottomley, were already well established with their constituents, the former having been elected during the war-time electoral truce and the latter having at one time been Liberal member for the area. Only in the Sowerby division of Yorkshire was an unaffiliated candidate, standing for the first time, victorious.

ii. *Left-Wing Parties*

1. *Communists.* In ten cases in 1922, 1923, and 1924 Communists stood in the absence of Labour candidates and polled substantial votes. One was elected in 1922 and one in 1924. There are only fourteen cases of a Communist securing as much as 20 per cent. of the vote in a contest in which Labour was involved.

> Greenock. 1924 (29%), 1929 (21%).
> West Fife. 1929 (20%), 1931 (22%), 1935 (38%, elected), 1945 (42%, elected), 1950 (22%).
> East Rhondda. 1931 (32%), 1933 by-election (34%), 1935 (38%), 1945 (43%).
> Mile End, Stepney. 1945 (47%, elected).
> Hornsey. 1945 (21%).
> South Hackney. 1945 (25%).

2. *Independent Labour Party.* The I.L.P.[1] secured substantial support in Glasgow in 1935 and four members were returned despite Labour opposition—all four had previously held their seats as Labour members. In two seats elsewhere former Labour members, defeated in 1931, contested their old divisions for the

[1] The I.L.P. broke away from the Labour party in 1932.

I.L.P., and, although defeated by Conservatives, won more votes 'than the official Labour candidate—Miss Jennie Lee in North Lanark (I.L.P. 37%, Lab. 15%), and Mr. F. W. Jowett in East Bradford (I.L.P. 27%, Lab. 22%). In 1935, too, an I.L.P. candidate in Merthyr won 32 per cent. of the vote in a straight fight with Labour.

During the war I.L.P. candidates on three occasions secured a substantial vote in the absence of a Labour candidate.[1] In 1945 2 of the 3 remaining I.L.P. members were returned comfortably without Labour opposition and 1 despite it (in Shettleston—I.L.P. 36%, Lab. 21%). But thereafter the party only once secured as much as a fifth of the votes, when in 1946 it narrowly retained Mr. Maxton's old seat, Bridgeton (I.L.P. 34%, Lab. 28%).

3. *Common Wealth.* During the war three Common Wealth members were returned at by-elections. But there is no doubt that their vote came primarily from Labour supporters deprived of a candidate by the party truce. In the general election of 1945 Common Wealth candidates polled substantial votes in seven seats where Labour did not stand and even won one of them—Chelmsford. But in all the sixteen cases where they opposed Labour candidates they lost their deposits.

III. *Independent Conservatives*

Independents proclaiming general sympathy with the Conservative party provide the largest group of unaffiliated candidates who have won a substantial vote. Between 1920 and 1922 an 'anti-waste' campaign was conducted by Mr. Horatio Bottomley and by the Harmsworth press. In five by-elections 'anti-waste' candidates went into battle against official Conservatives and on three of these occasions were victorious—each time in a straight fight. Another seat[2] was twice won in by-elections, but on neither occasion was there an official Conservative candidate. In the 1922 general election one[3] of the three successful

---

[1] One of these provides the perfect illustration of the way in which Independents could capture the Labour vote in war-time. In 1943 in the Bilston division of Wolverhampton the result was Cons. 51%, I.L.P. 49%. The same I.L.P. candidate stood again in 1945, but there was also a Labour candidate. The result was Lab. 67%, Cons. 31%, I.L.P. 2%.

[2] The Wrekin.   [3] Rear-Adm. M. F. Sueter, Hertford.

rebels stood as an official Conservative candidate, one[1] was quite heavily defeated, while the third[2] again routed the official candidate (after which he made his peace with the party and sat until 1929 as an orthodox Conservative). The revolt was concentrated mainly in the London area. In the 1922 general election there were three other independent Conservatives who made a good showing against official candidates. Mr. H. T. Becker won Richmond with twice as many votes as the retiring Conservative member, and in Putney and South Paddington independent Conservatives secured over one-quarter of the poll.

After 1922 the party confusion, for which the existence of a Coalition Government had been largely responsible, clarified itself and independent Conservative candidates died away.

However, in February 1924, Mr. Churchill, on his way back from the Liberal to the Conservative party, contested the Abbey division of Westminster as an Independent Anti-Socialist. He won 36 per cent. of the votes and was defeated by the official Conservative candidate by only forty-three votes. Since within nine months he was a member of a Conservative Government his candidature may fall within the Independent Conservative category.

In 1929, in Portsmouth South, a former city M.P. contested the sitting member's claim to the party nomination, and in a four-cornered fight won 23 per cent. as an Independent Conservative; however, the official candidate secured the seat with 37 per cent. of the vote.

In 1930 and 1931 there came the second major intrusion of independent Conservatives in by-elections. Lord Beaverbrook and Lord Rothermere, in pursuance of their campaign against Mr. Baldwin, launched candidates in four contests in the London area. Their nominee was a close third in a four-cornered fight in Bromley in September 1930. A month later they won South Paddington from the official Conservative. In February 1931, although defeated, their candidate led the official nominee in East Islington. The final battle came in March when there was a straight fight in St. George's, West-

---

[1] Sir T. A. Polson, Dover.
[2] Mr. J. M. M. Erskine, Westminster, St. George's.

minster. The official Conservative—who received support from both the Liberal and Labour parties—defeated the candidate of the Press Lords by a three-to-two majority.

There are four further examples of independent Conservatives who secured substantial support in their attempt to enter Parliament.[1] In 1932 in a straight fight an official Conservative only just held St. Marylebone (Con. 52%, Ind. Con. 48%). In 1935, in a by-election in the Wavertree division of Liverpool, Mr. Randolph Churchill split the Conservative vote (Lab. 35%, Con. 31%, Ind. Con. 24%, Lib. 10%). In 1937 Mr. Lipson, who felt that he should have had the Conservative nomination, stood as an Independent at Cheltenham and narrowly defeated the official candidate in a three-cornered fight. In 1940, in Newcastle-upon-Tyne North, after a disagreement about the party nomination, an independent Conservative easily defeated the son of the deceased member (Ind. Con. 71%, Con. 29%).

It is notable that few supporters of the other parties brought their disagreements to the polls and that none, apart from sitting members who had left the fold, secured any substantial support.

iv. *Nationalists*

Welsh and Scottish nationalism has never won many votes. Independents preaching Scottish nationalism won just over one-fifth of the poll in the Western Isles in 1923 and 1935; in a by-election early in 1945 one Scottish Nationalist secured 41 per cent. of the vote at Kirkcaldy (Lab. 52%, S. Nat. 41%, Ind. 7%). At the same time another Scottish Nationalist won Motherwell from Labour (S. Nat. 52%, Lab. 48%); however, at the general election three months later, when a Conservative also stood, the Scottish Nationalist secured only 26 per cent. of the vote and Labour regained the seat. Standing in Perth and East Perthshire the same candidate, Dr. McIntyre, won 23 per cent. of the poll both in 1955 and in 1959. In 1962 a Scottish Nationalist came second in West Lothian with 23 per cent. of the poll.

The first three examples of Welsh Nationalists securing a fifth

[1] Conservative M.P.s who later stood as Independents are dealt with later. See pp. 161–5.

of the vote were provided by by-elections. In 1945 one gained 25 per cent. of the vote in a straight fight with a Liberal in Caernarvon Boroughs; in 1946 another won 28 per cent. of the vote in Ogmore in a straight fight with Labour, while in the same year in Neath a Welsh Nationalist, fighting both Conservative and Labour, won 20 per cent. of the vote. In the 1955 General Election a Welsh Nationalist won 22 per cent. of the vote in Merioneth; in 1959 he raised it to 23 per cent. In 1959 a Welsh Nationalist in Caernarvon secured 21 per cent. of the vote.

Northern Ireland obviously provides much the largest group of Nationalist candidates. The counties of Fermanagh and Tyrone returned two Nationalists from 1922 to 1955 except for the 1924–9 Parliament. In almost all of the other ten seats Nationalists of some variety have at one time or another polled a substantial vote. Since 'the ordinary British political struggle has never been reproduced in Northern Ireland, and since partition and religion have always been the main issues, the size of the Nationalist vote there is hardly remarkable. But Irish Nationalism has not been confined to Ireland. From 1918 to 1929 Mr. T. P. O'Connor was returned unopposed from the Scotland division of Liverpool. In 1922 and 1923 the Irish Nationalists won 45 per cent. and 49 per cent. of the vote in straight fights with a Conservative in the Exchange division of Liverpool. However, a Labour member succeeded without opposition to Mr. O'Connor's seat, while in the Exchange division it is plain that after 1923 Labour inherited almost all the votes which had been given to these Nationalists.

v. *Independents*

There are very few instances of what may be called independent independents making much of a showing when they attempted to enter Parliament against the opposition of the major parties. Mr. Scrymgeour sat for Dundee as a Prohibitionist from 1922 to 1931, but it was a two-member seat in which it was usual for each of the parties to offer only one candidate. Mr. Scrymgeour virtually ran in harness with Labour against the Conservative and the Liberal candidates. Table 11 lists the sole examples of Independents winning 20 per cent. of the vote in face of major-party opponents in the inter-war years.

Only in the Isle of Wight in 1922 was the Independent vote won in the face of opposition from all three main parties. There was no Liberal in Rutland and Stamford in 1922 and no Conservative in the Isle of Ely in 1931, and the Independent vote may thereby have been very considerably swelled. There remain only the three examples where a local nonconformist with the support of a large congregation secured an appreciable vote.

TABLE 11. *Independents winning 20 per cent. of the Vote in face of Major-party Opponents*

Constituency	Candidate	Label	% of vote
1922 Rutland and Stamford	E. Clarke	Agricultural	20
1922 Isle of Wight .	Lt.-Col. A. C. T. Veasey	Independent	21
1929 Stirling Burghs .	A. Ratcliffe	Protestant	21
1931 Isle of Ely . .	J. H. Whitehead	Independent	22
1931 Liverpool, Kirkdale .	Rev. H. D. Longbottom	Protestant	25
1935 Liverpool, Kirkdale .	Rev. H. D. Longbottom	Protestant	25

During the war several Independents won large votes in the absence of major-party candidates and five were elected.[1]

VI. *Rebel M.P.s*

Much the largest and most interesting category of serious independent candidates is provided by those former members, who originally entered Parliament either as the candidate of one of the major parties or in the absence of such a candidate, and subsequently found themselves opposed by that party.

In 1922 Sir Owen Thomas, who in 1918 had been elected as Labour member for Anglesey, stood as an Independent and defeated a Liberal in a straight fight.

Sir Oswald Mosley, who in 1918 was elected for Harrow as a Conservative, stood as an Independent in 1922 and 1923 and easily defeated Conservative candidates in straight fights.

Mr. Austin Hopkinson was elected as a Coalition Liberal for Mossley in 1918. In 1922, 1923, and 1924 he was elected as an Independent—no Conservative opposing him. In 1929 a Labour candidate defeated him, but in 1931 he won back the seat,

[1] Namely, W. D. Kendall, Grantham, 1942; W. J. Brown, Rugby, 1942; G. L. Reakes, Wallasey, 1942; T. Driberg, Maldon, 1942; C. F. White, West Derbyshire, 1944. The last two were successful in 1945 as official Labour candidates. For the fate of the rest, see below, pp. 163 and 164.

defeating the Labour member and also, for the only time, a Conservative candidate (Ind. 36%, Lab. 34%, Con. 30%). In 1935 he won again with Conservative support, but in 1945, when he faced opposition from three major parties, his electors turned upon him and he secured only 8 per cent. of the vote.

Sir Thomas Robinson was elected for Stretford as a National Liberal in 1922, as a Liberal in 1923, as a Constitutionalist in 1924, and as an Independent in 1929, but he never had a Conservative opponent.

In 1926 Mr. J. M. Kenworthy (now Lord Strabolgi), who had sat as Liberal for Central Hull since 1919, winning each election in a straight fight with a Conservative, stood for re-election on joining the Labour party. The result (Lab. 53%, Con. 38%, Lib. 9%) suggests either that Mr. Kenworthy had an immense local following or, more probably, strong local sympathy for the Labour party which had had no previous chance of expression.

In 1927 Dr. Haden Guest, Labour member for Central Southwark, resigned from his party and stood for re-election with Conservative support. If the result (Lib. 44%, Lab. 37%, Ind. 19%) is compared with that in the general election two years later when Dr. Haden Guest was not standing (Lab. 46%, Lib. 44%, Con. 10%), some evidence of a personal following may be found.

In 1929 Sir Robert Newman, who had represented Exeter since 1918, rejected the Conservative whip and stood as an Independent; he won comfortably (Ind. 49%, Lab. 38%, Con. 23%).

In 1929 Mr. Pemberton Billing, who had sat as Independent M.P. for Hertford from 1916 to 1921, failed in his attempt to regain the seat, but at least he secured second place in a four-cornered fight (Con. 40%, Ind. 29%, Lib. 19%, Lab. 12%).

In the general election of 1931 four M.P.s who had been associated with Sir Oswald Mosley sought re-election, three of them as 'New Party' candidates. Sir Oswald Mosley, contesting Stoke, the seat his wife had represented for Labour, easily saved his deposit (Con. 46%, Lab. 30%, New Party 24%). The others were less fortunate. Mr. Dudgeon, who had represented Galloway as a Liberal, won only 3 per cent. of the vote. Dr. Forgan, Labour member for West Renfrew, won only 4 per cent. of the vote. Mr. John Strachey, Labour member for

Aston, won 10 per cent. of the vote when he stood for re-election as an Independent (having already left the New Party).

Early in 1931 Mr. Mardy Jones, Labour member for Pontypridd since 1922, resigned from Parliament upon being prosecuted for misuse of his railway warrant. In the general election in the autumn he stood again as an Independent and secured only 3 per cent. of the vote.

⁖ In 1935 there were two tests of whether the electorate was more faithful to individuals or to parties. At Shipley the sitting Conservative member stood as an Independent and barely saved his deposit (Lab. 36%, Lib. 26%, Con. 25%, Ind. 13%). In West Wolverhampton Mr. W. J. Brown, who had been Labour member from 1929 to 1931 and who in 1931 had led his local organization in rebellion against the Labour party (Con. 61%, Ind. 39), won a remarkable victory over the party machine, even though he was not elected (Con. 55%, Ind. 41%, Lab. 4%).

TABLE 12. *Independents successful in 1945*

Candidate	Label	Consti- tuency	First election circumstance	Previous result (%)	Result 1945 (%)
V. Bartlett	Ind.	Bridgwater	As Ind. with Lib. and Lab. support 1938	Ind. 53 Con. 47	Ind. 46 Con. 40 Lab. 14
W. J. Brown	Ind.	Rugby	As Ind. during party truce 1942	Ind. 52 Con. 48	Ind. 40 Con. 37 Lab. 23
W. D. Kendall	Ind.	Grantham	As Ind. during party truce 1942	Ind. 52 Con. 48	Ind. 58 Con. 26 Lab. 16
D. L. Lipson	Ind. Con.	Cheltenham	In party split 1937	Ind. 40 Con. 39 Lab. 21	Ind. 43 Lab. 30 Con. 27
J. H. McKie	Ind. Con.	Galloway	As official Con. 1935	Con. unop.	Ind. 41 Lab. 35 Con. 24
D. N. Pritt	Ind. Lab.	N. Hammersmith	As official Lab. 1935	Lab. 53 Con. 47	Ind. 64 Con. 25 Lab. 11
Rev. J. Little	Ind. Con.	County Down	As official Con. 1940	Con. unop.	1

¹ Mr. Little had two official Conservative opponents in a two-member

In 1939 the Duchess of Atholl resigned her seat (Kinross and Western) as a protest against the Government's Spanish policy. In the ensuing by-election she fought as an Independent with Liberal and Labour support. She was fairly narrowly defeated (Con. 53%, Ind. 47%). If the result is compared with that in the previous general election (Con. 60%, Lib. 40%), it does not appear that she carried many of her supporters with her in rebellion.

In the general election of 1945 there were many more successful fights against the established parties than in any other year. There were also five sitting members who vainly challenged the established parties.

TABLE 13. *Independent M.P.s defeated in 1945*

Candidate	Label	Consti- tuency	First election circumstance	Previous result (%)	Result 1945 (%)
A. S. Cunning- ham-Reid	Ind. Con.	St. Maryle- bone	As official Con. 1932	Con. 80 Lab. 20	Con. 48 Lab. 32 Ind. 12 Lib. 8
S. King-Hall	Ind.	Ormskirk	As official Nat. Lab. 1940	Nat. Lab. unop.	Lab. 46 Con. 36 Ind. 18
A. Maclaren	Ind.	Burslem	As official Lab. 1922	Lab. 54 Con. 46	Lab. 61 Con. 30 Ind. 9
T. Groves	Ind.	Stratford (West Ham)	As official Lab. 1922	Lab. 63 Con. 37	Lab. 75 Con. 20 Ind. 5
G. L. Reakes	Ind.	Wallasey	As Ind. dur- ing party truce 1942	Ind. 61 Con. 32 Ind. 7	Con. 43 Ind. 34 Lab. 23

In 1950 Independents fared much worse. Of those listed in Table 12, all but Mr. Bartlett and Mr. Little stood again. Mr. McKie was back in the Conservative fold. The fate of the others is simply revealed by the drop in their share of the poll.[1]

constituency. He won virtually as many votes as the two Conservatives combined and so his rebellion must apparently have received overwhelming support from Conservatives in the constituency.

[1] It must be noted that in each case constituency boundaries had been somewhat changed by the Representation of the People Act of 1948.

TABLE 14. *Independent M.P.s successful in 1945 but not in 1950*

	% of vote 1945	% of vote 1950
W. J. Brown	40	20
W. D. Kendall	58	28
D. L. Lipson	43	25
D. N. Pritt	64	25

Mr. Craven-Ellis, who from 1931 to 1945 had been Conservative member for Southampton, stood in 1950 for one division of the borough (which had been divided in 1948) as an Independent. He won only 2 per cent. of the vote.

There were four other party rebels who stood in 1950, all of them members who had been elected as Labour candidates in 1945. Mr. Edwards, who had been Labour member for East Middlesbrough since 1935, stood in 1950 as a Conservative; he secured a slightly smaller share of the vote than his Conservative opponent had five years ·before.[1] Three others who had been expelled from the Labour party for 'fellow-travelling' stood as Independents. Redistribution makes comparison with 1945 difficult, but the share of the vote falling to the official and the Independent Labour candidate is sufficiently revealing.

TABLE 15. *Rebel Labour M.P.s defeated in 1950*

		Rebel vote (%)	Official Labour vote (%)
K. Zilliacus	Gateshead East	15	45
J. Platts-Mills	Shoreditch and Finsbury	18	53
L. J. Solley	Thurrock	10	53

In 1951 there were no ex-M.P.s venturing to stand as party rebels in their old constituencies. In 1955 Sir Richard Acland, who had resigned from the Parliamentary Labour Party in protest against its hydrogen bomb policy, was heavily defeated in Gravesend (Con. 46%, Lab. 40%, Ind. 14%). In 1959 Sir David Robertson, who objected to the Government's Highland policy, was re-elected without Conservative opposition in Caithness and Sutherland.

---

[1] The constituency boundaries had been slightly altered.

Conclusion

If the university seats are excluded, fifty-nine Independent or minor-party M.P.s were elected in the 7,284 general and by-election contests in Great Britain between 1919 and 1959. In the same contests, a total of 195 Independent or minor-party candidates have secured more than a fifth of the votes in their constituency.[1] It is plain that the Independents' chances of election are small. None the less, they are markedly higher in some circumstances than in others. The following conditions seem to favour an independent candidate:

1. *Substitution.* There are cases where a local party has been willing not to contest a seat and to let an Independent 'cash in' on the vote which their candidate might expect to receive. This vacuum may be a matter of open co-operation—as, for example, in the case of Mr. A. D. Lindsay in Oxford in 1938—or the outcome of a party truce, as in the late war.

2. *By-elections.* A by-election presents a better opportunity than a general election for an Independent to enter Parliament for the first time. Since 1919 two Independents and four Communists have had their first success at a general election, while eighteen Independents have entered Parliament at by-elections (ten of these, it must be admitted, during the war-time truce). At a by-election the sense of choosing a Government and the force of party propaganda press less strongly upon the voter than at a general election, when all the weight of publicity drives him to vote for one of the established parties.

3. *Safe seats.* For the party rebel, a safe seat seems always to have offered a better chance of victory than a marginal one, perhaps because those who might support him have less fear of letting in the other side by a split vote. There have in fact only been four or five instances where a party split may have given the seat to the other side.[2] Of M.P.s who have left their party

[1] These figures differ from those on p. 155 through the exclusion of all contests in 1918 and of all contests in Northern Ireland.

[2] The by-elections in East Islington 1931 and Wavertree 1935 and the general election in Shipley in 1935 provide the only three clear-cut examples since the split between Liberals and National Liberals in 1922. East Islington and Shipley also provide the only two examples of an Independent Conservative securing as much as 20 per cent. of the vote in a seat which could not be regarded as safely Conservative.

and stood as Independents, only one has done so in what would be termed a marginal seat.[1]

4. *The London area.* In the only two peace-time periods when Independents have won substantial votes in a series of by-elections, the contests have been concentrated in the London area and the candidates have had strong newspaper support.

5. *Sitting members.* A sitting or a former M.P. had a much better chance of election as an Independent than an outsider. Since 1919 only three Independents and two Communists have entered Parliament for the first time in the face of opposition from both the Conservative and Labour parties. But, although his chances are slightly better than those of an outsider, an M.P. who has left his party has small hope of re-election as an Independent if his old party opposes him. Only five have been successful in such revolt, and only one (Sir Oswald Mosley) has performed the feat twice.

6. *The post-war period.* The confused aftermath of war seems to provide the best opportunity for the Independent candidate. Although only three were successful in 1918, many polled substantial votes. In 1945 more Independent candidates defeated both the major parties than in all the general elections since 1918 combined.

6. THE FORFEITURE OF DEPOSITS

THE Representation of the People Act of 1918 provided that every candidate should deposit £150 with the returning officer at the time of nomination, the money to be forfeited if he failed to secure one-eighth of the votes. The intention was to discourage freak and propaganda candidatures, and there can be little doubt that in recent years there would have been many more candidatures but for this limitation. However, the danger of losing £150 has not been sufficient to prevent a large number of hopeless attempts to enter Parliament. By 1959, 1,673 candidates had forfeited their deposits (thereby benefiting the Treasury by £250,950). As Table 16 on the following page shows, there has been a tendency for the number of forfeited deposits to increase.

[1] Mr. Lockwood in Shipley in 1935.

TABLE 16. *Forfeited Deposits*

Year	Con.	Lib.	Lab.	Comm.	Other	Total	% of all candidatures
General elections:							
1918 . .	3	46	13	..	73	135[1]	10·3
1922 . .	..	31	6	2	10	49	3·4
1923 . .	..	8	18	..	1	27	1·9
1924 . .	1	30	28	1	8	68	4·7
1929 . .	18	25	35	22	10	110	5·8
1931 . .	..	6	21	20	38	85	6·6
1935 . .	1	40	16	..	24	81	6·0
1945 . .	6	64	2	12	79	163	9·6
1950 . .	5	319	..	97	40	461	24·6
1951 . .	3	66	1	10	16	96	7·0
1955 . .	3	60	1	15	21	100	7·1
1959 . .	2	55	1	17	41	116	7·6
All general elections . .	42	750	142	196	361	1,491	8·2
By-elections:							
1919–24 .	1	5	3	. 1	7	17[1]	6·2
1924–35 .	..	17	5	11	14	47	11·2
1935–45 .	..	1	..	3	40	44	10·3
1945–50 .	2	11	1		20	36	24·8
1950–1 .	..	1	..	1	3	5	14·7
1951–5 .	..	7	..	1	6	14	12·9
1955–9 .	..	2	..	1	16	19	13·8
All by-elections	3	44	9	20	106	182	11·8
All elections .	45	794	151	216	467	1,673	8·5

7. THE COST OF ELECTIONS

THE cost of elections either to the nation or to the candidates cannot be accurately estimated. The official expenditure of the registration and returning officers may with difficulty be discovered, and the declared outlay of the candidates is readily available. But the administrative costs of an election must be greater than the returns suggest owing to the large-scale diversion of local government servants' time from routine work,[2] and the return of expenses made by candidates is a quite inadequate guide to the amount spent in promoting their election. There is no record of the expenditure by central party organizations, and in the

---

[1] 25 deposits forfeited in Ireland in 1918 and one in 1919 are excluded.
[2] There is also no separate estimate published for the cost to the Post Office of the free delivery of electoral communications.

constituencies only the money spent in the weeks immediately preceding the poll is made public. The amount devoted to nursing constituencies and preparing for elections remains unknown.

However, despite the fact that the figures are an under-estimate, and in some cases a very substantial under-estimate, it is worth setting out what is known about the cost of elections.

(a) *Annual Cost of compiling and printing the Electoral Register*

From 1918 to 1958 this was borne equally by the Treasury and the local authorities. Table 17 is based upon the Civil Estimates for specimen years. The actual expenditure seldom varied much from the estimate. These figures only include the expenses for which registration officers were responsible and the cost of printing the Voters' Lists which was arranged by the Stationery Office. Certain small expenses incurred by the Treasury, the County Courts, and the Post Office are not included here. By the Local Government Act of 1958 registration expenses were not included under the general grant paid to local authorities by the Government.

TABLE 17. *Cost of compiling and printing the Register*

Financial year	£	Registers annually	Method of registration
1922–3	1,020,000	Two	By canvass
1931–2	780,500	One	By canvass
1937–8	720,000	One	By canvass
1948–9	1,075,000	One	From Nat. Reg. records
1949–50	2,395,000	Two	By canvass
1951–2	1,720,000	One	By canvass
1961–2	2,360,000	One	By canvass

(b) *Returning Officers' Expenses at General Elections* (Chargeable to the Consolidated Fund)

TABLE 18. *Returning Officers' Expenses*

Year	£	Year	£
1922	280,138	1945	677,999
1923	324,566	1950	806,974
1924	339,028	1951	1,015,357
1929	422,244	1955	1,106,631
1931	305,945	1959	1,303,694
1935	314,500		

(c) *Candidates' Expenses*

Perhaps the most important figures about candidates' expenses are those which show the contrast between the parties. The official returns, of course, make no acknowledgement of the existence of parties, and it is a considerable task to calculate the

TABLE 19. *Candidates' Expenses*

Year	£	No. of candidates	£ per candidate
1922	1,018,196	1,442	706[1]
1923	982,340	1,446	685[1]
1924	921,165	1,428	645[1]
1929	1,213,507	1,730	701
1931	654,103	1,292	510[1]
1935	722,093	1,349	530[1]
1945	1,073,216	1,468	645
1950	1,170,114	1,868	628[2]
1951	946,013	1,376	688
1955	904,677	1,409	642
1959	1,051,217	1,536	684

figures for each party separately. Here it has been done for five of the general elections since 1918. In Table 20 all unopposed candidates and all candidates in university seats have been excluded from consideration.

TABLE 20. *Average Expenditure per Opposed Candidate*

Year	Con.	Lib.	Lab.	Comm.	Other
	£	£	£	£	£
1923	845	789	464	325	380
1929	905	782	452	247	442
1935	777	495	365	332	250
1945	780	532	593	656	424
1950	777	459	694	254	359
1951	773	488	658	585	286
1955	735	423	611.	342	641
1959	761	532	705	306	684

[1] The average expenditure per candidate for the years 1922, 1923, 1924, 1931, and 1935 is rather reduced by the fact that in these years a substantial number of seats (from 40 to 67) were uncontested. Unopposed candidates seldom spent more than £200.

[2] It should be remembered that in 1948 the expense maximum was substantially lowered (by about a third in the average constituency).

The three most notable features of this table only confirm what might have been expected. In every election the Conservatives have spent considerably more than their rivals. The Liberals were able to spend much more in the 1920's than they have since that time. Labour candidates since the last war have had much more money at their disposal.

There is no reason to suppose that there is a very close correlation between expenditure and success.[1] It may be that the Labour party would have fared better in the 1920's if they had been able to spend amounts comparable to their opponents. But certainly in the 1950's it was astonishing how few agents seemed to feel handicapped by the limitation on their expenditure.

8. PARTICIPATION IN ELECTIONS

OFTEN in the last thirty years there have been laments at the steady decline of interest in politics and some people have advocated the drastic remedy of compulsory voting. But as a matter of fact the figures for the percentage of the electorate voting show no very marked trend until the elections of 1950 and 1951 when there was a decided increase. After 1918 it is true that there was some falling off from the pre-war turnout, but that was only to be expected. The fact that all registration was not automatic before 1918 must have prevented some of the apathetic from being placed upon the register; the absence of women must have tended to increase the proportion voting;[2] and the much smaller electorate must have facilitated high-pressure canvassing.

It is, of course, misleading to regard all non-voters as apathetic. Death, illness, removal, and inaccuracies in the register would always prevent a 100 per cent. poll. Whatever may be achieved under totalitarian governments, experience in Belgium and Australia, where voting is compulsory, suggests that in democratic countries the effective maximum is a poll of about 90 per cent.

The figures normally given for the percentage of the electorate

[1] However, since 1922 Mr. Maxton is the only man to have won a contest in a territorial constituency on less than £100. He did this on three occasions, his record being in 1935 when he spent only £44.

[2] Cf. chapter iv of *Political Behaviour* by H. Tingsten (London, 1937) and the findings of public-opinion polls for overwhelming evidence of the greater tendency among women to abstain from voting than among men.

voting in Britain are exaggerated. Aĺl electors in the fifteen
double-member constituencies which survived the Act of 1918[1]
retained two votes. If both of these were used, they must have
swelled the total number of votes cast to over a million more
than the total number of electors voting. A few voters may have
'plumped' for one candidate, but an examination of the results
suggests that their number was small. If each vote in two-
member constituencies is counted as half a vote, the error in
estimates of electoral participation should be negligible.[2]

TABLE 21. *Electoral Participation*

Year	Total electorate	Votes cast as % of electorate in contested seats	Adjusted for two-member seats
1906	7,266,708	88·8	83·3
1910 (Jan.)	7,613,716	92·6	85·6
1910 (Dec.)	7,705,602	87·0	81·0
1918	21,392,322	58·9	57·6[3]
1922	21,127,663	75·4	71·3
1923	21,281,232	74·1	70·8
1924	21,731,320	80·6	76·6
1929	28,850,870	79·5	76·1
1931	29,960,071	79·8	76·3
1935	31,374,449	74·6	71·2
1945	33,194,436	75·9	72·7[3]
1950	34,412,255	84·0	84·0
1951	34,937,865	82·5	82·5
1955	34,858,263	76·7	76·7
1959	35,397,080	78·7	78·7

It will be seen that this adjustment shows the turnout in the
inter-war period to have been about 3 per cent. less than the
crude figures suggest. Before 1914 the difference is much
greater, but then there were twenty-four two-member constituencies, compared with fifteen subsequently.

[1] In 1928 only thirteen double-member territorial constituencies were
left. But three two-member counties were created in Northern Ireland in
1922.

[2] Professor H. F. Gosnell in *Why Europe Votes* (Chicago, 1930), p. 5,
provides the only figures in which allowance for two-member seats is made.
Up to 1929 the last column in Table 21 is taken from his work.

[3] The registers in 1918 and to a lesser extent in 1945 were notoriously bad.
If they had been as efficient as in normal peace-time elections there can be
no doubt that the percentage voting would have been appreciably higher in
both these years.

9. THE RESULTS OF ELECTIONS, 1918–59

I T is very hard to know what election results mean as expressions of public opinion. It is not even easy to discover what election results have been; nowhere are the figures of recent general elections collected and set out on a single page. From various works of reference it is possible to discover the crude totals of seats and votes won (although the various sources are seldom in exact agreement), but there appears never to have been an attempt to make the simple adjustments which are prerequisite to effective comparison of the results. Therefore it seems worth while, firstly, to present the crude results of the last nine general elections in a consolidated table; secondly, to adjust these results to eliminate the distorting effect produced by the varying number of candidates and other factors; thirdly, by a detailed comparison of the results in a limited number of constituencies, to trace more precisely what may have happened in certain elections; and, lastly, by an examination of by-election results, to trace the movement of opinion during the life of certain Parliaments.

1. *The Actual Results*

TABLE 22. *Results of General Elections, 1922–59*[1]

Year	Seats					Votes %			
	Total	*Con.*	*Lib.*	*Lab.*	*Other*	*Con.*	*Lib.*	*Lab.*	*Other*
1922	615	346	115	142	12	38·2	29·1	29·5	3·2
1923	615	258	159	191	7	38·1	29·6	30·5	1·8
1924	615	419	40	151	5	48·3	17·6	33·0	1·1
1929	615	260	59	288	8	38·2	23·4	37·0	1·4
1931	615	521	37	.52	5	67·1		30·7	2·2
1935	615	431	21	154	9	53·6	6·6	37·8	2·0
1945	640	212	12	394	22	39·8	9·0	47·8	3·4
1950	625	298	9	315	3	43·5	9·1	46·1	1·3
1951	625	321	6	295	3	48·0	2·6	48·8	0·6
1955	630	344	6	277	3	49·7	2·7	46·4	1·2
1959	630	365	6	258	1	49·4	5·9	43·4	0·9

[1] In 1922 Liberal and National Liberal are classed together. In 1924 Constitutionalists are included with Conservatives. In 1931 Liberal National and National Labour members are classed with Conservatives. The votes for all candidates supporting the National Government are classed together.

11. *The Results Adjusted*

Three adjustments seem necessary before the results can be intelligently compared.

The exclusion of university seats. The franchise, the system of voting, and the candidatures in university constituencies were on a different basis from ordinary constituencies. An attempt to trace the movement of national opinion is probably only confused by the inclusion of these twelve seats in which the electors were almost all plural voters.[1]

Allowance for two-member seats. Thirteen two-member boroughs were preserved in 1918. Cork City's representation ended in 1922, but three two-member counties were then created in N. Ireland. In them each elector was entitled to two votes. This meant that at every election until 1950 the number of electors apparently using their votes has been exaggerated by nearly 1 million votes. It has also made the national strength of the parties which happened to be strongest in those seats seem slightly greater than it really was. The simplest way of allowing for this is to count every vote in these seats as half a vote.

Allowance for the varying number of candidates. A change in the share of the national vote won by a party may be as much due to a change in the number of seats it chooses to contest as to any movement in public support. There is, for instance, no doubt that there are some Liberals in every constituency. If the Liberal party had always contested every seat, it would have won an increased number of votes even though there had been no increase in the number of its sympathizers. The average percentage of the vote won by each candidate is probably a more accurate guide to the division of sympathy between the parties than their percentage share of the total national vote.

This method of calculation is by no means perfect. It is almost impossible to make any allowance for those votes cast for other parties as a *pis aller* by electors with no candidate of their own persuasion, still less for those votes cast for another party on the ground that the voter's preferred candidate had no chance of success. Nor is it practicable to allow for the way in which a

---

[1] For a detailed examination of the votes cast in university seats see p. 149 above.

party's average vote per candidate was reduced by its decision to contest an increased number of hopeless seats. It is difficult, too, to discount the distortion caused by unopposed returns.[1]

With all these limitations in mind, it is none the less suggested that the following figures throw a light upon the movements in political opinion since 1922 which is different from that offered by the more conventional figures in Table 22, and that they probably present a more accurate picture of what happened.

Three notable points emerge from a comparison between the figures in Tables 22 and 23. Diagrams I and II which provide a graphic representation of Table 23 serve to underline these points.

The decline in the Conservative vote between 1922 and 1923. Those who advocate proportional representation have long been accustomed to point to the elections of 1922 and 1923 as a demonstration of the fact that the electoral system is a complete gamble. Table 22 illustrates their argument; with an average change of well under 1 per cent. in the share of the votes won by each party the Conservatives lost eighty-eight seats. However, in 1922 the Liberal vote was split in a number of seats and, much more important, in 1923 the Conservatives contested sixty-four more seats than a year before. This increase in the number of candidates swelled their total vote enough to cancel their decline in the constituencies they had fought in 1922. They lost seats in

---

[1] This certainly cannot be done, as the *Constitutional Year Book* tried, by assuming that every elector in an unopposed seat would have voted for the successful candidate; nor even as *The Times House of Commons* for 1931 and 1935, with slightly greater realism, attempted, by assuming that the same number of electors would have voted in the unopposed as in the opposed constituencies and that they would have been unanimous in support of the victor. It would be much more accurate to assume that the swing in the constituency resembled that in the rest of the country and then to calculate from the last contested election what the outcome of a contest would have been. The uncertainty of such a calculation, particularly in cases where a constituency was uncontested for several elections in succession, makes the labour it would involve unjustified. Only in 1931 does it appear that allowance for unopposed seats would noticeably modify the party percentages. The election of 1918, although omitted from these calculations, provides another example. Coalition candidates secured only 48 per cent. of the votes cast. It was suggested by some that the Coalition's overwhelming victory was only due to the split votes of its adversaries. But the great majority of the 107 uncontested seats fell to Coalition candidates, and there is little doubt that had every seat been fought, the Coalition candidates would have secured well over 50 per cent. of the total vote.

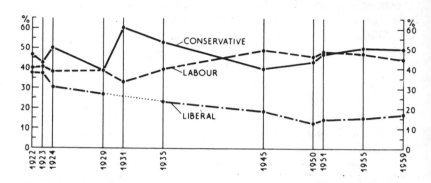

DIAGRAM I. Votes, 1922–59. (Average percentage vote per candidate.)

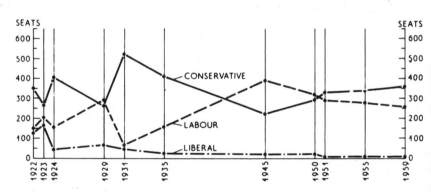

DIAGRAM II. Seats, 1922–59.

1923 not through fortuitous machinations of the electoral system but because they had lost some public support.

The steady decline in Liberal support from 1922 to 1951. In Table 22 the variations in the number of candidatures served to conceal to some extent the Liberal decline, particularly in the elections of

TABLE 23. *Average Vote for Candidates of each Party in General Elections, 1922–59 (calculated as a percentage of the average vote cast in each constituency at each election)*

Year	Opposed candidates			Average % vote per candidate		
	Con.	Lib.	Lab.	Con.	Lib.	Lab.
1922	435	415[1]	409	48·6	38·4	40·0
1923	499	438	417	42·6	37·8	41·0
1924	528	329	500	51·9	30·9	38·2
1929	576	507	567	39·4	27·7	39·3
1931	540[2]		509	67·4		33·0
1935	551	160	535	54·8	23·9	40·3
1945	618	304	599	40·1	18·6	50·4
1950	618	475	617	43·7	11·8	46·7
1951	613	109	617	48·6	14·7	49·2
1955	623	110	620	50·2	15·1	47·3
1959	625	216	621	49·6	16·9	44·5

1945 and 1950. But in fact up to 1950, excluding only the special case of 1931, Liberal candidates won on the average a smaller and smaller share of the poll in their constituencies at each successive contest. This decline in strength may be a little deceptive as far as 1929 in concerned since the average Liberal vote was also reduced by a sharp rise in the number of hopeless seats contested. On the other hand, the apparent increase in 1951 is equally deceptive. The Liberals in 1951 concentrated on their few best opportunities. In the 103 seats they fought both in 1950 and

[1] This figure represents the number of contested constituencies where Liberal or National Liberal candidates were standing. The number of candidates was somewhat larger but there were some constituencies where the vote was split.

[2] This figure represents the number of contested constituencies where a supporter of the National Government was standing. The number of candidates was somewhat larger but there were a few constituencies where the vote was split.

1951 their poll fell substantially. But the improvement shown between 1955 and 1959 underrates the real gain in Liberal strength since they were fighting on twice as broad a front.

The steadiness of the Labour vote between 1922 and 1935. If 1931 is excluded, the average vote for each Labour candidate hardly fluctuated in this period. Only between 1923 and 1924 was there more than the very slightest change—and that may be accounted for quite largely by the increase in the number of hopeless seats contested. In general it may be said that the changes in Labour party strength in the House of Commons were due to changes in the relative strength of the Conservative and Liberal parties more than to variations in its own support.

III. *A Comparison of Selected Results*

The uncertainties of the foregoing calculations are appreciable and it therefore seems worth while to investigate what happened between one election and the next in a series of directly comparable contests. This provides a rough check on earlier findings and may also offer some answer to wider questions.

TABLE 24. *Seats fought by all Three Parties both in 1923 and 1924* (Seats involved: 121)

Year	Con. %	Lib. %	Lab. %
1923	38·2	34·6	27·2
1924	45·4	23·6	31·0
Change	+7·2	−11·0	+3·8

The elections of 1923 and 1924 are most suited to such detailed examination and comparison. Each was contested on a large scale by the three main parties and no others, and movements of population can have had little importance in the ten months between December 1923 and October 1924. Moreover, the answer to the question of how votes moved between the contests is of some importance in view of the argument that the Zinovieff letter campaign has always provoked. It is interesting to study the change of opinion in those constituencies which were fought by all three parties at each election and in those constituencies which had similar straight fights on each occasion.

TABLE 25. *Seats fought by Two Parties only both in 1923 and 1924*

Conservative and Labour (Seats involved: 79)			Conservative and Liberal (Seats involved: 38)			Liberal and Labour (Seats involved: 22)		
Year	Con. %	Lab. %	Year	Con. %	Lib. %	Year	Lib. %	Lab. %
1923	46·8	53·2	1923	49·0	51·0	1923	47·8	52·2
1924	51·3	48·7	1924	57·6	42·4	1924	47·5	52·5
Change	+4·5	−4·5	Change	+8·6	−8·6	Change	−0·3	+0·3

From these figures it would appear that the decline in the Liberal vote was more than anything else responsible for the 'landslide' of the 1924 election in which the Conservatives made a gain of 161 seats.

It is worth while, using similar but less elaborate analysis, to follow the fate of the Liberal party in subsequent elections. For this purpose an examination has been made of the results in those seats which were fought by the three main parties and no others, both in 1924 and 1929, both in 1929 and 1935, both in 1935 and 1945, both in 1945 and 1950, and both in 1950 and 1951.

The main value of these figures is that, with one exception, they confirm the steady ebb in Liberal strength apparent in Table 23 but not in Table 22. Support for the Liberal party seems to have dropped steadily from 1929 to 1951 despite the fact that in 1945 and 1950 the increased number of candidates they put in the field prevented this from being visible in the aggregate Liberal vote. But these figures also suggest that the Liberals did recover a little between 1924 and 1929; the crude figures in Table 22 give an altogether exaggerated picture of this recovery, but the adjusted figures in Table 23 are in this one case almost equally deceptive. An increase of almost 200 in their candidatures in 1929 swelled their total vote in 1929 but, since many were in absolutely hopeless seats, reduced their average vote per candidate; however, in comparable constituencies their candidates appear to have fared rather better in 1929 than in 1924. In a similar way, but to a lesser degree, the decline in the average vote per candidate in 1950 exaggerated the falling off of Liberal support, because many of their 475 candidates were

TABLE 26. *Seats fought by Three Parties in Two General Elections*

1924 and 1929 (Seats involved: 196)				1929 and 1935 (Seats involved: 112)			
Year	Con. %	Lib. %	Lab. %	Year	Con. %	Lib. %	Lab. %
1924	47·1	24·7	28·2	1929	39·1	30·5	30·4
1929	38·0	28·2	33·8	1935	51·3	18·8	29·9
Change	−9·1	+3·5	+5·6	Change	+12·2	−11·7	−0·5

1935 and 1945 (Seats involved: 72)				1945 and 1950[1] (Seats involved: 21)			
Year	Con. %	Lib. %	Lab. %	Year	Con. %	Lib. %	Lab. %
1935	51·2	21·8	27·0	1945	40·5	18·2	41·3
1945	40·4	19·2	40·4	1950	46·3	14·6	39·1
Change	−10·8	−2·6	+13·4	Change	+5·8	−3·6	−2·2

1950 and 1951 (Seats involved: 76)				1951 and 1955 (Seats involved: 35)			
Year	Con. %	Lib. %	Lab. %	Year	Con. %	Lib. %	Lab. %
1950	44·5	16·9	38·6	1951	51·7	14·9	33·4
1951	48·1	12·4	39·5	1955	52·2	15·9	31·9
Change	+3·6	−4·5	+0·9	Change	+0·5	+1·0	−1·5

1955 and 1959 (Seats involved: 76)			
Year	Con. %	Lib. %	Lab. %
1955	51·5	14·3	34·2
1959	50·5	18·2	31·3
Change	−1·0	+3·9	−2·9

contesting areas which had not been thought worth fighting for twenty years or more. In 1951 a drastic reduction in the number of Liberal candidates increased the average vote per candidate, but, as Table 26 shows, the vote in seats fought both in 1950 and 1951 fell sharply. Their recovery between 1955 and 1959 is shown more sharply by Table 26 than it was by Table 23.

The uncertainties of these figures serve to illustrate the limita-

[1] Only eighty seats were left with unchanged boundaries after the 1948 Act. These were largely in the London area where the swing to the Conservatives was above the average.

tions of this type of analysis. But there is no doubt that it can throw considerable light on the verdict of elections, light of a kind useful both for politicians and historians. The examination of results attempted here is not exhaustive; no attempt, for example, has been made to trace the regional variations underlying the national trends; further detailed comparisons of the results in groups of individual contests may well do much to clarify the way in which opinion moved between the parties in successive general elections.

IV. *By-election Results*[1]

It has always been customary for by-election results to be seized upon and more or less wishfully interpreted as guides to the public attitude towards the Government of the day. But how far reliance can be placed upon by-election results and what their relation is to the outcome of subsequent general elections have been surprisingly little examined. There are many uncertainties involved and no laws of by-election behaviour can be laid down, but the extent to which the results fall into patterns is remarkable.

It is, of course, very hard to assess the special local conditions which may influence individual by-elections but which in a general election may be assumed to cancel out. The turnout in by-elections has usually been 10 per cent. to 20 per cent. less than at a general election. In addition it must be remembered that at a by-election the citizen can register a protest vote against the Government without having to consider whether he would prefer to have the other party in power; it is notable how by-elections have usually tended to be more anti-government than subsequent general elections.

Interest in by-elections naturally tends to focus on who wins, although the turnover in votes is a much more significant indication of the movement of popular sympathy. For a study of the turnover in votes, it is necessary to concentrate attention on those by-elections fought by the same parties which contested the seat in the previous or subsequent general election. It is worth considering these results year by year, whenever there

[1] Much of the substance of this section has been published previously under the title 'Trends in British By-elections', in the spring 1949 issue of the *Journal of Politics*, p. 396.

were sufficient comparable by-elections to prevent the chance circumstances of an individual contest from distorting the picture too violently. The 1924–9 Parliament provides the first opportunity for this. From 1919 to 1924 there were never more than two comparable by-elections in any one year which were suitable for such analysis.[1]

TABLE 27. *By-elections 1925–9 compared with the General Election of 1929*[2]

Year	Number of contests involved	By-election results: % of votes won by each party			1929 General Election results in the same constituencies: % of votes won by each party			By-election (%) advantage over 1929 results		
		Con.	Lab.	Lib.	Con.	Lab.	Lib.	Con.	Lab.	Lib.
1925–6	7	41·2	36·8	22·0	37·5	39·4	23·1	3·7	−2·6	−1·1
1926–7	10·	37·9	33·6	28·5	35·3	33·3	31·4	2·6	0·3	−2·9
1928	15	39·8	30·5	29·7	40·9	30·5	28·6	−1·1	0·0	1·1
1929	5	33·6	44·6	21·8	37·5	41·4	21·1	−3·9	3·2	0·7

Table 27 gives a picture of the fairly steady loss of support by the Conservatives. Further light is offered by contrasting the parties in pairs to see their net loss and gain, relative to each other, when compared with the 1929 results in the same constituencies.

TABLE 28. *By-election Advantage between Parties, 1925–9*
Compared to 1929 result in the same constituencies

	Conservative advantage over Labour (%)	Conservative advantage over Liberal (%)	Labour advantage over Liberal (%)
1925–6	+6·3	+4·8	−1·5
1926–7	+2·3	+5·5	+3·2
1928	−1·1	−2·2	−1·1
1929	−7·1	−4·6	+2·5

[1] Except in 1922 when four straight fights between Conservative and Labour produced results 4·5 per cent. more favourable to Labour than in the same constituencies in the general election at the end of that year.

[2] There were 59 contested by-elections in non-university constituencies between the 1924 and 1929 general elections. In this table only the 37 which were fought both in the by-elections and in 1929 by the three main parties and no others are considered. There were only 4 by-elections in 1925 and only 5 in 1927. Therefore the years 1925–7 are divided at 3 May 1926, the date of the General Strike.

Table 28 shows strikingly how by-election results may be much more anti-Government than those in a nearby general election. All the five 1929 by-elections considered here took place in February or March, that is to say within four months of the general election. Those four months saw no very startling

TABLE 29. *By-elections 1930–1 compared with the 1929 General Election*[1]

Year	Number of contests involved	By-election results: % of vote won by each party			1929 General Election results in the same constituencies: % of votes won by each party			By-election advantage over 1929 results (%)		
		Con.	Lab.	Lib.	Con.	Lab.	Lib.	Con.	Lab.	Lib.
1930–1	8	42·8	35·3	21·9	35·9	36·3	27·8	6·9	−1·0	−5·9

change in the national political scene. It is hard to avoid the conclusion either that the contented stayed away at the by-elections, or, more probably, that some Conservative electors, since they were not choosing the Government, took the opportunity to register a protest vote.

TABLE 30. *By-election Advantage between Parties, 1930–1*

Compared to 1929 result in the same constituencies

Year	Conservative advantage over Labour (%)	Conservative advantage over Liberal (%)	Labour advantage over Liberal (%)
1930–1	+7·9	+12·8	+4·9

It is hard to pursue the trend through the 1929–31 Parliament, for few by-elections were fought on a comparable basis. But, although the sample is small, the attempt is made in Tables 29 and 30.

The number of by-elections which have to be excluded from consideration must make any conclusions from these figures rather tentative, but they do point strongly to one fact—the

[1] There were twenty-nine contested by-elections during the 1929–31 Parliament but only six (one in 1930 and five in 1931) were fought by all three parties on a strictly comparable basis to 1929. Two other by-elections in 1930 in which a Communist intervened and received only a negligible number of votes are also included here.

rapid decline of the Liberal party after its relative failure in 1929. The full extent of this decline was never put to the test, for the Liberals fought the 1931 election largely in alliance with the Conservatives, but it seems plain that that temporary loss of independence was not alone responsible for the transformation of the Liberals from being a major party in 1929 to being a minor party in 1935. Even during the 1929–31 Parliament their fortunes had slumped severely.

The absence of change in Labour's fortunes revealed by these results is the more remarkable when the results of the seven

TABLE 31. *By-elections in 1932 compared with the 1931 General Election*

Year	No. of conests involved	By-election results: % of major-party vote		1931 General Election results in the same constituencies: % of major-party vote		Labour's by-election advantage over 1931 (%)
		Con.	Lab.	Con.	Lab.	
1932	7	55·9	44·1	69·5	30·5	13·6

1932 by-elections considered in Table 31 are compared with the outcome in the same constituencies in 1931.

After the 1945 'landslide' it was widely said that an anti-Conservative swing had long been brewing and that a normal general election held in 1940 would have shown substantial Labour gains. The by-election results run counter to this contention. Once the electorate had recovered from the shock of 1931 there appears to have been a very sharp swing in favour of the Labour party, but from 1933 onwards their support seems, if anything, to have declined. The reason for the belief that the Labour party was gaining ground presumably lies in the fact that between 1935 and 1939 it won twelve seats from the Conservatives in by-elections. But a study of the votes cast does not suggest any trend in its favour. It might be said to have won by-elections only because it had fared so ill in the general election. The fact that it won nearly 6 per cent. more of the vote in by-elections in both 1935 and 1936 than it did in the same constituencies in the general election of November 1935 is most significant. As in 1929 and 1950 the Government appears to have fared much better in a national contest deciding which party should rule than in individual by-elections where no such portentous issue faced the voter.

TABLE 32. *By-elections 1932–9 compared with the 1935 General Election*[1]

Year	No. of contests involved	By-election results: % of major-party votes		1935 General Election results in the same constituencies: % of major-party votes		Labour's by-election advantage over 1935 (%)
		Con.	Lab.	Con.	Lab.	
1932	7	55·9	44·1	58·9	41·1	3·0
1933	8	46·7	53·3	52·6	47·4	5·9
1934	12	56·9	43·1	62·4	37·6	5·5
1935	6	58·9	41·1	64·7	35·3	5·8
1936	10	51·4	48·6	57·5	42·5	6·1
1937	19	58·4	41·6	62·5	37·5	4·1
1938	13	51·4	48·6	56·4	43·6	5·0
1939	12	50·8	49·2	54·9	45·1	4·1

During the war-time party truce no by-elections were fought on a basis comparable to the general elections either of 1935 or 1945. But from 1941 a very mixed series of more or less left-wing independents stood almost every time a Conservative seat fell vacant. Although the quality of these independents varied greatly, it is worth comparing the Conservative share of the vote in these years with the share they secured in the same constituencies in 1935 and 1945.

These figures are not reliable enough to be treated as anything more than a bare suggestion of the way in which the swing between 1935 and 1945 was concentrated into the war years, with 1941–2 as the decisive period.

[1] The seats included here are those which were contested between 1932 and the outbreak of war by both a National Government and a Labour candidate, both in the general election of 1935 and in a by-election, excluding only the considerable number where the intrusion of a third or fourth party candidate appears substantially to have affected the division of the major-party vote.

TABLE 33. *By-elections 1941–5 compared with the General Elections of 1935 and 1945*[1]

Year	No. of contests involved	Conservative share of vote (%)			Conservative by-election (%) compared with	
		1935	By-election	1945	1935	1945
1941	9	60·3	61·2	45·7	+0·9	+15·5
1942	9	62·4	52·4	41·8	−10·0	+10·6
1943	14	59·7	55·7	41·7	−4·0	+14·0
1944	3	67·1	53·5	48·7	−13·6	+4·8
1945	2	60·7	44·7	39·0	−16·0	+5·7

A rather clearer pattern emerges from a study of the by-elections in the 1945–50 Parliament. The figures in Table 34 speak for themselves, but two comments are worth making. The fact that the victorious party did better rather than worse in the by-elections which immediately followed the general

TABLE 34. *By-elections 1945–9 compared with the 1945 General Election*[2]

Year	No. of contests involved	By-election results: % of major-party vote		1945 General Election results in the same constituencies: % of major-party vote		Conservatives' by-election advantage over 1945 (%)
		Con.	Lab.	Con.	Lab.	
1945	7	47·2	52·8	48·8	51·2	−1·6
1946	8	42·8	57·2	41·8	58·2	1·0
1947	7	49·8	50·2	42·2	57·8	7·6
1948	8	48·2	51·8	40·3	59·7	7·9
1949	3	44·6	55·4	38·5	61·5	6·1

[1] This table includes all Conservative-held seats which fell vacant between 1941 and 1945 (and which were contested in both 1935 and 1945 as well as in the war-time by-election).

[2] There were 50 non-university by-elections during the 1945–50 Parliament. Only 16 of them were fought on the same party basis as in the 1945 general election; however, if all interventions of minor-party candidates who forfeited their deposits are ignored, it is only necessary to exclude 17 by-elections from consideration on the ground that they were not comparable.

election of 1945 is in sharp contrast to previous experience; the holding of an early election may have been wise strategy for the Conservatives for the figures plainly suggest that they would have fared even worse if it had been put off until the autumn. Secondly, the 1949 figures are significant; the boundary changes under the 1948 Act make impossible any direct comparison between these by-elections and the results in the same constituencies in 1950. However, the 1949 by-elections showed a swing of over 6 per cent. against Labour since 1945, while in the 1950 general election the swing over the whole country was little more than 3 per cent. Again, by-election results were more anti-Government than those of a general election.

In 1950–1 the pattern recurred, as Table 35 shows. The Government fared worse in by-elections than in their nation-wide appeals.

TABLE 35. *By-elections 1950–1 compared with the 1950 and 1951 General Elections in the same constituencies*

Year	No. of contests involved	1950 General Election results: % of major-party vote		By-election results: % of major-party vote		1951 General Election results: % of major-party vote		Conservatives' by-election advantage over (%)	
		Con.	Lab.	Con.	Lab.	Con.	Lab.	1950	1951
1950	9	41·6	58·4	45·3	54·7	43·2	56·8	3·7	2·1
1951	5	53·4	46·6	58·9	41·1	54·7	45·3	5·5	4·2

Boundary changes render difficult any systematic comparison of the 1955 results with the preceding by-elections. However, in the three by-elections in January–March 1955 where exact comparison with the May General Election is possible the Conservatives fared only 0·5 per cent. worse—a marked contrast to every other pre-election period in the last forty years.

In the by-elections of 1959 the old pattern reasserted itself. The Government fared $3\frac{1}{2}$ per cent. worse than when the October General Election occurred.

TABLE 36. *By-elections 1951–5 compared with the 1951 General Election*[1]

Year	No. of contests involved	By-election results: % of major-party vote		1951 General Election results in the same constituencies: % of major-party vote		Conservatives' by-election advantage over 1951 (%)
		Con.	Lab.	Con.	Lab.	
1952	6	52·6	47·4	53·9	46·1	−1·3
1953	8	48·5	51·5	45·9	54·1	−2·6
1954	14	52·0	48·0	52·2	47·8	−0·2
1955	6	54·4	45·6	54·0	45·0	+0·4

The by-elections since 1959 have been marked by a spectacular increase in the Liberal vote and the results have to be presented in a different manner. Since 35 of the 40 by-elections up

TABLE 37. *By-elections 1955–9 compared with the 1955 and 1959 General Elections in the same constituencies*[2]

Year	No. of contests involved	1955 General Election results: % of major-party vote		By-election results: % of major-party vote		1959 General Election results: % of major-party vote		Conservatives' by-election advantage over (%)	
		Con.	Lab.	Con.	Lab.	Con.	Lab.	1955	1959
1955	3	52·6	47·4	50·8	49·2	48·7	51·3	−1·8	+2·1
1956	7	52·9	47·1	44·8	55·2	53·2	46·8	−8·1	−8·4
1957	7	67·3	32·7	60·4	39·6	68·5	31·5	−6·9	−8·1
1958	7	51·1	48·9	47·0	53·0	50·8	49·2	−4·1	−3·8
1959	5	51·0	49·0	47·7	52·3	51·1	48·9	−3·3	−3·4

to the end of 1962 had candidates from the three leading parties, straightforward Conservative-Labour contrasts are positively misleading. In 15 contests direct comparison with 1959 can be made, but the remaining 20 have to be treated separately because

[1] There were 48 by-elections during the Parliament, but 14 have to be excluded because third party intervention or withdrawal was on a scale to vitiate any contrast.

[2] There were 52 by-elections during the Parliament. Of these, 4 are excluded because either the Conservative or the Labour party was not involved; a further 19 have to be excluded because the effect of third party intervention or withdrawal was on a scale to render any contrast misleading.

the Liberals had not fought previously. The Liberal revival is the most striking by-election trend manifested in more than forty years.

TABLE 38 A. *By-elections 1960–2 in seats fought by Liberals in the by-election but not in 1959*

Year	No. of contests involved	1959 (%) Con.	1959 (%) Lab.	By-election (%) Con.	By-election (%) Lab.	By-election (%) Lib.	Con. loss	Lab. loss
1960	5	53·6	46·4	41·3	36·8	21·9	−12·3	−9·6
1961	7	53·6	46·4	35·2	38·1	26·7	−18·4	−6·3
1962	8	47·4	52·6	27·4	48·1	24·5	−20·0	−4·5

TABLE 38 B. *By-elections 1960–2 in seats fought by three leading parties both in 1959 and the by-election*

Year	No. of contests involved	1959 Con.	1959 Lab.	1959 Lib.	By-election Con.	By-election Lab.	By-election Lib.	By-election advantage over 1959 result Con.	By-election advantage over 1959 result Lab.	By-election advantage over 1959 result Lib.
1960	4	54·0	29·0	17·0	49·1	21·5	29·4	−4·9	−7·5	+12·4
1961	3	51·1	33·0	15·9	42·3	31·5	26·2	−8·8	−1·5	+10·3
1962	8	51·3	31·1	17·6	35·1	30·4	34·5	−16·2	−0·7	+16·9

In both these tables votes for fourth parties and independents are ignored

The tendency manifest before every general election except 1955 should underline the danger of comparing by-election results directly with general election results. There are more valid ways of drawing conclusions from by-elections than can be offered by a simple computation of the change that has taken place in a constituency since the last general election. If the result is put beside that in previous by-elections and a comparison is made to see what is the *trend of difference* from the general election results, it is possible to draw far more reliable conclusions.

10. THE CONSEQUENCES OF PROPORTIONAL REPRE-
SENTATION AND THE ALTERNATIVE VOTE

Proportional representation. Under a different electoral system the number of seats won by each of the parties in British general elections might have been very different. Calculations have been

published in several places showing what the consequences of
proportional representation might have been in every contest
since 1918.[1] These calculations are rather unsatisfactory for
various reasons. The most important is that under a different
electoral system many people would have cast their votes
differently. More candidates would have presented themselves,
and electors, with the assurance that their votes would not be
wasted, would have been more willing to give their first endorsement to forlorn hopes. But even if votes had been divided between the parties in just the same proportions as they were
under the existing system, there is no guarantee that P.R. would
have distributed seats in exactly the same ratio as votes. The
correlation would undoubtedly have been much closer than it
in fact was, but even under P.R. there is a wide margin of error.
The single transferable vote in a five-member constituency[2] is
not likely to help a party unless it secures at least 16 per cent.
of the first preferences. In 1950, for example, it has been calculated that on the votes cast the Liberals would have gained
only 16 seats under P.R. instead of the 9 which in fact fell to
them, giving them barely 2½ per cent. of the seats in Parliament,
although they won 9 per cent. of the votes. There is no reason
to suppose that in any election in the 1950's P.R. would have led
to the election of a single Independent or Communist candidate.

However, since any speculations about the consequences of
P.R. are so uncertain, it is perhaps unnecessary to make any
detailed adjustments to allow for such imperfections in the
system. Table 39 shows simply how Parliaments from 1922
to 1959 would have been composed if seats had been distributed in the same proportion as the votes that were in fact
cast.

These figures probably under-estimate the strength of the
Liberal party in all years and of the Labour party up to 1935,
simply because they left so many seats uncontested. The Conservatives, having always a fuller list of candidates, probably
received a total vote nearer to that which they would have

---

[1] See e.g. R. W. G. Mackay, *Coupon or Free?* (London, 1943), p. 38. J. F. S.
Ross, *Parliamentary Representation*, 2nd ed. (London, 1948), pp. 89–93, is also
of interest.
[2] The only system seriously advocated in Britain.

secured under P.R. than either of the other parties. It is perhaps unlikely that under the single transferable vote so many Independents would have succeeded.

The precise results of P.R. might well have been far from these figures. But it is fairly clear that only two elections in the

TABLE 39. *The Consequences of Proportional Representation*

Under P.R.				Year	Actual result			
Con.	Lib.	Lab.	Other		Con.	Lib.	Lab.	Other
235	179	181	20	1922	346	115	142	12
234	182	188	11	1923	258	159	191	7
298	108	202	7	1924	419	40	151	5
235	143	228	9	1929	260	59	288	8
413		189	13	1931	521	37	52	5
330	41	232	12	1935	431	21	154	9
254	58	306	22	1945	212	12	394	22
272	57	288	8	1950	298	9	315	3
300	16	304	5	1951	321	6	295	3
314	17	292	7	1955	344	6	277	3
311	37	276	6	1959	365	6	258	1

last ten would have been likely to return a party with a clear working majority. The fears constantly expressed by critics of P.R. would have been realized. Strong majority governments would have been rare. Elections would not have decided which party should form the Cabinet or what general policy it should follow. Responsible government and the power of the ordinary elector would thereby have been weakened. At the same time, it is far from certain that the quality or independence of M.P.s would have risen, for the independent candidate would only have had a very limited chance of success and there is no strong reason to suppose that the electors would have placed the candidates of each party in the order most appropriate to their abilities as public servants.

On the other hand, the advantages of strong government may be exaggerated. The necessity of coalition might have made Parliament a more genuinely deliberative body. P.R. would have given fairer representation to minority parties and it would have averted the unbalanced Houses of Commons with overwhelming majorities which were so characteristic of the period. It may be a virtue of the existing system that it gives the governing party a working lead in the House of Commons; but in six of the last twelve elections the Government has had a majority so much greater than was necessary for the control of legislation and policy that it ran the danger of riding roughshod over an Opposition too weak adequately to do its job.

The case for and against P.R. is argued too often in absolute terms. It must be decided afresh for each country and each period of history. In some instances it may make little difference and in others much. In Great Britain in the last forty years the statistician can say with little fear of contradiction that it would have made minority government the rule and not the exception. The student of politics can assert with almost equal confidence that it would have had a drastic, if largely incalculable, influence upon the structure and programmes of the parties and upon the conduct and thought of politicians.

The alternative vote. The consequences of the introduction of the alternative vote would have been less revolutionary than those of P.R. but almost as uncertain. Obviously, if there had been no danger of wasting their vote, many people would have cast their first preferences differently; assumptions about their second preferences must be purely speculative. None the less, it seems worth while to examine what the effect of the alternative vote would have been in the last seven general elections, assuming first preferences to be divided as in fact they were and making certain arbitrary guesses about the disposition of second preferences. The result may serve as a guide, if not to the precise consequences of the alternative vote, at least to their possible order of magnitude. For the purposes of these calculations it is assumed:

1. If the votes of a Conservative candidate were redistributed between Liberal and Labour candidates, the Liberal would have gained a majority of 80 per cent. (i.e. 90% — 10%).
2. If the votes of a Labour candidate were redistributed between Conservative and Liberal candidates, the Liberal would have gained a majority of 80 per cent. (i.e. 90% — 10%).

3. If the votes of a Communist candidate were redistributed between Labour and Liberal or Labour and Conservative candidates, the Labour candidate would have gained a majority of 80 per cent. (i.e. 90%—10%).

4. If the votes for an Independent of known right-wing or left-wing views were redistributed, a majority of 80 per cent. would have gone to the Conservative or Labour candidate respectively.

5. If the votes of a Liberal candidate were redistributed between Conservative and Labour candidates, the following hypotheses are made for different years:

1923	Conservative 33·3 per cent.,		Labour 66·6 per cent.			
1924 (*a*)	,,	66·6	,,	,,	33·3	,,
(*b*)	,,	33·3	,,	,,	66·6	,,
1929	,,	33·3	,,	,,	66·6	,,
1931	,,	66·6	,,	,,	33·3	,,
1935 (*a*)	,,	66·6	,,	,,	33·3	,,
(*b*)	,,	33·3	,,	,,	66·6	,,
1945	,,	33·3	,,	,,	66·6	,,
1950	,,	66·6	,,	,,	33·3	,,
1951	,,	66·6	,,	,,	33·3	,,
1955	,,	66·6	,,	,,	33·3	,,
1959	,,	66·6	,,	,,	33·3	,,

From Table 40 it is plain that, on these assumptions, the alternative vote would in no case have changed a decisive result into an indecisive one. In some cases the majority would have been reduced, but it would have remained adequate; in 1945 it seems likely that it would have been further exaggerated. In three of the four cases where an election did not in fact produce a very clear decision, it does, however, seem that the situation would have been materially changed. In 1950 a narrow majority might well have been turned into a minority by the alternative vote, and in 1923 and 1929 the Liberals would have held a much more influential position in the deadlock of parties.

It appears that in all elections since 1923 the alternative vote would have given a rather more proportionate number of seats to the Libreals. But it would hardly have ensured fair representation all round, and it would not have prevented a party with less than 50 per cent. of the votes from obtaining a potentially tyrannical parliamentary majority. It might well have given the ordinary elector a greater sense of freedom of choice, but it would have done little to clarify the relation between seats and votes in the country as a whole. It would have been

TABLE 40. *The Consequences of the Alternative Vote*

Under alternative vote				Year	Actual result			
Con.	Lib.	Lab.	Other		Con.	Lib.	Lab.	Other
195	217	196	7	1923	258	159	191	7
403 ⎫ 371 ⎭	74	⎧133⎫ ⎩165⎭	.5	(a) (b) 1924	419	40	151	5
167	137	301	10	1929¹	260	59	288	8
513	42	55	5	1931	521	37	52	5
430 ⎫ 416 ⎭	24	⎧151⎫ ⎩165⎭	10	(a) (b) 1935	431	21	154	9
171	22	426	21	1945	212	12	394	22
309	16	297	3	1950	298	9	315	3
323	11	288	3	1951	321	6	295	3
340	11	276	3	1955	344	6	277	3
375	10	244	1	1959	365	6	258	1

as likely to multiply as to reduce the protests at the 'injustice' of the electoral system.

11. SEATS AND VOTES

THE British electoral system is not a gamble. Fortuitous biases have been manifest in its operation, but the relation between a party's representation in Parliament and its support in the country is almost as predictable as it would be under proportional representation. The theoretical possibility of quite haphazard results arising from any given division of votes is undeniable; the practical improbability is so great under present conditions that it need not be considered. The electoral system would not have survived unchanged for so long if it had been the complete gamble which advocates of proportional representation have alleged. It has produced greatly exaggerated

---

¹ In a careful examination of the 1929 results in the *Political Quarterly* for April 1931 (p. 251) the conclusion is reached that the alternative vote would have given the Conservative 270 seats, the Liberals 94, and Labour 253.

parliamentary majorities and it has been very hard on minor parties—but even a cursory glance at past results shows there to have been a definite relationship between the aggregate of votes won by each party and the division of seats in the House of Commons. The existence of some such relationship might *a priori* have been anticipated; detailed examination shows it in fact to have been surprisingly consistent.

Casino proprietors know that while a single throw is exposed to the full range of chance, there is little uncertainty about the outcome of a large number. Similarly, even if the result in a single constituency were a complete gamble, some pattern might be expected to underlie the outcome in 600 constituencies. Both before and after the era in which the existence of three major parties complicated the issue, formulas were suggested which roughly related seats and votes. In 1898 Professor Edgeworth pioneered the subject;[1] he was followed in 1909 by Mr. James Parker Smith who argued before the Royal Commission on Electoral Systems that if votes were divided between the parties in the ratio $A:B$, seats would be divided in the ratio $A^3:B^3$.[2] There the subject was left until in 1945 the present writer approached it in a more empirical way by calculating how many seats would have changed hands in 1935 and 1945 for any given swing away from the actual results of these elections.[3] In 1950 a similar but simpler empirical formula was devised.[4] The percentage majority of every M.P. was calculated. Since obviously the transfer of half that percentage to the other side would cause defeat, the number of seats which would have been won or lost by any evenly spread change in the national division of the vote could be surmised. The results of the 1951 election confirmed the calculations made after the 1950 election;[5] it makes virtually no

[1] F. Y. Edgeworth, 'Miscellaneous Applications of the Calculus of Probabilities', *Journal of the Royal Statistical Society*, vol. lxi, p. 534.

[2] *Cd. 5352/1910*, p. 81. For a recent mathematical justification of this formula see M. G. Kendall and A. Stuart, 'The Law of Cubic Proportion in Election Results', *British Journal of Sociology*, vol. i, No. 3, p. 183.

[3] See *The British General Election of 1945* (Oxford, 1947), by R. B. McCallum and A. Readman, pp. 277 et seq.

[4] See *The British General Election of 1950* (London, 1951), by H. G. Nicholas, pp. 327 et seq.

[5] See *The British General Election of 1951* (London, 1952), by D. E. Butler, pp. 275–7.

The Working of the System

difference which of the two elections is used as the basis for assessing the current relation between seats and votes. Table 41 and Diagram III in fact show that relation as calculated from the outcome in 1951.

TABLE 41. *The Relation between Seats and Votes in 1951*[1]

	Conservative lead over Labour in % of votes							Labour lead over Conservative in % of votes						
	20%	15%	10%	5%	2%	1%	0%	1%	2%	5%	10%	15%	20%	
Conserva-tive seats	475	443	412	375	346	337	329	320	310	281	234	188	152	Conserva-tive seats
Labour seats	141	173	204	241	270	279	287	296	306	335	382	428	464	Labour seats
Majority	334	270	208	134	76	58	42	24	4	54	148	240	312	Majority
	Conservative lead over Labour in seats							Labour lead over Conservative in seats						

It is plain that in 1951, as in 1950, the Conservatives would have won more seats than Labour for any given percentage of the total vote. To secure a majority over the Conservatives the Labour party needed to get 2 per cent. more of the vote than them, or, to put it the other way round, the Conservatives stood to win more seats than the Labour party even though they were as much as 2 per cent.—or about 500,000 votes—behind them in the popular poll. Thus in 1951 when they were in a minority of about 200,000—0·6 per cent.—they secured a majority of 26 seats over Labour. It seems that the Conservatives require to get 1 per cent. more of the popular vote than Labour to obtain a majority of 50 seats; Labour, to obtain a similar majority, require to get nearly 5 per cent. more of the popular vote than the Conservatives. There is plainly an appreciable Conservative bias in the system today. In 1945 there seems to have been an almost equal bias in favour of the Labour party. If such biases can exist, some explanation is needed for the accuracy of so simple a relation as the $A^3 : B^3$ formula. It makes no allowance for biases, yet it fits the results in 1931 with an error of only one seat, in 1935 with no error at all, and in 1945 with an error of 6 seats. In 1950 the error was 18 seats and in 1951 21 seats; even these are small differences when 625 seats are at stake. What

[1] The nine seats which were won by Liberals or Anti-partitionists are ignored in this table.

are the cancelling biases which allow such surprising precision? The conditions necessary to such a clear and steady relationship between seats and votes seem to fall under three heads.

1. *Political homogeneity.* So regular a relation between seats and votes could only exist in a relatively homogeneous country

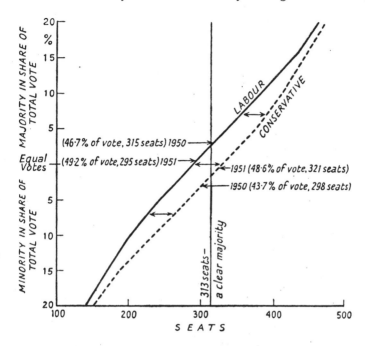

DIAGRAM III. The relation between seats and votes in 1951

whose politics were fought predominantly on national issues to which the different constituencies reacted in a fairly similar way. The empirical formulas which have been mentioned are based on the assumption of universal and equal swings from one party to another in all constituencies. Upon investigation this assumption is found to be satisfied to a remarkable extent,[1] although the turnover in votes between one constituency and the next is by no means completely uniform. Strictly speaking, however, the empirical formulas only require that there should be no substantial

[1] See Butler, op. cit., pp. 268–70.

correlation between current swing and previous majority in each constituency; such variations in swing as do occur may then be assumed to cancel out. It is theoretically possible that the national swing should be concentrated in the marginal constituencies held by one party; it is politically and statistically highly improbable, and it has not happened in practice.

2. *Fair and equal constituencies.* Although there has certainly been no deliberate gerrymandering in the drawing of boundaries, there are two ways in which the constituency map can bias the relation between seats and votes in favour of one side or the other.

Boundaries can never be drawn so that each constituency contains exactly the same number of electors. If there happens to be some correlation between party sympathy and size of electorate, the party whose support tends to be drawn from the smaller constituencies is obviously likely to get more members for a given number of votes than its rival. In 1950, just after a general redistribution, this was a negligible factor; the average Conservative constituency had 55,270 electors compared with the 55,161 of the average Labour constituency—a difference fully accounted for by chance alone. But in 1945 the situation was very different. There had been no general redistribution for twenty-seven years and the depopulated constituencies—many of them in East London—tended to be in areas where the Labour party was strong. As a result, in the 1945 election constituencies won by the Conservative party contained an average of 56,713 electors compared with an average of 50,785 in those won by the Labour party. If, all other things being equal, there had been no such variation, the Labour party would have won fifteen fewer seats. This does much to explain the bias towards Labour which existed in the system in 1945. The institution of regular redistribution makes it unlikely that this cause of bias will be of great importance in the future, but it may have had an appreciable effect in past elections.

The other bias that may arise from the nature of the constituency map is less eradicable. If the supporters of one party tend to be more concentrated than those of the other, the former may squander many more votes than the latter in building up huge majorities in safe seats. Such a phenomenon can be simply demonstrated on the basis of the results in 1950. Of the majorities over 20,000, 42 were secured by Labour candidates and only 8 by Conservatives. Percentagewise, of the 60 biggest majorities 50 were Labour and 10 Conservative. The point about this unproductive show of strength can be made in another way. Over the whole country the median percentage support for the Conservative party (that is its strength in that constituency which ranked midway between its safest and its most hopeless) was 44·7 per cent., while the mean Conservative vote was 43·7 per cent. The median Labour vote was 45·8 per cent.; the mean 46·7 per cent. In other words, more than half the Conservative candidates secured more than the national average support for their party while more than half the Labour candidates secured less. Since almost all victorious candidates are among those who do better than average, the implication is that Conservative support was more effectively distributed about the country from the point of view of winning seats. The misfortune of the Labour party in having their strength concentrated to such an extent in safe constituencies meant that in 1950 and 1951 they needed 2 per cent. more of the aggregate vote than the Conservatives to secure any given number of seats—that they entered the election with a handicap of something like half a million votes. If majorities had been evenly distributed the Labour party would probably have secured about eighteen additional seats. In the long run substantial changes in the geography of party support may occur, but in the past swings in opinion have tended to be very evenly spread about the country and the political map has only changed very slowly. There is, therefore, nothing ephemeral about the consequences of this local concentration of one party's supporters. It imparts an unavoidable, but not an unpredictable, type of bias to the working of the electoral system.

3. *A two-party system.* There are difficulties in analysing the relation between seats and votes in a period when three major parties were involved in the contest. The relation between seats and votes in successive elections can only be similar if the elections are fought on a comparable basis. But in the period up to 1929 the number of seats contested by each party varied very considerably. The number of seats a party wins depends hardly

at all upon the number of its candidates, for it is certain to fight virtually all seats in which it has a serious chance of success; but the number of votes it wins depends greatly upon this factor.[1] Therefore substantial adjustments would be needed before any attempt could be made to link the aggregates of votes in the 1920's to the division of seats.

There is another difficulty in dealing with three parties: a formula covering three variables must be more intricate than one which covers only two. Although no attempt will be made to devise one here, it must be pointed out that it is theoretically quite practicable; if a relationship can be shown to exist between seats and votes when there are two major parties, there is no logical reason why the intrusion of a third party should throw the electoral system completely to the mercy of chance. It is worth observing that only once in the three-party period did a major party with more votes than one of its rivals secure fewer seats.[2]

Some of the special difficulties involved in devising a formula to relate seats and votes in a period when there were three major parties are also relevant when there are only two major parties. It has never yet happened that two major parties have contested every constituency. Seats which are unopposed, and seats where a third party provides a major candidate, are liable to distort the simple relation between seats and votes. The intrusion of hopeless minor-party candidates could have a similar effect. However, the number of uncontested seats has declined considerably, and by 1950 the number of seats in which the Conservative and Labour parties did not jointly dominate the field was not great; only 2 seats were uncontested and all but 12 had candidates from both the Conservative and Labour parties.[3] The aggregate vote for these parties might, therefore, be taken as a more or less accurate index to their true strength in the country. But if in the future any substantial number of seats is left unfought by a major party, the relation between seats won and aggregate

---

[1] See p. 174 above.

[2] In 1929 the Labour party with 37·0 per cent. of the total vote won 288 seats, while the Conservatives with 38·2 per cent. of the vote secured only 260 seats.

[3] In 1951 4 seats were uncontested and all but 16 had candidates from both the Conservative and Labour parties.

votes may be altered. It might then be more appropriate to investigate the relation between seats and votes only in the fully contested constituencies.

It might seem that allowance for minor-party candidates was essential to a formula relating the seats and votes won by the major parties. But assuming the intrusion of a third-party candidate to draw significantly different percentages of the electorate away from the two major parties, the net effect may be likened to that which would result from those proportions of their supporters abstaining altogether from voting. However many minor-party candidates decide to stand or not to stand, the number of seats each of the major parties wins is likely to be related to the number of votes it actually secures in just the same way as before. As long as minor-party candidatures are evenly scattered and not concentrated in marginal constituencies, they may be ignored.

If there are some constituencies in which minor parties have a serious chance of victory, they may, of course, affect the balance. But in 1945 there were only 66 constituencies in which the major parties did not provide the top two at the poll; by 1950 this number had fallen to 37 and by 1951 to 26. Few of these could remotely be regarded as marginal seats, and, moreover, they were so divided between the parties that anything happening in them would be most unlikely to have a noticeable net effect on the size of the majority in Parliament.

Conclusion. The major parties seem likely to receive roughly equal and predictable treatment at the hands of the electoral system:

(*a*) when two parties are predominant in all constituencies,

(*b*) when any variations in the swing between them are distributed at random in relation to the majorities,

(*c*) when there is no party bias in the size of constituencies,

(*d*) when there is no especial concentration of vote-splitting third-party candidates in marginal seats, and

(*e*) when neither party's support is more concentrated in safe constituencies than the other's.

The major biases in the working of the system which it has been possible to trace arise from failure to satisfy these conditions. Hitherto the biases have cancelled each other out to a surprising extent. In 1950 and 1951 they had for the most part disappeared, although perhaps only temporarily; the only bias that seems to have been of importance was the unequal distribution of huge majorities. Its total effect does not appear to have been very great—twenty seats at most. It is seldom that such a number would have been of decisive importance in the composition of the House of Commons.

One of the main virtues of the British electoral system is that it produces clear parliamentary majorities; one of its main weaknesses is that it produces excessive parliamentary majorities. In 1950—and to a lesser extent in 1951—it did neither. Votes happened to be divided at precisely the point which produced a hairbreadth majority. But nothing that happened in those elections gives reason to doubt the tendency of the system to translate even a narrow majority in popular votes into a majority large enough to make strong government possible. As both the $A^3:B^3$ formula and the examination of recent results suggest, a swing of 1 per cent. in votes is likely to cause about 18 seats to change hands—making a difference of 36 in a parliamentary division. A 2 per cent. swing is, therefore, more than enough to make the difference between a comfortable majority for one party and a comfortable majority for the other. Only if the division of votes happens to be within 1 per cent. of the critical point is there serious danger of indecisive results.

Especially when there is an overwhelming two-party dominance, the working of the electoral system seems to be one of the more certain things among the uncertainties of politics. But no attempt to analyse the relation between seats and votes must be pressed too far. The whole approach to the problem is based on the assumption that the future will resemble the past and that there will be no drastic changes in electoral behaviour or the structure of parties. That assumption may always be invalidated by the emergence of new biases, and, even if it continues to hold good, minor chances will always arise; arithmetic must not be pressed too far and no formula can be expected to relate votes cast and seats won without an appreciable margin of error. Yet this error is not on a scale sufficient to justify the assertion that the British electoral system is a gamble. It does in fact work reasonably systematically.

Postscript 1962. The foregoing section stands as it was written in 1952. Nothing in the results of the 1955 or 1959 elections invalidates the general argument, although ten years later it might be presented with some additional reservations. The swing between 1951 and 1955, and still more between 1955 and 1959, was rather more uneven than the swing between 1950 and 1951, but it was still remarkably regular. Moreover, there were some signs that the two-party domination of the scene was being threatened; the number of seats where Conservative and Labour failed to provide the first two candidates rose from 26 in 1951 to 31 in 1955 and to 41 in 1959.

None the less the general relationship between seats and votes held to the formulae set out here; about 18 seats changed hands for every 1 per cent. swing between Conservative and Labour—and there continued to be a bias in the system in favour of the Conservatives, owing to the disadvantageous way in which Labour strength was concentrated in safe seats. This bias seems to have been rather less than the 2 per cent. suggested by the results in 1950 and 1951. In both 1955 and 1959 the figure appears to have been very close to $1\frac{1}{2}$ per cent. The explanation for this difference lies mainly in the fact that in 1955 and 1959 the Conservatives fought every seat in Northern Ireland for the first time and so did more than before to redress the balance of wasted votes in safe seats.

In 1955 the Labour party held on to about 6 seats which, on the assumption of universal and equal swing, would have been lost; it was then thought that sitting members might have an advantage which would damp down the effect of any swing. But 1959 provided no support for this hypothesis—any more than 1951 had done.[1]

With the experience of two more general elections, it can be stated more confidently than ever that in the conditions of mid-century Britain, so long as two parties dominate the scene as they did in the 1950's, the electoral system works with predictable regularity in relating seats to votes.

The resurgence of the Liberal party in the by-elections of

[1] For a fuller discussion of this see *The British General Election of 1955* (London, 1955) by D. E. Butler, pp. 202–9, and *The British General Election of 1959* (London, 1960) by D. E. Butler and R. Rose, pp. 235–40.

1961 and 1962[1] does of course reopen the question of what would happen in a genuinely three-party situation. Provided that each party fights almost all seats (or rather, provided that the seats any one party leaves unfought are randomly distributed) there is no reason to suppose that the relation between seats and votes will cease to follow a fairly regular pattern. But this pattern will be much more complicated. Decisions about intervening in particular marginal seats might have a crucial influence. Moreover, if a third party were to arise which seemed to draw its strength more evenly from all areas of the country than the Conservative and Labour parties have done, then the tendency of the system to translate small changes in votes into large changes in seats could be exaggerated. This book is concerned with fact rather than hypothesis. The elections of 1923 and 1929 hardly provided the basis for an empirical theory of the relation between seats and votes in a three-party situation—nor would such a theory necessarily apply to a new situation in the 1960's with a different geographic distribution of party strength. The results of those elections were far from being entirely capricious: but they were certainly such that anyone translating opinion poll percentages into forecasts of House of Commons membership would demand a much wider margin of error than was required in the 1950's.

12. CONCLUSION. THE INTERPRETATION OF ELECTION RESULTS

ELECTIONS are focal points in the working of British democracy, and, though the system under which they operate has of late been accepted and left substantially unchanged, their results have remained a constant subject of comment. But the analysis has always tended to be superficial. In the foregoing pages certain special aspects of the question have been examined, such as the consequences of the full enfranchisement of women and of the business vote, and an attempt has been made to set the aggregate voting statistics in a more balanced light, by means of certain simple adjustments. Much more refined and elaborate calculations would undoubtedly be possible, but it is doubtful whether the labour would be justified since the raw material is so uncertain.

It seems worth while to end this study with an inquiry into

[1] See p. 189.

the nature of that uncertainty and with an exposition of some of the reservations which must be borne in mind in interpreting election results.

It is hard to assess what is signified by the individual vote, which constitutes the foundation of all electoral analysis. A vote is too easily taken as a declaration of unwavering faith in the preferred candidate, in his party, and in every item in its programme. But it may, of course, be an expression of anything from a mere whim to a deep-rooted prejudice, or from a reasoned assessment of the lesser evil to a confident assertion of political faith. It may be cast by a person who dislikes all existing parties, by one who has no representative of his own party standing, or by one who votes against his convictions recognizing that his preferred candidate has no chance. It may be influenced by the personality of the candidate or by some local issue quite extraneous to the national struggle. But whatever its motivation, every vote looks alike in a table of figures. Therefore if any meaning is to be drawn from election results certain minimum assumptions have to be made about the behaviour of voters. It has at least to be assumed that wholly irrational voters tend to cancel each other out and that, whether as the fruit of conscientious reflection or of mere prejudice, a vote represents a definite expression of preference between the general outlook of the contending parties.[1]

By and large, these assumptions lead to few difficulties. They are not susceptible of proof, but they do not seem unrealistic. However unthinking many electors may be, their votes do seem on balance to represent a general judgement between the merits of the national parties. The most notable lesson offered by a comparison of election results is the similarity of behaviour between different constituencies. In the last five general elections scarcely a single seat has changed hands in a direction opposite to the national trend; if the percentage swings in votes are considered, the differences between neighbouring constituencies were surprisingly small. It would appear that neither the quality

[1] It also has to be assumed, to a large extent, that the *pis aller* voter who would have acted differently had another party been standing—or had his preferred candidate had a chance of success—can be ignored. In a sense this may be justified on the ground that almost every vote is in the nature of a *pis aller*; few can regard their party or its local representatives as the epitome of perfection. Every voter has to make do with what he is offered.

of the candidate, nor the efficiency of his organization, nor the special local issues which may have arisen, were capable of affecting the result to anything like the same degree as the national party struggle.

Since elections are so predominantly fought on the merits of the parties as a whole to the exclusion of local issues, the problem of interpreting the results should be much simpler than in a more diverse country, such as the United States. But it is complicated enough and provokes many erroneous statements. The main sources of confusion can be roughly classified.

1. *Votes and seats.* There is a natural tendency in commenting upon elections to focus attention upon victories and defeats to the exclusion of the turnover in votes. This is quite proper if interest is confined to the affairs of the House of Commons, but all too often interpretations of the public mood are also based upon the number of seats which have changed hands rather than upon the losses and gains in votes. After each election it is salutary to remember how many people supported the minority party. In 1945, for example, so much was written about the 'landslide' that it was sometimes forgotten that less than 5 out of every 10 voters had supported the Labour party and that virtually 4 out of every 10 had supported the Conservatives. In both 1950 and 1951, if over the whole country 1 voter in 100 had changed his mind in one direction or 2 voters in 100 in the other, the outcome would have been decisive and 'the clear verdict of the British people' would have been discussed. Overmuch attention to the winning and losing of seats has repeatedly led commentators into wildly excessive generalizations about the meaning of election results as expressions of the public mood.

2. *Candidatures.* Comparisons between the share of the national vote secured by a party in successive elections may be largely vitiated by failure to consider changes in the number of candidates put forward. In individual constituencies too, when a new contestant appears or an old one withdraws, allowance is not always made for the ways in which their supporters may have been distributed between the other parties.

3. *Turnout.* The full electorate never votes. The causes of most non-voting have no direct connexion with political conviction, but a reduction in turnout may none the less affect the

fortunes of the parties. There is good reason to believe that the upper classes are more conscientious about exercising their franchise than the lower.[1] This factor is not of such great importance in general elections where a high proportion of the potential voters has always voted. But in by-elections the turnout fluctuates much more and the apparent swing of opinion may be as much due to this selective apathy as to any change of heart. Therefore those who try to draw conclusions from elections in which the poll has dropped substantially may be misled.

4. *By-elections and general elections.* Variations in turnout are not the only or even the main cause for the misinterpretation of by-election results. Irrespective of turnout there has been a general tendency for by-elections to go more against the Government than general elections. While this tendency continues crude forecasts based upon by-elections may prove most deceptive.

5. *Majorities.* In individual contests excessive attention is often paid to the victor's lead in votes. An increase·in the numerical majority is regarded as a triumph and a reduction as a defeat. But the majority may vary in a manner quite opposite to the swing in opinion owing to a fall in turnout or to the intrusion or withdrawl of an extra candidate. By the use of percentages some, though not all, of this confusion can be avoided.

6. *Conclusion.* In addition to these causes for the misunderstanding of election results, which relate to factors partially capable of statistical demonstration, there are other illusions which are largely due to verbal confusion.

The 'personification' of the electorate is perhaps the most outstanding example. Speaking after the results in 1950, Mr. Morrison provided an admirable instance of this almost universal tendency:

The British electorate has a habit of knowing what it wants and has a habit of overdoing the getting of what it wants . . . this time I think it wanted Labour back with a smaller majority but . . . it said it in italics instead of roman and the result is that it has got a tighter situation than it meant.[2]

[1] This is illustrated by the way in which, from 1946 to 1951, the Conservatives regularly fared better in local elections where the turnout was normally in the region of 40 per cent. than in parliamentary elections in the same areas when the turnout tended to be twice as great.

[2] *Manchester Guardian*, 28 Feb. 1950.

The dangers of presenting the change of mind of a small proportion of the population as though it represented the considered decision of the whole have only to be pointed out to become obvious.

There are several similar and widespread confusions; some, for instance, are fostered by the excessive use of the analogies of war in the description of the electoral process and some by the use of unexamined clichés such as 'the floating voter' or 'the balancing power of the middle class'. But there is no point in pursuing too far this analysis of the errors with which electoral commentaries habitually abound. Many foolish things have been said and will continue to be said about the meaning of elections; they may be traced almost entirely to two causes—the comparison of figures which are not comparable, and the thoughtless acceptance of unsupported generalizations about voting behaviour. Since relatively few election statistics are strictly comparable between one election and the next, and since there has been so little systematic investigation of voting behaviour, commenting on elections is naturally hazardous. But with the aid of research and reflection the hazards can be greatly reduced.

APPENDIX I

DEVELOPMENTS SINCE 1951

IN the nineteen-fifties redistribution was the only aspect of the electoral system to provoke major controversy; the debates on this are dealt with in Appendix II.

However, a number of minor issues arose.

University representation. Faint echoes were heard of the dispute over university representation. Its restoration had been promised in the Conservative manifesto of 1951 and demands that this pledge should be fulfilled were heard from time to time. In the debate on the Address in November 1951 Mr. Churchill said:

> For the Government to add to their majority in Parliament already elected would create a questionable precedent. . . . Any alteration of the franchise should follow the normal course of franchise measures and be operative only at the Dissolution. . . . We have in no way departed from our intention to restore the University franchise, but the measure is no longer urgent.[1]

A year later[2] he reiterated the Government's intention of taking action, but on 21 October 1953 he announced that the question was to be dropped. Thenceforth, the issue was plainly a dead one, although in Parliament—and still more in *The Times* correspondence columns—wistful pleas continued to be heard from time to time.

Voting Systems. Although the Labour party made remarkably little complaint about the 1951 election result (when, despite getting more votes, they lost power to the Conservatives), Liberals and others protested periodically about the working of the electoral system. Mr. Churchill seems to have had some sympathy with their demands for reform and on 3 February 1953 he received a Liberal deputation on the subject: he told them that, while legislation was impossible in the current Parliament, an inquiry would be considered.[3] Lady Violet Bonham Carter told the Liberal Assembly[4] that the Prime Minister still favoured Proportional Representation, in spite of his followers. But the lack of enthusiasm in the Conservative party was complete; and on 27 July 1954 the Prime Minister indicated that there was little hope even of a factual inquiry.[5] On 22 November 1954 an all-party campaign for an inquiry on voting systems was announced but hardly anything more was heard of the matter.

[1] *H.C. Deb. 491* c. 71.　　　　[2] *H.C. Deb. 507* c. 1869.
[3] *The Times*, 4 February 1953.　　[4] *The Times*, 11 April 1953
[5] *H.C. Deb. 531* c. 233–5.

Cars. The limitations on the use of cars imposed by the 1948 Act excited continuing criticism from the Conservatives. Resolutions for their abolition were put down before every Conservative Conference and in 1955, 1956, and 1958 they were debated and carried. Until 1958 successive Home Secretaries announced that the time for amendment was not ripe, but then Mr. Butler relented and during the 1958–9 session the Representation of the People (Amendment) Act[1] found its way on to the Statute Book. It was a simple one-clause Act repealing Section 88 of the 1949 Act. The debates on its passage[2] were marked by much party wrangling. Labour complaints of the partisan nature of the Bill were countered by the Government argument that the spread of car ownership[3] not only reduced any partisan advantage the Conservatives might once have had, but also increased the likelihood of the law being evaded and brought into contempt.[4] Experience in the 1959 election seemed to confirm that there is no likelihood of restrictions being reimposed.[5]

Postal Voting. The innovation of the postal vote in 1948 had had drastic electoral consequences. The number of electors taking advantage of it was greater than expected.

TABLE 42. *Postal Votes 1950*

	No. of votes cast by post	% of total vote
1950	471,088	1·6
1951	756,956	2·6
1955	526,904	2·0
1959	598,559	2·1

There is no doubt that the great majority of these votes went to Conservative candidates. If the ratio between Conservative and Labour was 75:25, it has been calculated that the Conservatives may

[1] 7 Eliz. 2, ch. 9.
[2] 2nd Reading *H.C. Deb. 594* c. 954–1076; Committee 595 c. 1030–118; 3rd Reading 596 c. 225–316.
[3] It was pointed out during the debates that the number of cars had risen from 2 m. in 1948 to 4½ m. in 1958. A Gallup poll suggested that in 1958 60 per cent. of the cars were owned by Conservatives and 19 per cent. by Labour supporters.
[4] The Home Secretary made play with the fact that of the 20 convictions under Section 88, 18 had involved Labour supporters and only 2 Conservatives (*H.C. Deb. 594* c. 960).
[5] See *The British General Election of 1959*, by D. E. Butler and R. Rose, pp. 141–2.

have owed 12 seats to the postal vote in 1950, 10 in 1951, 9 in 1955, and 11 in 1959. No complaints were heard, however, about the partisan impact of the postal vote, even if suggestions for its extension came primarily from Conservatives. After each election, and at several Conservative Annual Conferences, demands were made for a widening of the categories allowed to vote by post—particularly on behalf of those on holiday. Successive Home Secretaries rejected such demands on the grounds of administrative inconvenience and of the dangers to the secrecy of the ballot.

Election Expenses. Despite the change in the value of money, no substantial demands for an increase in candidate's permitted expenses were voiced. But party and business expenditure on the national level attracted increasing criticism. In the two years before the 1959 election, private enterprise appears to have spent at least £1½ million pounds on anti-socialist propaganda while the Conservatives spent £½ million on more direct party propaganda. All this expenditure fell outside the scope of the existing law.[1] Complaints were voiced before and during the election, and on 21 July 1960 the House of Commons, after an undistinguished debate,[2] rejected a Labour motion for a Government inquiry into political expenditures.[3] But the last has plainly not been heard of this issue.

Broadcasting. The rapid growth in the electoral importance of television raised acute problems, both of law and of fairness. Do the broadcasting authorities, when they spend money on presenting party programmes during an election, contravene the Representation of the People Act? How much time should the broadcasting authorities allot to minor parties? Should there be any restrictions on the form or content of political broadcasts? These and other complicated questions came to the fore in 1959 when broadcasting authorities took a far more active role than hitherto in presenting both news and discussions of electoral speeches and issues. The B.B.C. Charter, the Television Act of 1954, and the understandings between the broadcasting authorities and the parties all came under some criticism

---

[1] It was almost all stopped in September 1959 on the announcement of the election. The private enterprise campaign might well have been legal even if it had continued up to polling day, since it seldom mentioned parties explicitly, and, since in the leading (Tronoh-Malayan Mines) case in 1952, the Courts had ruled that advertising not directed towards the election of a specific candidate was permissible.

[2] For a full discussion of the situation which provoked this debate see *The British General Election of 1959*, by D. E. Butler and R. Rose, pp. 17–34, 241–55, 280–1. For possible remedies see 'Money and Election Law' by R. Rose, *Political Studies*, pp. 1–15, February 1961.

[3] *H.C. Deb. 627* c. 733–804.

before and after the election.[1] Unfortunately public discussion of these issues was short-lived and they were almost completely neglected by the Pilkington Committee in its far-reaching examination of broadcasting in 1960–2.[2]

[1] See *The British General Election of 1959*, by D. E. Butler and R. Rose, pp. 75–77, 96–97.

[2] *Cmd. 1757/1962.* However, see pp. 92–95.

APPENDIX II

REDISTRIBUTION

THE principles of redistribution now accepted have only gradually been formulated. The changes in 1832 and 1867 were merely palliative measures under which the worst anomalies of representation were attacked. The constituencies with the smallest electorates were wholly or partly disfranchised and the extra seats were given to the areas most under-represented; but huge discrepancies in the size of constituencies were allowed to continue, and on both occasions it was only a minority of seats whose representation was disturbed.[1] In 1886 redistribution was reluctantly accepted by the Liberals as a necessary price to pay for the extension of the franchise. The principle of equality in the size of constituencies was specifically rejected,[2] but none the less anomalies were dealt with much more vigorously than formerly and no constituency was left with more than eight times the electorate of any other.[3]

There were many complaints about the anomalies left in 1885, and in 1905 the Local Government Board published redistribution proposals which were hardly very radical.[4] Boroughs were to have one seat for each 65,000 members of the population. If they had less than 18,500 population they were to lose their separate representation. Two-member seats with less than 75,000 population were to lose one seat. Nothing was done to carry out these proposals.

The Speaker's Conference of 1917 made much more far-reaching recommendations which were implemented in the Representation of the People Act of 1918. Seats with less than 50,000 population were

[1] The actual number of seats involved was 143 in 1832 and 52 in 1867.
[2] See C. S. Seymour, *Electoral Reform in England and Wales* (New Haven, 1915), pp. 506 et seq.
[3] The following table shows the approximate ratios between the largest and smallest electorates in territorial constituencies after each of the five major redistributions.

Year	U.K.	England only
1832	100 to 1	60 to 1
1868	150 to 1	80 to 1
1885	8 to 1	7 to 1
1918	5 to 1	3 to 1
1948	3 to 1	2 to 1

[4] *Cd. 2602/1905.*

disfranchised and one member was given to a county or borough for each 70,000 of its population. But there was still a suggestion of patchwork about the redistribution; it did not start from scratch but only dealt with all cases where existing constituencies did not conform to certain reasonably narrow limits.

The Speaker's Conference of 1944 provided an agreed basis for a permanent approach to the problem and the main recommendations of the conference were embodied in the House of Commons (Redistribution of Seats) Act, 1944. By that Act permanent Boundary Commissions for England, Wales, Scotland, and Northern Ireland were set up with instructions to keep under continuous review the representation in the House of Commons of the area with which they were concerned, and to make periodical reports concerning the whole of that area. The Commissions were also given power to make recommendations at any time relating to a particular constituency or constituencies.

One of the rules for redistribution to be observed by the Commissions provided that the electorate of a constituency should not be greater or less than the electoral quota (a figure obtained by dividing the electorate of Great Britain by the number of constituencies existing on a prescribed date) by more than approximately 25 per cent.[1] In practice this limitation was found to be far too rigid and to produce results which in some instances cut right across local unities; in 1946 the Government decided to replace it by a more elastic instruction that 'the electorate of any constituency shall be as near the electoral quota as is practicable, having regard to [the rules about respecting local boundaries]'.[2]

The acceptance of approximate numerical equality as the essential basis of redistribution led to some extent to the abandonment of an old-established principle of representation—the identification of constituencies with communities. In the redistribution of the nineteenth century, county and borough boundaries had always been respected. But in 1917 the Boundary Commissioners for the first time were merely instructed that parliamentary boundaries should '*as far as practicable* coincide with the boundaries of administrative areas'.[3] However, only seventy-eight rural districts were divided and no boroughs or urban districts.[4] Again in 1944 the Act setting up the

---

[1] Compared with roughly 30 per cent. below and 70 per cent. above in 1917.

[2] See *Cmd. 7260*/1947, p. 9.

[3] *Cd. 8756*/1917, p. 14.

[4] As time went on, of course, many local boundaries were changed by Private Acts, while parliamentary boundaries remained unchanged. By 1939

Boundary Commissions provided that 'as far as practicable' local administrative areas should not be divided between constituencies. In 1947 the Commissioners recommended the division of only forty-one English rural districts; they also proposed that three London constituencies should contain one borough and part of another; that parts of adjacent rural districts should be added to three provincial boroughs, and that the parliamentary counties of East and West Suffolk should be merged. On the whole, thanks to the relaxation of the rules in 1946, the Commissioners were extremely successful in avoiding conflict between local and parliamentary boundaries.

Apart from the attempt to respect local boundaries, two other exceptions have been made to the principle of numerical equality. The first is the special treatment accorded to Wales, Scotland, and Ireland. The national pride of these areas has been very sensitive to any reduction in representation. In 1917 the problem was met by the creation of extra seats; Scotland and Wales were at the time over-represented; however, as 29 more seats were given to England, but only 1 to Scotland and 1 to Wales, England ended by being only slightly under-represented.[1] Ireland was, for obvious reasons, allowed to retain the 100 seats granted in 1801, although, on the basis of electorate, it should have had no more than 63. When the Northern Ireland Government was set up in 1920 there was a further departure from numerical equality, although in the other direction. Northern Ireland, having a Parliament of its own, was thought to need less representation at Westminster and was only allotted 12 territorial seats instead of the 17 to which it would have been entitled by its electorate.

Scotland and Wales received more favoured treatment in 1944. It was provided that the total number of M.P.s should be 'not substantially greater or less' than it then was, but that there should be no reduction in the representation of Scotland or Wales, although that gave Scotland one member for 46,693 electors and Wales one for 51,333, compared with one for 55,693 for England.[2] In the 1948 redistribution the contrast would, owing to population movements, have been even greater but for the fact that Parliament decided to

very few parliamentary boroughs outside London still coincided exactly with municipal boroughs. One of the great advantages of the permanent Boundary Commissions set up in 1944 is that such anomalies can be prevented at the outset. Between 1948 and 1951 the boundaries of thirty-eight constituencies were modified by Order in Council for this reason.

[1] On a strictly proportionate distribution of the seats in Great Britain, England should have had 488 seats and not 485.

[2] On the basis of the 1945 register.

give England twenty-one more seats than had been envisaged in 1944.[1]

These advantages for Scotland and Wales, although zealously demanded by nationalists, could to a certain extent be justified by the other agreed exception to the principle of numerical equality. It has been generally accepted that remote rural areas cannot be treated on just the same basis as the rest of the country. In 1917 the Speaker's Conference recommended the segregation as far as possible of adjacent industrial and rural areas, and Parliament further permitted the Boundary Commissioners to depart from their instructions where these would lead 'to the formation of constituencies inconvenient in size or character'.[2] The 1944 Act provided that the Boundary Commissioners might depart from their instructions 'if special geographical considerations including, in particular, the area, shape and accessibility of a constituency'[3] appeared to render this desirable. In Scotland and Wales there are about a dozen constituencies which it would be very hard to force into the normal arithmetical mould, and both in 1917 and 1948 these were allowed to survive, although some had barely half the electors required by the national quota.[4] But in general the Boundary Commissioners have been inclined to treat even relatively compact rural areas more generously than urban ones. In England in 1918 the average county constituency had 31,594 electors, compared to the 34,009 of the average borough. In 1947 the Commissioners' recommendations averaged 55,360 and 61,442 respectively. The difference was subsequently halved when Parliament created seventeen extra borough seats, but it remained appreciable.[5]

Population changes are relatively rapid, and, although the 1918

[1] The average electorates under the 1949 register were in fact:

England	56,073
Wales .	50,061
Scotland	47,465
Northern Ireland .	72,090

Using these figures, if the seats in Great Britain had been distributed on a strictly proportionate basis, England would have had 12 more (518 not 506), Wales 3 fewer (33 not 36), and Scotland 9 fewer (62 not 71).

[2] *H.C. Deb. 94*, c. 1495.

[3] *Cmd. 7260/1947*, p. 9.

[4] The Western Isles division provides the extreme example:

	G.B. electoral quota	Western Isles electorate
1918	32,784	18,237
1949	54,723	28,290

[5] See p. 127 above.

redistribution was thorough, anomalies grew up quickly. In 1918 only a handful of electorates were as much as a third above or below the national average. But by 1939, 119 seats were outside the limits suggested in 1917;[1] 87 seats no longer justified their existence, while 32 were entitled to increased representation. In the London area there were huge contrasts. Hendon and Romford had four times the quota, and four other seats had more than two and a half times the quota; on the other hand, there were half a dozen constituencies in the East End which had barely a third of the quota. The situation in the depopulated constituencies was in many cases aggravated by bombing. For a large part of the country, of course, there were no great movements of population in the inter-war period, but even in constituencies where numbers remained more constant boundary revision became overdue, both to check small discrepancies in numbers from growing into bigger ones, and to keep pace with local boundary changes. There was no disagreement when the Vivian Committee suggested, and the Speaker's Conference endorsed, the idea of making redistribution a continuous process instead of an occasional one; nor was there much opposition to the temporary creation of 25 extra seats to deal with the most overgrown constituencies while waiting for the general redistribution.

The procedure by which the Boundary Commissioners worked in 1947 seemed uncontentious enough. The Commissions—made up of the Speaker, the Registrar-General, the Director-General of the Ordnance Survey,[2] and two other senior Government officials—made an *a priori* distribution of seats in accordance with the quota. They then published their proposals for each district in the local press and invited representations to be made to them. If there was a serious protest an Assistant Commissioner was appointed to hold a local inquiry. The Commissioners would then, if it seemed to them desirable, modify their recommendations in the light of his report. The first general redistribution by the permanent Commissions was effected by a Schedule at the end of the Representation of the People Act of 1948. But subsequent minor adjustments and future general redistribution were to be made by Order in Council subject to affirmative resolutions in both Houses.

The idea that routine redistributions once in the life of every Parliament would serve as a painless check on the growth of anomalies was ill-founded. The first attempt to apply the provisions of the House of Commons (Redistribution of Seats) Act of 1949 provoked

---

[1] i.e. roughly below 70 per cent. or above 170 per cent. of the quota.
[2] In Northern Ireland the Commissioner of Valuation.

greater irritation over redistribution than ever before, although far fewer seats were involved than in the general redistribution of 1948. The Boundary Commissioners were slow in starting their first periodic revision in 1953 and the changes they proposed were carried through in a rushed and controversial manner. During 1954 their provisional recommendations aroused a fair amount of comment as they emerged one by one and a number of local inquiries were held to satisfy objectors. But more serious trouble arose in December when their final recommendations were published[1] and the Statutory Orders giving effect to the changes came before Parliament.[2] Unsuccessful attempts were made in the Courts to enjoin the Home Secretary from acting upon recommendations that, allegedly, ran counter to the Boundary Commissioners' Statutory Terms of Reference.[3] The problems involved in this controversy have been dealt with exhaustively elsewhere;[4] but they can be summarized.

1. There was no administrative procedure for appeal from the Commissioners' revised recommendations.
2. The English Boundary Commissioners (unlike the others) failed to explain their decisions.
3. The redistribution took place too soon. There were few gross anomalies, but the rigorous pursuit of mathematical equality meant that, after only 5 years, 170 constituencies had their boundaries altered, often drastically.
4. There was no real possibility of Parliament or the Government altering the Commissioners' recommendations, so that the debates on them became farcical.
5. In several major respects, the rules laid down for the Boundary Commission were ambiguous, contradictory, or inadequate.
   (a) The Commissioners were instructed to allocate seats on the basis of a quota for Great Britain, yet they were also to leave Scotland and Wales with at least 106 seats and they were not to increase substantially the total number of seats. In practice, therefore, they had either to sanction an increase of 13 seats (which they decided was too substantial) or they had to disobey the instruction to distribute English seats according to the quota for Great Britain.
   (b) The Commissioners were given no clear guidance on how far they should take imminent population changes into account (they did in practice do so to a small extent—in contrast to 1947).

---

[1] *Cmd. 9311–9314/1954.*
[2] *H.C. Deb. 535* cc. 1780–1940, 1987–2228; *536* c. 180–382.
[3] See *The Times,* December 1955.
[4] See 'The Redistribution of Seats' by D. E. Butler, *Public Administration,* Summer 1955, pp. 123–47.

(c) The Commissioners had difficulty in interpreting what was involved in respecting local government boundaries 'as far as practicable'.

(d) The Commissioners had no clear guidance on how strictly to adhere to the quota; an excessive devotion to numerical equality could produce seemingly gratuitous upheavals.

(e) The Commissioners' mandate to depart from the quota if 'special geographical conditions' rendered it desirable did not make clear whether it was intended in general to give county seats a lower quota than borough seats.

During the debates on the 1954 recommendations, general agreement was expressed on most of these points, despite some partisan argument about the application of the quota for Great Britain to English seats: Labour spokesmen alleged that the Conservatives were seeking their own advantage by refusing to increase further the number of English seats.[1]

In 1956 and 1957 there was some inter-party consultation and as a result the House of Commons (Redistribution of Seats) Act[2] was passed in 1958, substantially as an agreed measure. Its only seriously controversial provision was the alteration by which seats in England were to be redistributed on a quota calculated from the electorate of England, not of Great Britain: Labour spokesmen would have preferred more seats to have been created for England. Labour attempts to include formal instructions that county seats should have no advantage over boroughs were also rebuffed. The main changes provided for in the Act were an increase in the interval between general redistributions from 3–7 years to 10–15 years; a greater latitude for the Commissioners to depart from the quota in order to leave constituencies undisturbed; more opportunity for the hearing of local objections to proposed changes; and changes in the composition of the Commissions.[3]

There is no doubt that these amendments should smooth the

---

[1] Comparable complaints were heard (see pp. 127–30, 134 above) about the 17 extra seats created during the passage of the 1948 Act. In fact, just as those 17 seats seem to have made a negligible difference (two seats at most) to the Conservative-Labour balance in the 1950 and 1951 elections, so in 1955 the boundary alterations had scarcely any effect on the overall fortunes of the parties.

[2] 6 & 7 Eliz. 2, ch. 26. For debates see *H.C. Deb. 582* c. 226–301, *585* cc. 599–700, 1297–1305.

[3] A High Court Judge was to become the Deputy Chairman of each Commission and the Commissions were to be reduced from five members (besides the Speaker as Chairman) to three, through transforming the Registrars-General and the Directors of the Ordnance Survey from Commissioners into Assessors.

process of redistribution. But in view of the wholly unforeseen difficulties of 1954 it would be rash to suggest that it will ever be a trouble-free process. The neutrality of the Boundary Commissioners is beyond question but the consequences of redistribution are not necessarily neutral. There is always a chance that there will be some correlation between movements of population and social class—and, therefore, with party sympathy. By 1945 the depopulation of central city areas led to the average Labour seat having 50,785 electors, compared with 56,713 in the average Conservative seat. A tribute to the fairness of the 1948 redistribution is perhaps to be found in the fact that in 1950 the average electorate in seats won by the Conservatives was only a fraction more than in seats won by the Labour party (55,270 compared to 55,161). Estimates made by the parties and a careful check of individual boundary changes suggest that the 1948 redistribution may have cost the Labour party thirty seats [1] One of the major benefits of continuous redistribution is that no party is likely to suffer so sharply in future.

It is not, of course, within the Boundary Commissioners' powers to eliminate all biases in the distribution of seats. They can ensure the approximate equality of electoral districts, but there is no way in which they can counter the geographical chance which may lead to the strength of one party being more favourably distributed for the winning of seats than that of its rivals. [2]

[1] See *The British General Election of 1950* by H. G. Nicholas (London, 1951), p. 4.
[2] See pp. 194–204 above.

BIBLIOGRAPHICAL NOTE

THE contemporary historian normally suffers from a profusion of very inadequate sources; but upon a subject as peripheral as the electoral system, even profusion is lacking. Before 1918 an appreciable quantity of material on the subject was to be found in the press, in parliamentary papers, and in biographical works; but after 1918 the published sources which are of any use are very few. If the evidence of *Hansard* and the Statute Book is to be supplemented, it is necessary to turn primarily to the uncertain memories of surviving politicians.

1. *Government publications*

Parliamentary Debates. Official Report. 5th Series.
Parliamentary Papers (for Bills and Proceedings of Standing Committees).
Public General Acts.

Reports:

Cd. 5163/1910. The Royal Commission on Electoral Systems (see *Cd. 5352/1910* for minutes of evidence).
Cd. 8463/1917. Speaker's Conference on Electoral Reform.
Cmd. 3636/1930. Ullswater Committee on Electoral Reform.
Parliamentary Papers 1938–9, vol. vii, p. 215. Select Committee on Mr. Speaker's seat.
Cmd. 6408/1942. Committee on Electoral Machinery.
Cmd. 6534/1944 and *Cmd. 6543/1944*. Speaker's Conference on Electoral Machinery and Redistribution of Seats.
Cmd. 6606/1945 and *Cmd. 7286/1947*. Committee on Electoral Law Reform.
Cmd. 7004/1946. Committee on Electoral Registration.
Cmd. 7260/1947, *Cmd. 5311/1954*, Boundary Commission for England; *Cmd. 7274/1947*, *Cmd. 5312/1954*, for Wales; *Cmd. 7270/1947*, *Cmd. 5313/1954*, for Scotland; *Cmd. 7231/1947*, *Cmd. 5314/1954*, for Northern Ireland.
Official Returns of candidates' expenses, published as Parliamentary Papers after each general election except that of 1918.
Official Returns of the number of electors in each constituency, published occasionally as Command Papers, and reproduced in the Annual Reports of the Registrars-General for England and Wales and for Scotland.

2. *Reference books*

The returns of election expenses which provide the only official source of information about election results are of limited use to the student as they ignore the existence of political parties. There are, however, two indispensable sources for voting figures, which, although not always in complete agreement, either with each other or with official returns, are accurate enough for all practical purposes. These are:

The Constitutional Year Book (published annually 1885–1939).

The Times House of Commons (published after the elections of 1918, 1929, 1931, 1935, 1945, 1950, 1951, 1955, and 1959).

Election results are available in summary form in *British Political Facts 1900–1960* by D. E. BUTLER and J. FREEMAN, London, 1963.

3. *Works on the electoral system.*

Books:

D. E. BUTLER. *The British General Election of 1951.* London, 1952.

—— *The British General Election of 1955.* London, 1955.

—— and R. ROSE, *The British General Election of 1959.* London, 1960.

J. CADART. *Régime électoral et régime parlementaire en Grande-Bretagne.* Paris, 1948.

S. R. DANIELS. *The Case for Electoral Reform.* London, 1938.

I. R. M. DAVIES. *Trial by Ballot.* London, 1950.

M. DUVERGER, ed. *L'influence des systèmes électoraux sur la vie politique.* Paris, 1950.

H. F. GOSNELL. *Why Europe Votes.* Chicago, 1930.

F. A. HERMENS. *Democracy or Anarchy?* Notre Dame, 1941.

C. G. HOAG and G. H. HALLETT. *Proportional Representation.* New York, 1926.

J. HOGAN. *Election and Representation.* Cork, 1945.

G. HORWILL. *Proportional Representation. Its Dangers and Defects.* London, 1925.

T. LLOYD HUMBERSTONE. *University Representation.* London, 1951.

E. G. LEWIS. *British By-Elections as a Reflection of Public Opinion.* California, 1943.

E. LAKEMAN and J. D. LAMBERT, *Voting in Democracies.* London, 1955.

R. B. MᶜCALLUM and A. READMAN. *The British General Election of 1945.* Oxford, 1947.

R. W. G. MACKAY. *Coupon or Free?* London, 1943.

H. L. MORRIS. *Parliamentary Franchise Reform in England from 1885 to 1918.* New York, 1921.

H. G. NICHOLAS. *The British General Election of 1950.* London, 1951.

C. O'LEARY. *The Elimination of Corrupt Practices in British Elections, 1868–1911.* Oxford, 1962.

Parker's Election Agent and Returning Officer, 5th ed. London, 1950.

J. M. ROBERTSON. *Electoral Justice.* London, 1931.

J. F. S. ROSS. *Parliamentary Representation*, 2nd ed. London, 1948.

—— *Elections and Electors.* London, 1955.

C. S. SEYMOUR. *Electoral Reform in England and Wales.* New Haven, 1915.

H. TINGSTEN. *Political Behaviour.* Stockholm, 1937.

4. *Newspapers*

The news, editorial, and correspondence columns of the press were astonishingly barren of comment on electoral matters during these years. For this book the files of *The Times* and *The Economist* were thoroughly searched, while most other national daily and weekly papers were explored at the periods when the electoral system was receiving parliamentary attention.

5. *Ancillary sources*

Apart from one or two passages which have been quoted in the text, the biographies and autobiographies of politicians active in this period yield no material on electoral matters. This book owes far more to the personal recollections of the surviving protagonists than to any published lives or histories; and full acknowledgement must be made here of the assistance rendered by the many politicians and officials who, in interviews, or by correspondence, or by loan of private papers, supplied much invaluable background information.

INDEX